Beyond Theology | *The Autobiography*
of Edward Scribner Ames

Beyond Theology

The Autobiography
of Edward Scribner Ames

EDITED BY VAN METER AMES

THE UNIVERSITY OF CHICAGO PRESS

Library of Congress Catalog Number: 59-10483

The University of Chicago Press, Chicago 37
Cambridge University Press, London, N.W. 1, England
The University of Toronto Press, Toronto 5, Canada

© 1959 by The University of Chicago
Published 1959. Composed and printed by
The University of Chicago Press
Chicago, Illinois, U.S.A.

Library of Congress Catalog Number: 59-10763

The University of Chicago Press, Chicago 37
Cambridge University Press, London, N.W. 1, England
The University of Toronto Press, Toronto 5, Canada

Foreword

On July 6, 1893, my father (1870–1958) married my mother, Mabel Van Meter (1869–1953), descendant of a
Van Metre who came from Holland to New Amsterdam. My
mother's father, Hugo Grotius, followed a pioneering brother to
Dallas County in Iowa, where they set up a flour mill on the
Raccoon River, near De Soto. Hugo Grotius married Damaris
Dodge in 1867, after sending her for a year to Abingdon College.
My mother was born in the Brick House by the mill, where she
and my father returned for some summers with their children:
Van Meter, Damaris, Adelaide, and Polly. In 1908 we moved into
the big house at 5722 Kimbark Avenue, and there my mother died
on June 21, 1953, two weeks before the sixtieth wedding anniversary, which also would have been the sixty-sixth anniversary of
the day when my father first saw her at the Brick House.

After all their strenuous activity it was good to see them in their
late years relaxing at Pentwater. Watching the waves or branches
in the wind, my father said he was "cultivating vacuity." He
spoke of "the solace in the great processes of nature" which reach
out and can be relied upon. At Pentwater the golden wedding was
celebrated in 1943, as were nine more anniversaries of the sixth
of July, with children and grandchildren present.

The last time my father and mother came to Cincinnati was for
Christmas, 1949. His book *Religion* had just been brought out in
the third printing (by John O. Pyle), and he wrote in a copy for
each of his grandchildren in his clear hand: for Sanford, "Morning
dawns upon new days all over the world, and the light may show
more and more splendor until the evening of life brings out the

15761

v

stars"; for Christine, "Listening and thinking and working for lovelier and happier things helps bring them to be"; for Damaris, "Songs give wings and beauty to words that make them heard far away and long remembered."

My father's most important books were *The Psychology of Religious Experience* (Houghton Mifflin, 1910) and *Religion* (Henry Holt, 1929). His other books were: *The Higher Individualism, The Divinity of Christ, The New Orthodoxy, Letters to God and the Devil*. These and his published articles and pamphlets, up to 1940, are in the Bibliography of a volume in his honor: *Faith of the Free*, edited by W. E. Garrison (Willett, Clark & Co.). Three addresses given in 1943, before the Convention of the Disciples of Christ of Northern California at San Jose, were privately printed that year in a pamphlet with the title "The Disciples of Christ: Their Growth, Their Heritage, Their Timeliness." This went through several editions and was bought by many churches for their members as a good, concise introduction to the Disciples.

He began his autobiography in 1935, the year he retired from teaching in the University of Chicago, where he was then chairman of the department of philosophy (which had conferred upon him its first Ph.D. degree in 1895). He finished the book in 1940, when he retired from his forty-year pastorate at the University Church of the Disciples of Christ (originally the Hyde Park Church). In 1945 he retired as dean of the Disciples Divinity House, although he continued to be a member of its board of trustees. In 1951 he gave up editing the *Scroll*. He scarcely touched the autobiography after 1940, when he had given the chapters as sermons. Some other autobiographical writings have now been worked in, with the benefit of personal files—including the first chapter, which was printed in the Spring, 1958, *Scroll*. The memorial service for him appeared in the Autumn, 1958, issue.

The last twenty years have seen a reaction against the liberal thinking represented by my father, a return to something like the theology he had worked away from. But what he would say is clear enough in what he said. Already there is beginning a fresh appreciation of his thrust into the future and of his confidence that he was following the creative advance of the Disciple movement itself. He wrote: "We live forward. Change is of the very nature of things and of ourselves. . . . The future into which we go is uncharted. . . . We must make of it an adventure and deal with the days as they come and with the situations they bring. . . . Christianity now faces the alternative of becoming a religion of this world or of having no appeal to this age."[1]

VAN METER AMES

[1] "Theory in Practice," in *Contemporary American Theology: Theological Autobiographies* (2d ser.), ed. Vergilius Ferm (New York: Round Table Press, 1933), pp. 14, 12.

Preface

My purpose is to give a somewhat intimate and informal account of my religious experience from childhood to the development of my later views. I am led to do this in the hope that it may be of interest and value to others who are also concerned about the achievement of a vital, working religion in the present age, in the midst of many perplexing problems both in theory and in daily living.

Since man became even dimly aware of his simplest needs, and of the dangers surrounding his life, he has been engaged upon a great quest. Through its urgency he has built altars and temples in every land; he has written sacred books in all languages; he has danced and marched for his gods in every age; he has made himself drunk with wine and loosed his elemental passions in a feverish hope; and has crucified his flesh with terrible torments of ascetic discipline. It has been thought that the coming of civilization, and especially of science, would dissuade or deflect man from this quest, but he returns to it with calmer and wider vision. Vast numbers of persons still remain within the old faiths, unaware of the changed world of ideas. Others keep their old beliefs securely apart from their intellectual life. But a rapidly increasing company fearlessly seeks to understand and to realize the most intimate religious ideals with all possible knowledge and experience. They are ready to forego some forms of consolation and incentive, if necessary, on behalf of more practical and consistent ideals. Such persons are unwilling to rest upon the opinion of majorities or upon the authority of long-established custom. Their search is for self-evidencing and socially verifiable values.

Men who have lived in the currents of the world's thought during the last fifty years, and who have clung to the religious life, have epitomized in their personal experience a profound transformation. This inner history doubtless never has been just the same for any two individuals; yet those who have shared it will not fail to recognize a genuine spiritual kinship with anyone who expresses it. Others who are striving for clear discernment of the meaning of life and of the deeper satisfactions may find interest and perhaps encouragement in one more friendly soul's self-revelation. No unique value is claimed for the experience here recited. Whatever significance it has lies in its general and representative features, not in its peculiarities. The justification for so personal a story may lie in the interest which belongs to an intimate narrative and in the atmosphere of reality and authenticity which a personal statement conveys.

Contents

Chapter i | Childhood

My father, Lucius Bowles Ames (1834–1913),
was reared in a suburb of Boston where the family had been for
several generations. He learned to be a shoemaker before going to
college at New Hampton, New Hampshire. To defray his expenses he taught singing classes in neighboring towns, one of
which was Plattsburg, New York, across Lake Champlain, where
he met my mother, Adaline Scribner, as his pupil. They both
came of deeply religious Calvinistic ancestors. My father became
acquainted with the Disciples of Christ in West Rupert, Vermont,
united with their church, and became their pastor in 1864. He
found in the views of Alexander Campbell and other Disciple
leaders a refreshing freedom from creeds and sectarianism, and he
caught the passion for union among all Christians. He welcomed
the idea of understanding the Bible in a common-sense way, without the need of an emotional conversion. From my childhood I
retain a vivid sense of his release in coming to the simple and
reasonable faith of the Disciples.

My father preached in many places for short stretches. I was
born in Eau Claire, Wisconsin, where relatives had encouraged
him to move from New England at the close of the Civil War.
For a time we lived on a fruit farm near Benton Harbor, Michigan,
where I locate my earliest memories. One is of breaking a tooth
on a hard green peach in an orchard; another is of standing by a
horse the family drove. He towered hugely above me, filling me
with intense curiosity and fear. I also recall a storm on Lake
Michigan when we were crossing to Chicago. I have been told
that we were aboard a little steamer, the *Corona*. Even now I can

feel her roll and the shuddering strain of her timbers. But most vivid is the deep sense of security which quieted all fear when my father took me in his strong arms and soothed me. No symbol of a kindly Providence has ever been so real to me as that simple, natural act. The wind and waves had not ceased to beat with fury upon us, but my father was a guarantee of safety against all.

The fruit farm was not to his liking, so he took us to Chicago to stay with Aunt Emma and Uncle Sanford Scribner until he could locate a place for us to live. There was a large oak center table in the living room, which had a wooden ball fitted as an ornament into the place where the legs took off. The story my brother likes to tell is that one day Aunt Emma called to Mother to come and see what "Eddie" was doing with the ball. I was told to let it alone, but, as soon as Mother's back was turned, I would be at it again until I dislodged the ball from the socket. Every time I could get to the table alone, I would repeat the performance, working hard to get the ball loose. When my brother speaks of this, he always says it was the beginning of the show of determination which helped me to get along in life. He also remembers that my mother's brothers were very strong Baptists who were much upset that my mother married a "Campbellite" and so left the Baptist fold too.

My father found a Disciple church needing a pastor near Decatur, Illinois. We moved next to Walnut, and then settled in Toulon, Illinois, where he had a pastorate for four years, the longest of his life. Perhaps I remained forty years in the same pulpit to make up for all the moving my father did! We lived afterward in Marion, Monticello, and Davenport, Iowa, but Toulon was the home of my happy childhood days. We had a little story-and-a-half house on the edge of town, with a nice garden plot and an open meadow stretching into the country. There more connected and clearly remembered events began to happen. A row of fine old maple trees graced the front yard. They cast a deep shade over our playground, where I learned to throw curves and to catch the ball with my bare hands. The lightning played over those trees in the fierce thunderstorms I loved. The wind swayed them with mysterious power and a moaning sound.

It was a great day for me when I entered the first grade of school at the age of six. The teacher was a gracious, understanding person who made her room a happy, companionable place and the first steps in study a delight. Her interest followed her pupils into all the successive stages of education. When I visited her last, she was an old lady with snow-white hair but with the same sprightly interest in how life was going with the man who had been a little freckled boy in her school forty years before.

Being the youngest of four children, and five years younger than my brother who was nearest me, I was taken to church on all occasions. I am inclined to think that the greatest religious influence of my childhood was the mood of piety in home and church. The church building was a little one-room brick structure in the heart of Toulon. The congregation of fifty or sixty people came in from the village and the country with faithful devotion Sunday morning and evening, and for prayer meeting on Thursday night. All the minister's family attended as a matter of course and sat together in a front pew. Many faces of that company are vivid in my memory. I can both see and hear them sing. I can still feel their mood of devotion and recall their reverent manner, their confidence in the faith they cherished. The quality of their worship and in their mutual greetings after the service impressed even a restless boy. Scarcely any specific teaching remains clear in retrospect, but the sense of something of great importance is deep and abiding.

Perhaps it came with the sound and rhythm of the singing, but I am sure it came also with the warmth of bodily comfort as I sat close to my mother and touched her hand. And it came with the quiet and expectant air of the whole company dressed in their Sunday best, away from their everyday toil and anxiety, and played upon by the dreams and aspirations of their religious faith. They were in an uncommon reach of thought and intention. They felt themselves somehow identified with a great cause coming down from the days of Christ and the Apostles, a cause in which even in that little town and gathering they could take a real part and further by their zeal. They even felt some responsibility for the redemption of all mankind. In their missionary enthusiasm they could sing:

> From Greenland's icy mountains,
> From India's coral strand,
> Where Afric's sunny fountains

Roll down their golden sand,
From many an ancient river,
From many a palmy plain,
They call us to deliver
Their land from error's chain.

The leader of the volunteer choir was a stalwart farmer, John Brown, with a deep bass voice. He had the qualities of leadership and sang the hymns with beaming face and soulful sincerity. I remember little of the Sunday school except that an organ was used. That was momentous. Some advocated its use in the church service also, but a few older people prevented that with their conscientious objections. (In Iowa my future wife's church had no organ until after her grandfather's death. When one was rented for Christmas exercises, which he regarded as pagan, he saw it in a back room, said Beelzebub was there and that he would break it up with an ax if he saw it again, because he could pay for it.) At last a Sunday came in Toulon when the innovation was introduced in the morning service. As the organ tones filled the church, an aged elder rose from his pew and walked brokenly down the aisle, out the door. He was the type of man who has made churches of many denominations subject to the will of small minorities. Claims of conscience and piety have too often been allowed to hamper the progress which equally religious and more adaptable souls have desired.

My father's sermons have left no clear imprint upon my early years except for their quality of earnestness and lofty faith. But the Sunday dinners with parishioners, especially with those who lived in the country, were memorable occasions to a small boy. The fried chicken, the preserves, the wonderful cakes and pies, for a healthy appetite made feasts for kings. After dinner there would be excursions about the place to see the fat hogs, the sleek horses, the colts and calves, and the watchful dogs. The great haymows of the barns were fragrant with mystery and adventure. There could be no keener joy than on rainy days to burrow into the hay and lie listening to the patter on the roof, the warmth and comfort magnified by thought of the cold and damp without. But the most impressive thing of all was the spirit of the people in their hearty hospitality and religious enthusiasm. In their homes and at social gatherings there seemed to be comradeship and friendliness of a unique quality and degree. This gave me in early childhood the feeling that religion bound people together in closer bonds than any other interest.

In our home religion pervaded the whole of life. Always there was grace at table. After breakfast we sat in a circle in the living room to read a chapter from the Bible, each reading two verses. As soon as I could do so at all, I took my turn. Often the story was quite lost to me in my effort to count ahead and find the lines which would fall to me next. When the reading was finished, we sang a familiar hymn, which my father loved to do as a former singing teacher, playing the accompaniment on a small reed organ. Sometimes he would strike a tuning fork to pitch the tune, and we would all join in two or three verses of "Nearer, My God, to Thee," "My Soul, Be on Thy Guard," "Grace, 'Tis a Charming Sound," "Awake My Soul, Stretch Every Nerve," "Hail to the Brightness of Zion's Glad Morning," "From Every Stormy Wind That Blows," "Sweet Hour of Prayer," "How Firm a Foundation," "O Thou Fount of Every Blessing," "Joy to the World!" or "I Love to Tell the Story."

Then we knelt down at the chairs where we had been sitting, and Father or Mother led us in prayer. He often began with these words: "Our Father, we are grateful to Thee that there is no visible mark of Thy displeasure resting upon us." Mother, when alone with us children, began: "O God, Thou knowest that we are as prone to do evil as the sparks to fly upward." But such phrases were used with no intentional reference to the Calvinistic training of her youth. Like most children, at bedtime we always said: "Now I lay me down to sleep and pray the Lord my soul to keep. And if I die before I wake, I pray the Lord my soul to take. Amen."

Father believed profoundly in prayer. It was for him the audience of the soul with God, as direct and natural as for a man talking with his friend. Nothing could be too large and nothing too small for Father to present before his God. After ascriptions of praise to Almighty God, praise for the glories of creation, praise for our human existence and for the redemptive work of Christ, he prayed for the nation and for the church, for the sick and the distressed, and for the family, for our health and success and ultimate salvation. He prayed for the culmination of Christ's kingdom in the day of judgment and for the glorious reign of the redeemed in heavenly bliss.

This ritual of morning prayers was more or less irksome, especially to us boys, but to a remarkable degree we took it as a matter of course and never thought of trying to run away from it, no matter how urgent the call of play or work. Here was an influence strengthened by the realization that it was sustained by the sincerest motives and beliefs. Sometimes I heard Father praying alone, and there came over me a sense of awe. He literally went into his closet and shut the door and prayed in secret.

But our religion had its happiest expression in singing hymns. Frequently on Sunday afternoon or during an evening the whole family would gather about the organ. Father played and sang, leading us with the range of his baritone voice and knowledge of music. He never was happier than at such moments. It was our habit to begin with the first hymns in the book and sing all our favorites to the last page. Looking back with better understanding of the responsibilities and anxieties he had to bear, I am sure those hours of song meant far more than any of us children could imagine. Sometimes I noticed that Mother would slip aside into a chair and rock quietly, as if thinking of other scenes or wondering what the years would bring to us. But her heart was entirely with us, and she sang as long as her strength and voice permitted. Often at her work she hummed the same hymns softly, with almost unconscious fidelity to their spirit and meaning.

The shadow of deep and unrelenting poverty always hung over our home. I never cease wondering how a family of six could contrive to achieve so much comfort and happiness on the minister's salary of six hundred dollars a year, very irregularly paid. My mother, never in vigorous health, did an appalling amount of work, with such help as any of us could give, and she seems to me now to have done all the worrying by herself. Father had marvelous faith that the Lord would provide. It often happened that, when food was scarce, some farmer would bring in a supply of potatoes, apples, and meat that would for the time being prove the strange ways of divine providence. Now and then this providence took the form of a "pound social," when members of the church would surprise us with a party, each bringing a pound of coffee or fruit, butter or eggs, cake or homemade candy.

I had the good fortune to know that my father had other interests and capacities than those which showed in his sermons or in his religious moods at home. Somehow his religion is more significant to me because of enjoying experiences with him which were more within my boyish appreciation. To others he may have seemed too serious and preoccupied with his professional concerns. But in summer he taught me to make kites and went with me to a big pasture where he helped to fly them. He would send up "messages" with as much zest as any boy. In winter he made figure-four traps to set for rabbits. When the telephone first began to be talked of, he helped us boys string a line of cord taut from the house to the barn, with tin cans at the ends, so that we realized for ourselves that sound waves could be transmitted a great distance.

There was, after all, genuine comfort in the plain, happy home of my childhood. Among its delights were days when I was not quite well enough to go to school but not ill enough to be kept in bed. Then I could lie on the couch in the living room and talk with Mother as she moved about her duties, or I could read the stories in the back of the school reader which had not been spoiled yet by being given as lessons. On such a day a great event occurred. It was winter. Snow covered the ground and a driving sleet would cut the face. As I lay in the quiet house, I heard a low whine and something scratching at the door. When I opened it I found a little yellow dog crying with cold and hunger. Mother had no heart to refuse my wish to take him in. So we got the ice off his coat and fed him and let him lie under the stove. From that day we were fast friends. We belonged to each other. He had come to me and I had rescued him from a cold and cruel world. Who can tell what a faithful dog means to a young boy, especially when in spite of all love and human companionship he feels that something is lacking? He can tell things to his dog which no one else could understand. The dog will respond with secure silence and with his best caresses. So my dog Trip filled a real place in my soul and remains yet the symbol of dumb affection and good fellowship.

I do not remember any pronounced fears in those early years. The sharpest were connected with the disapproval of my parents or teachers. But I do recall great pleasure in one thing generally

frightful to children. A thunderstorm induced a strange excitement, but I did not feel impelled to run from it or to shut my eyes
against it. I have the recollection of a powerful fascination in
watching the black clouds fill the sky and seeing them swept by
great sheets or chains of lightning. The booming thunder brought
a kind of glee, and when the rain broke over the house in torrents
I reveled in the sound of it on the windows and roof. It seems to
me I had imbibed a kind of fatalism which made me feel that if
the lightning were to strike there was nothing I could do to ward
it off. There were lightning rods on the house, and we had prayed
God to keep us safe, and the storm was a grand sight to see!

Like every child of such an environment, I prayed earnestly for
things I wanted. An aching void of unfulfilled dreams remains
from one unanswered prayer which I often repeated as I fell
asleep: a prayer that I might find tied to the hitching post in front
of the house next morning a pony all bridled and saddled.

There were impulses quite at variance with the prevailing attitude of the household. One was the idea of trying to set up communication with "familiar spirits." The suggestion came from the
biblical account of Saul's interview with the Witch of Endor. I
teased my father by hinting that there might be something in it
and gave the impression, as nearly as I could without actually
lying, that I thought I had established connections with a spirit I
called Mike. My elders were afraid I might become obsessed with
such foolishness. There were times, too, when I drew my father
into arguments about some passage in the Bible. A favorite text for
this was the one which says that God hardened Pharaoh's heart
and punished him for having a hard heart and refusing to let the
children of Israel go. It was there in the Bible, but it did not seem
fair and does not to this day, taken in the simple meaning of the
phrases.

My considerable curiosity once might have been the undoing
of us all. In the floor of an upper room I found a knothole and
felt a great desire to see what was down in the dark below. I
smuggled matches from the kitchen, lighted one, and dropped it
down that hole. It made a momentary illumination which showed
the plaster through the lath and gave me some idea of how the
house was put together. But I wanted more light. After having
several matches go out I tried to get the pile of them to burn,

thinking they would make a sufficient blaze to enable me to see into the farthest corner. It never occurred to me that the house might burn down, but I regarded the performance as my secret and did not confide it to any member of the family until many years after we had removed from that home.

During my early years there were increasing tokens of connections our family had with people in other places. Letters came from my mother's relatives in Chicago and from my father's in Wisconsin and Boston. These were often read aloud and led to conversations about various uncles and aunts and cousins who seemed to live in a remote and mysterious world. Those most frequently mentioned lived in the city, and their mode and scale of life reflected a very different existence. There was the handsome house with its grand staircase, and the table with the ball under it, of my Aunt Emma and Uncle Sanford Scribner. I sensed that it had embarrassed my mother to be taken in by them at a time when my father was without a pulpit. When visits were planned they were topics of interest for months, and preparations in our house went on for weeks in anticipation of them. When my mother's sister Elizabeth (Mrs. Alexander Vaughan) came, she brought her boy of my own age (Sanford Scribner Vaughan, called "Sannie"), and we had rare times together in forms of play entirely new to him. One delight was to go into the garden, select a hidden spot in the tall corn, build an oven of bricks, and make a real fire. We baked potatoes in clay and roasted ears of corn. Dressed up as Indians, we pretended mighty adventures of hunting and fighting or more serenely gathered berries and went into the woods for nuts or for strips of slippery elm, which it was fun to chew. Return visits to Chicago were as full of novelty and excitement to me as the country was for my cousin. The polar bear in Union Park and the strange creatures in Lincoln Park were objects of insatiable curiosity. We climbed the old water tower for a view of the city and the lake. A lasting memory is that of the odor of tar used in laying cedar-block pavement. The faintest smell of tar still brings back the city streets of those far-off days.

After one or two short periods of residence in other towns, the family settled in Davenport, Iowa, when I was eleven. Although it was larger than the other places where we had lived, what impressed me were the river and the hills. The fascination of the mighty Mississippi never lessened. A family with whom I often played lived on the bluffs overlooking miles of the valley. During the long days of the summer vacation we spent hours under the spell of that scene. Steamboats plied up and down the river, and we boys gathered about the docks to see them come in and to watch the gangs of Negroes handle cargoes. They worked to the rhythm of their songs, deft and apparently contented. When the cables were loosened at the capstans, every boy of us felt an unspeakable longing to journey up or down winding miles of beauty and surprise.

I cannot forget the fate of a boat which was lost in the raging waters one spring. The news spread through town that a steamer going upstream had just passed the bridge when her engine broke, and she drifted helpless in the swift current down against the stone pier and sank. The crew were lost. All that day at school my mind hovered over the disaster. In the late afternoon I went with other boys and stood on the bank, wondering and depressed. The feeling was the same as once before when I had stood on the shore of another river, watching the angry water swirl over the place where a man and his horse had drowned the night before. In neither case did the river change its mood. It rushed on with the same roar. How strange that there was no sign of change! That life had disappeared there made no more difference to the stream than the submerging of logs broken loose from a raft.

The reading of my childhood had small range. Juvenile books were not plentiful, and the available fiction was under suspicion. Dime novels were taboo. But in my father's library, among lives of saints and commentaries, I found two volumes which fed my imagination. These were Dr. Kane's *Arctic Explorations*. The simple woodcuts stirred my soul: great ice fields and glaring snow, dog sleds and fur-covered men. The pictures bore out stories of hardship and privation. Unexpected openings would appear in the ice, necessitating long detours and threatening to set men adrift. Perhaps men, dogs, and sleds would have to be drawn up icy walls to a plateau. I was filled with admiration. Nothing in the literature of travel and exploration has had quite the same fascination for me.

In the year before I was twelve my older sister brought her dying husband back from Colorado and California, where they had gone for his health. Day after day he sat in his invalid's chair, helpless but patient, supported to the last by unflagging love and devotion. We understood that it was God's will and that no one could explain why it should be so. Here was a mystery. We realized that terrible things could happen to our family.

Another experience had the same effect. A fellow from the other side of town provoked me into a fight at school. He was more experienced than I and left no doubt of his victory. Seeing that I had got my punishment, the principal did not add to it except to send me home with a note to my parents, telling them what had happened. My mother was brokenhearted. Her keen family pride was wounded beyond expression. I felt I had brought disgrace upon us all. The immediate result was a little better control of a hasty temper and a more wholesome respect for the other fellow. Both these experiences helped me toward the next step.

In June, after I was twelve, I went with my father one weekend to a little town where we had lived and where he was preaching. It was a glorious Sunday. As I sat by an open window in the church, the beauty of the world grew on me and a religious mood deepened in me. On the way I had told my father that I had decided to join the church. At the close of the sermon, when the customary "invitation" was given, I went forward. He asked me the one simple question: "Do you believe in Jesus Christ?" My father was very happy and moved. That afternoon we went out in the country where I had hunted, to the river where I had gone fishing and swimming, and I was baptized. Peace and happiness filled me, and a new comradeship with my father. My sins were washed away. Perhaps they were not great, but to me release from them was salvation. I cannot remember any perceptible change in my manner of life. But I had done what my parents wished, and I had the sense of putting myself right with God and the universe. I felt closer to Christ and to all the good spirits who had fought and labored in his cause. I had responded to a great summons. It was June, and I was setting forth upon a far journey.

Chapter ii | Youth

Two years later, when I was fourteen, we were living in Toulon again, my father having been recalled there for a second pastorate. He was thinking of locating later in a college community for the education of my sister Mattie and me. My brother Charlie was away on his first job (which he had from the age of sixteen to twenty) as a telegrapher with the Chicago, Milwaukee, and St. Paul Railroad, at several different stations, but mostly at Anamosa and Cedar Rapids, Iowa. He worked all night from 7 P.M. to 7 A.M., beginning at forty-five dollars a month and sending home ten dollars after each payday. So I felt it was up to me to get a job. I had worked the previous summer in a grocery store for fifteen dollars a month. For the last month the proprietor had offered me my choice of the money or a watch. I took the big gold Elgin and still carry it. Now I contracted to work for a year in a general store for seventeen dollars a month. That store gave me as much education as any year of schooling I ever had.

There were four brothers in the firm, and I was the only hired help. I was the boy of all work, opening the store every morning at six in summer, seven in winter, sweeping out, scrubbing the floor twice a week, selling plug tobacco to farmers and calico to their wives and daughters, and delivering orders about town. We carried all lines of merchandise: groceries, tobacco, dry goods, clothing, notions, and some hardware. Traveling salesmen brought the breath of a wider world, and unpacking new shipments was like opening prize boxes at a party. Farmers often brought in butter and eggs to trade for sugar and coffee and the rest. The butter had to be graded and packed in small casks called firkins. Eggs needed to be candled and put in cases. And in winter I was responsible for the furnace. These tasks kept me many hours in the dark cellar. Once a customer brought in a brown jug and asked to have it filled with sorghum. I took it below, filled it full from the keg, and jammed the cork down hard. That split the jug and splattered the sticky stuff over my clothes and the floor.

I was strong, and, except in such a crisis, the exertion was not irksome. But the barrels of salt were about all I could handle, and I had to have help on the barrels of sugar, molasses, and kerosene. Fifty-pound sacks of flour became much heavier toward the end of a wagonload, as we carried them in to stack in the stockroom. It was fun to sell goods. When a housewife came in from the country, it was often to do her shopping on a grand scale. It gave me a real sense of importance to go from counter to counter, making up the order. It was a trick to make a neat package of ten pounds of granulated sugar poured upon a flat piece of paper, for there were no ready-made bags of all sizes at hand in those days. But if the customer did not know what she wanted, or came just to see the goods, it was hard for the clerk to hide his irritation. So I have always had keen sympathy for the person behind the counter who is asked to show quantities of things, only to be told, "Well, I really did not want to buy today; I was just looking around."

That store remains for me the symbol of system, of tireless energy, speed, and good-natured contact with a very mixed procession of human beings. The members of the firm were keen, fair men, giving just measure and price, and generous but rigorous treatment of the many charge accounts. They bought shrewdly and they made a good, reasonable profit. The cost price of everything was marked in the letters of a code, the key to which was not given to me at first. I felt promoted the day they took me into their confidence and gave me the key. It enabled me to see for myself the gross profit, but it took some time to get the idea of overhead costs and to realize the losses from bad accounts, leftover goods, and other risks of the trade. I learned for the first time the more important lessons of enterprise, hard work, patience, and courtesy in practical dealings.

Shortly after I engaged with this firm, another offered me better wages for the same kind of work, and I found out what it meant to keep a contract when an apparent advantage could be gained by breaking it. Another impression which that year's work helped to define later on concerned the byplay of social life and fellow feeling which attends business. We were a kind of natural group, not only we who worked together and cherished certain trade secrets, but along with us the customers and advertisers and traveling salesmen. The customers were zealously cultivated, and new people coming in were treated with a degree of self-conscious attention as possible patrons. The farmers were more leisurely than the townspeople and inclined more to a friendly chat. There were no loafers, but since the store was open until nine o'clock every evening there were some quiet hours at noon or suppertime which invited sociability.

In one year of work, and living at home, I saved a hundred dollars. On that hundred dollars I went to college for ten years. At least it was the beginning and the working capital. In 1885, in the spring of my fifteenth birthday, my family located in Des Moines, so that my sister Mattie and I might attend Drake University. I had to spend a year in the preparatory department completing entrance requirements, since I had not had much more than the equivalent of a year of high school. In five years at Drake I finished the college course and took a year of graduate work.

In the summers there continued the education through efforts at self-support. I teamed up with another student in my situation—living at home and needing to do what he could to pay his way—Will Reynolds. Our first venture was to sell Kilbourn Brothers' stereoscopes and views. The method we followed was to go into one little town after another in northern Iowa, find a place to board with a family, and draw lots for the sides of the town we were to canvass. No one who has not done such a thing can imagine the trepidation with which we set out to approach strangers. But expense had been incurred. Our cherished dream of an education depended upon success. We had the emotions of boys of sixteen aware of our inexperience, with our future at stake. Homesickness threatened us. But here and there we found purchasers. At night in our room we compared the results of the day and learned from each other's ups and downs. With gradually increasing confidence and skill, we got larger orders. Will was more deliberate and tenacious. He often made a sale after overcoming much argument and hesitation. I tried to put everything into my first words and then foster every sign of interest until assent was secured. Once a person had refused to buy, I seldom could overcome his objections. So I learned to head off a decisive answer until I had got my whole story out. Often, after talking to a wife, we had to go out to field or shop or office to get the deal approved by the husband. Eventually it became clear to us that our visits were pleasant interruptions of routine for a farmer or merchant and that our boyish procedure awakened other than strictly business attitudes. It was among immigrants that the most hearty interest developed, since frequently the views were of places in the old country which brought back the scenes of youth. Servant girls were likely to buy the most pictures.

Another vacation was given to establishing circulating libraries in villages by selling memberships. For two dollars a member could have the use of at least two hundred volumes. Of course it was first necessary to secure a certain number of subscriptions in a place. This enterprise was more congenial to academic youth and gave us a sense of being missionaries of culture. We got lists of names and started out, walking as much as ten or twelve miles a day, occasionally going on horseback or getting a lift on a wagon or hiring a rig, and sometimes coming back on a freight train. It would cost seventy-five cents a day for a hotel. Five or six orders made a fair day, but some days I got only two or three, now and then ten or twelve, and twenty orders made the greatest day on record. Later on I learned the reward and satisfaction of being a general agent receiving a commission from the labor of other fellows. I could even take a day off and still know that money would be coming in. But in one town I met with suspicion and envy. When I had collected the money from my days of work there, a few citizens conferred and decided that two hundred dollars was more than the books would cost if ordered direct from dealers. They did not appreciate that they had never thought of pooling their money for such a purpose. They did not realize that if the missionary-agent had not come they would have gone on without the standard works of literature. It was only afterward that I learned of the citizens' indignation and that they had sent the sheriff to a neighboring town to arrest me, where he missed me, without my knowing that I was eluding him.

Then a strange and wonderful event occurred which came near to making me believe in premonitions. After I had canvassed the village of De Soto, I was given the names of a few persons living out a way who might be willing to join the library association. It was on the morning of July 6, 1887, that I rode out into the country on a farmer's hay wagon. I got off where he turned into a hay field and walked on. As the road turned, I saw a brick house in the shade of maple trees. I had a presentiment that there I would meet my fate, a lovely and happy fate. When I had concluded my interview with the lady of the house, her daughter entered the room and I was introduced. She was to enter Drake that autumn. Three years of college courtship were to follow, then three years of engagement before we were married on July 6, 1893, in the Brick House.

Drake was one of the many denominational colleges founded primarily for the training of the ministry. It also provided for children of the Disciples and others a general education within the atmosphere and influence of the church. Drake was founded in 1881 by a gift of twenty thousand dollars from General Francis Drake and land provided by the citizens of Des Moines. There was one brick building and a frame structure called the Students' Home. The tuition was thirty-six dollars a year. It was coeducational. The president often explained that it was a university not in the German sense of advanced graduate instruction but in the English sense of a group of schools offering college courses and training for the professions. None of the professional training called for the prerequisite of graduation from college, but it included elementary work for prospective ministers, business and normal instruction, fine arts, music, and elocution.

The faculty were honest, determined men who had for the most part come out of similar institutions. They used the textbook method. There were no library facilities beyond an encyclopedia, numerous government reports, and some miscellaneous volumes from the libraries of deceased ministers and laymen. No journals or magazines were available for leisure reading. No one fully realized the poverty of the situation, but everyone looked forward to great developments in the future, in anticipation of which all made the best of the present and worked industriously, in a good spirit.

The faculty taught from twenty to thirty hours a week, and the best paid did not receive more than a thousand dollars a year.

I took the classical course, which meant Greek, Latin, mathematics, history, literature, logic, morals, and history of philosophy. But the work was all very elementary, superficial, and hurried. Language study consisted largely in labored translations of sentences, word by word, with slight regard for the thread of what was being said. This was encouraged as "mental discipline." In mathematics I got on fairly well but stopped with analytic geometry. I gathered later that if I had only gone on to calculus I would have found out what all the previous courses were about! But my mathematics remains still much in the state of those early exercises in the classics—rather blind efforts to follow the rules without getting the larger bearings or the sense of real power. In the study of English, especially in courses in composition and in Shakespeare, there was more satisfaction. Just after I had made myself familiar with *Othello* and had written a class paper on it, I saw the play given by Booth and Barrett. That was momentous in my intellectual and emotional life, setting up at a stroke a kind of enduring standard.

The really live and truly educative things in my college course were activities outside the classroom. Most important was the Philomathian Literary Society, which met every Saturday night. There would be a program of declamations, readings, orations, impromptu speeches, essays, music, and a debate. Then in closed session came the business meeting, where parliamentary law reigned over every detail, down to the item of unfinished or new business, when the excitement began. New members were chosen with care and "rushed" furiously. We did not merely deliberate but had property and practical affairs to administer, all through the proper procedure. For the purchase of a carpet, pictures, curtains, chairs, a committee had to be appointed to investigate and report. Funds had to be raised and assessments were often heavy to bear. Discussions were vociferous and votes were taken in tense silence. The glorious Saturday nights in old Philo were the hot and formative times of our young lives. Studies in English were the only ones which had vital and constant significance for that real world.

The sole intercollegiate events of those days were the oratorical contests. We had no organized athletics. A physical director, much less a coach, was undreamed of. Orations were the manly exercises. We labored long and hard for the "home contest." Success there in my senior year brought me the honor of representing Drake in the state contest, where winning third place made me a delegate to the interstate contest, including colleges of several of the central states. This was stimulating and gave some opportunity to get the measure of other men and colleges.

Another highly educative opportunity was that of editing the college paper, the *Delphic*. Not only did we seek to gather news and to cultivate literary interest among the students, but we took the editorial office with a seriousness which now seems ludicrous. Through the exchange department we were in touch with many colleges in all parts of the country, and this led to my resolution to go to one of the great Eastern universities for postgraduate study.

The social life of the students was pitifully limited. Dancing was taboo. But there were sleighing and skating parties. The faculty had no resources of money or experience to provide adequate social recreation. The graces of hospitality and entertainment were rare in the surrounding community of families who had come for their children's education. Occasional "socials" were held, but the stiff awkwardness of the overworked professors and the shy students was painful. Yet the demands of the young could not be entirely defeated. In the literary societies and in the casual contacts of the day we became acquainted. We formed opinions of one another and of the world we lived in. At evening the favorite walks were haunted by strolling couples, talking of little nothings while living great emotions and having half-uttered dreams. In such tender hours of companionship many found their comrades for life.

I was not especially concerned with religious thought and activity during the college years. I took no courses in religion, but we all went to daily chapel and attended church on Sunday. Nonchurch members were regarded with mixed feelings of curiosity and suspicion. They were outsiders. One professor held aloof from church membership though he regularly attended. His attitude furnished the topic for animated discussions. I felt a peculiar unrest in reference to him. Why didn't he join the church? Where would he go when he died? Yet I had a secret admiration for his standing out against the whole community and calmly taking his chances. Late in my stay another professor came who taught science and had the reputation of being a great man; his students got much from him, but when he became ill and died the question was asked in subdued tones whether there could be any hope for the future of a man like that. I had a revulsion against the prevailing sentiment. I said to myself and to some friends that if such a man could not go to heaven I did not care to go there either.

I sang in the large choir and always sat by my chum, Will, of the summer business partnership. We listened to the sermons and were loyal to the cause. In four years we heard different types of pastors. One was a pompous, self-conscious, but capable man whose dogmatism could not be excelled. He relieved his ponderous style with quaint humor. But he was too argumentative, didactic, and lacking in feeling. Another was a veteran of the Civil War who had been a prisoner at Andersonville, about which he told an amusing and pathetic story. His army life seemed to have given a practical and direct quality to his preaching. Although dramatic, his sermons were simple and genuine, with the note of reality and sanity. A third preacher who often came had a poet's sensitiveness and imagination. In his youth he had been plunged into infidelity for a time by his inability to be converted in the usual way. But he had finally discovered that it is not necessary to have a strange experience of conversion in order to be right religiously. That discovery released him from the doctrines of predestination and fatalism. He could become excited during his sermons and was often carried away in impassioned flights.

During my sophomore year an evangelist of wide reputation came to Des Moines and held special meetings for three months. He could quote chapters from the Bible and long passages of poetry impressively. He dressed eccentrically and had odd mannerisms. But he held the attention of large audiences and influenced hundreds of persons to unite with the church. Numbers of students were among his converts, and he left the impress of his personality and gestures upon the whole body of ministerial students. He advocated a reasonable kind of religion, insisting that emotion could not be a safe guide or test. I remember his saying, "Some people say they know they are saved because they feel good, but we feel good because we are saved." He contended that one may be guided in religion by the teaching of the Scriptures and the example of Christ, and that for one who follows that guidance peace and satisfaction naturally follow.

In certain respects I found myself controlled by very conservative attitudes. While I had not been subjected to the strictest interpretation of Sunday observance, I was disturbed that my bride-to-be often returned on Sunday evening from a weekend at home. I was amazed one Sunday night, after going to church, when a ministerial friend invited me to a restaurant for ice cream. The idea of a theater or a ball game on Sunday would have been intolerable. To make Sunday a holiday of games and sports, as in a German community I had known, was to me the extreme of sacrilege. For a long time I was suspicious of Roman Catholics, thinking they were idolaters who put the Pope in the place of God. And I thought Unitarians were equally hopeless. I once went to a Unitarian church and listened intently to make sure whether the divinity of Christ was being denied. My astonishment at what I took to be a display of irreverence culminated when the minister finished the closing prayer without mentioning Christ, instead of saying, "We ask all this in the name and for the sake of Jesus Christ." Surely such a prayer was worse than none.

A student who boldly proclaimed himself a believer in the doctrines of Robert Ingersoll scandalized all who heard him. For a long time I could think of him only as a man who deliberately turned away from what he really believed, parading his infidelity from a spirit of sheer bravado and perversity. The ease with which I could attribute to good people the wilful rejection of what they knew to be the truth is now beyond my comprehension.

In the religious services I sometimes experienced deep emotion. This frequently grew out of reflection upon the practical enterprises of the church. The union of Christendom seemed a great and appealing task. To overcome the friction and waste of divisiveness and combine the strength of the whole church upon the vital needs of mankind was an ideal to move the heart and imagination. When this dream was presented by an earnest and eloquent preacher, it was confirmed by the enthusiastic acceptance of a large congregation. And the missionary cause had persuasive spokesmen, with romance about them from having lived in China

or Japan or India. Their heroism and devotion stirred youthful
souls to emulate them. But I reflected when alone that if their undertaking was so great only persons of the best possible equipment
should go into it. As I thought of the preparation called for, I was
not sure that such vast religious responsibility was for me. My
dominant attitude was that I was too young and that in any event
years of study were still ahead of me.

At the same time there were profound experiences of nature.
The far-spread sky lifted my whole being into rapturous wonder
and awe. I had little accurate knowledge in that direction, but two
verses of the eighth Psalm expressed what I felt: "When I consider
thy heavens, the work of thy fingers, the moon and the stars,
which thou hast ordained; What is man, that thou art mindful of
him? and the son of man, that thou visitest him?" (Ps. 8:3–4).
Watching the stars on clear summer nights, I tried to imagine their
number, distance, and age. One evening I was waiting for a train
at a little station out on the vast level prairie. I was alone. The
elation of healthful energy welled up in me, and my soul sang
within me. I was remote from home and friends. Great white
cloud banks covered the western sky. The sun went down, touching the rim of the clouds with bands of gold, as if they were the
very isles of the blessed. Perhaps for all who had lived on earth it
was given at such moments to see the glory of the life beyond.
Any such cloud effect will still carry me back to that quiet evening when heaven came down and my heart was lifted up.

In 1889, at nineteen, I graduated from college. My work had
been graded high. Of such honors as there were I had received my
share. But I was not satisfied. I felt impelled to study in other
places. I had the boldness peculiar to timid people. Being diffident
and fearful of the world, I constantly craved such discipline and
advantages as would give me the sense of being able to cope with
other men and play my part with them. I anxiously thought of the
future, wondering what work I could best do, restlessly turning
from one profession to another, and also considering "practical
pursuits." I had been in too great a hurry to finish my course. I
was too serious, in a way. I should have had more recreations,
more interests, wider reading, and richer social contacts. It would
have been a great boon if I could have been trained in music, if
only in listening to more of it, or if I had known more about

painting and drama. But I was really happy and grateful that so many opportunities had come within my reach.

I had come through college absolutely free from the vices to which youth is easily subject. I was not profane or lazy or dissipated, although my virtues were doubtless quite negative, owing to the fact that there was no gambling, drinking, smoking, or sexual indulgence among my friends and intimates. Perhaps we were priggish and naïve, but no one accused us of it. Nor were we altogether sheltered. In our own sphere, in the activities set for us, we experienced real struggle and felt the strain of powerful forces. We were eagerly bent upon finding out the truth about life and were determined to live by it with all devotion.

My chum, Will, and I often reviewed the possibilities. Our business ventures had given me a sense of independence, and I might have continued in some partnership with him. It was a bit uncomfortable that other people had already made up their minds that I would go into the ministry, but neither at home nor elsewhere was any effort made to persuade me. Still undecided, I entered upon a year of graduate work at Drake, electing to study church history, Greek, and Hebrew, with a view to either teaching or preaching. But in the midst of that academic year, in January, 1890, an incident occurred which was decisive.

I went for a weekend at Prairie City, Iowa, where my father had taken a pastorate. When I got there on Saturday, I found that he was ill and unable to preach the next day. On the impulse of the moment I asked him if he would like to have me preach for him. He was surprised and a little doubtful of my seriousness, not to say of my ability, and replied, without any show of enthusiasm, that I might do so if I wished. His hesitation about turning me loose in his pulpit, when I had never conducted a public service, was natural enough. But it was just the tone to make me want to prove to him what I could do.

So I set about preparing my first sermon overnight. After struggling a long time to create something of my own, I finally resorted to putting together what I could remember of a sermon I had recently heard in the college chapel by one of the professors. The text was Psalm 17:15: "As for me, I will behold thy face in righteousness: I shall be satisfied, when I awake, with thy likeness." But I do not recall anything that the professor or I said about it. In the pulpit Sunday morning I realized that I would be expected to preach again that day. When the moment came for announcements, I bravely said the subject of the afternoon sermon would be "Hope." I found enough to say on that theme, and the congregation was considerate.

Back in class on Monday morning, I had a feeling that the die was cast for my life work, but I did not confess it to anyone. Then I was invited to preach in another town the next Sunday. Since I now had the rough outlines of two sermons, I accepted and made them do duty again. I preached a few more Sundays that winter and one day was surprised to receive a letter offering me the pastorate of the church at Perry, Iowa, to begin when classes were over in June. I accepted the call. I was without special training for it, and I had not been ordained. But among the Disciples the local church manages its own affairs. If this church wanted me for its pastor, there was no one but me to consult. It was in this rather informal and unexpected manner that I became a minister of a sort. Yet it was not until ten years later that I really thought of myself as a minister, and many events intervened.

The church at Perry had a congregation of about one hundred members in a relatively new town of 2,500 people, a division station of the Northwestern Railroad, whose employees were a considerable factor in the membership. They accepted the young minister with friendliness and curiosity. We got on well together and began to have dreams of growth. I was ordained in June, with my father one of the officiating ministers. He and I were both very happy.

In July I became engaged to the slip of a girl I had met three years before when soliciting her mother to become a member of the circulating library association. Then in September of that year, 1890, when I was twenty, I was suddenly shaken out of my work by a scare over my health. I had gone to the county seat to attend the union meeting, where I was to speak in the afternoon. A slight bronchial hemorrhage prevented me. Although frightened, I went back to Perry, hoping to be all right. But I had a recurrence of the hemorrhage and went to Des Moines, where the physicians disagreed about the thing to do, and so I took the advice I preferred (of Dr. Woods Hutchinson), to go to Texas for the winter and live outdoors.

It was a tug to leave home and my promised bride. I had a lump in my throat when I bought a ticket which would take me a thousand miles. My imagination was filled with exaggerations of the southwestern state of Texas, still abounding with the spirit of the frontier, with big tall men dead in earnest. The first snow was on the ground when I left on the ninth of November, dreading tuberculosis, which had taken my brother-in-law after a vain search for recovery in the West.

Soon I was settled in beautiful hill country forty miles northwest of Austin, in the little town of Burnet, where I engaged to preach every other Sunday for six months. The other Sundays I preached in the neighboring town of Bertram, going back and forth on the train. In Bertram the little church was unfinished and I raised the money to put a roof on it. Probably it still stands. I was glad of the dry, clear air and the cedar trees of the land. I spent my free time walking in the healing sunshine or riding in the buggy with Dr. James S. Watson on his calls in the country—a very intelligent and capable man.

I was staying with his dear old mother, who had a deaf-mute son married to a deaf-mute. A young woman friend of the wife was also one. I learned to talk on my hands but not to read the sign language, since they had been taught to speak, though their voices were very strange. The friend was an educated woman who had studied in Washington, D.C., had read Darwin and Spencer, and considered herself an agnostic. She was much interested in religious problems, probably the more because she had reason to think she had not long to live. She was attracted by my simple, creedless, democratic faith, read the books I gave her, and finally was convinced by the arguments I had learned. Then she came to me with what proved to be a decisive inquiry. She wanted to know whether I thought that if she died that day she would go to hell! Without hesitating, in a casual manner I said, "Yes." That shocked her, but it worked. It "converted" her. It turned her around in her attitude toward religion, and she joined the church. When she stood before the congregation to make the confession, I questioned her in finger signs amid deep silence. I explained the symbolism of baptism by immersion, and I baptized her in a nearby stream. She told me later how happy she had been since the event

and how she had often gone alone to look upon the place of her
baptism as the grave of her old self.

There was no dearth of happenings, important or not, to put in
letters. One day at the church, when we were fixing the Christmas
tree, I made the mistake of playing a little tune on the organ. Although people urged me after that when I was near an organ, I
refused to play again, choosing to leave them in ignorance as to
my musical ability. Now and then in the evening I would get out
my flute, shut the windows, and play "Home, Sweet Home." It
was a comfort to think that the same moon would be shining in
Iowa. Picking out the hymns for a Sunday, I was glad to come
upon the one called "Iowa."

A memorable Texas night I spent with a good farm family with
ten children. There did not seem to be a bed for me. After dinner
they began putting the children to bed, the youngest first. As
soon as one was asleep, he was rolled on to the floor, and the next
was tucked into the only bed. At last it was my turn!

I was always writing letters—until time to take a train, or before
the dinner bell stopped me or the oil was low in my lamp. I wrote
so much to my father and mother that they must have thought I
loved them more, and maybe I did. I wrote to my brother and
sister, to Will, and endlessly to my future wife, who was in her
senior year at Drake. I had no sooner sent her a letter than I began
another, even a third on the same day. It was painful when there
was nothing at the post office from her, which would happen on a
Wednesday. We knew that, even if I got well soon, our marriage
would be long deferred by our plans for further study in the East.
I braced this purpose with catalogues beside me and by continuing
to read. We had the thought of our college courtship to share,
our Christian commitment, our dreams. We read the same chapter
in the New Testament each day, we met in prayer, and we sat
down to write each other at the same hour. We counted the
months since our separation and before our reunion in June. We
prayed that after long years of toil and discipline we might come
together in love's eternal ties.

I had wanted to visit Mexico before coming home. I got as far
as San Antonio. When I went from the train to a hotel, the clerk
asked me my profession. Hearing "preacher," he said, "God, I
thought you were a gambler!" In those days one might be taken

for the other, because the uniform of both was the Prince Albert suit and derby hat. And I was betting on the long chance of going to Yale. I could believe that luck had made the sight of blood frighten me and my friends into giving up my first pastorate. As a slender youth of twenty I had simply taken on too much in college, especially in extracurricular activities. In Texas it had not hurt my lungs to preach twice on a Sunday. My illness had freed me to try my luck in a larger world, to prepare better for my life work.

I had debated whether to go to Harvard or Yale, both of which had attracted me through their student publications that had come as exchanges to the office of the Drake paper. So I had some idea of what was going on there, and I had used textbooks by Yale professors. It was my youthful conservatism that decided for Yale. Harvard was a Unitarian institution, and Yale was of the more conservative Congregational tradition. Yale became for me the symbol of the great traditions of scholarship and of New England culture and religious leadership.

It is a matter of regret to this day that I could get no positive encouragement from the leaders of my own denomination to make such a venture. At that time it was something scarcely any of them had done, and a thing for which they did not see the need. Perhaps they felt a reflection upon the university whose courses I had taken; perhaps it was just tender-minded provincialism. The financial difficulties seemed the most insurmountable. But my sister Minnie offered to lend me the necessary funds. This, together with a provision in the Yale Divinity School for a hundred dollars a year for any student who neded it, brought my dream within reach. Then there was an invitation to supply the pulpit of the Central Christian Church in Des Moines during the summer of 1891, while the pastor, Dr. Breeden, was on vacation. Here was not only real encouragement but a return to my fiancée. It was a time of high rejoicing to be near her again and restored to health by the sojourn in Texas.

The trip east in the autumn, enabling me to visit Washington, Philadelphia, and New York, opened my eyes upon historic places and the wonder of cities dominant in American political and commercial life. In spite of all indifference and opposition I entered the Yale Divinity School. Because of the graduate work I had had, and some experience in the ministry, I was admitted to the senior class. It would have been better if I had been required to enter the first- or second-year class, for my previous training was lacking in many ways, I discovered. But the courses were not exacting. I was also able to enter a course in the philosophy of religion in the department of philosophy, which proved to be most significant. There I wrote a paper which gave me a new outlook upon religion and upon the Hebrew religion in particular.

In reading for that paper I came upon the idea that this religion had developed through natural processes from very humble beginnings to the heights of the great prophets. This revolutionary conception displaced in my mind the idea of a supernatural, miraculously inspired religion, providing instead the more interesting and fruitful notion of a religion growing up with the life of a people and being modified by their changing experiences. Reading Otto Pfleiderer's *The Philosophy of Religion*, the section on "The Historical Development of the Religious Consciousness," stays with me as crucial in changing my outlook. I have just looked in my library for this passage, which is marked:

> But he who seeks to understand the history of religion must possess the faculty of putting off the modern habit of thought, and placing himself inside the spirit of those times and peoples, to whom that was still becoming which reaches us as a thing finished, with whom accordingly creative fancy, working in the service of the heart, still ranked before the intellect with its objective thinking.[1]

The application of this method put many historical characters and events in new light. For example, Pfleiderer said: "The traditional reference of most of the Psalms to David is based on the quite unhistorical legend, which makes a pious singer of the warlike king, the celebrated hero of patriotic story, who certainly was far from a fine-strung nature; just as it makes of his splendour-loving son Solomon a philosopher."[2] The work of Pfleiderer placed

[1] Otto Pfleiderer, *The Philosophy of Religion on the Basis of Its History*, trans. from the German of the second edition by Allan Menzies (London: Williams & Norgate, 1888), III, 152.

[2] *Ibid.*, p. 155.

all Semitic religions, including Judaism and Islam, in the same unfolding process of human experience and idealism, alongside the development of the religious consciousness in Brahmanism, Buddhism, Zarathustrianism, in the religion of the Greeks and Romans, and in Christianity. This view did not reduce them all to the same level, but it saw them growing up in a similar way in their different environments and all of them striving for a representation and control of the great crises and destiny of mankind.

This made a very different approach and a very different method for the study of Christianity. It had been assumed in my religious background, at home and in college, that there was one true religion and that all the rest were false or at least faulty. This true religion came by direct revelation and alone offered absolute and complete redemption for the world. The great task of the church was to evangelize all peoples and convert them to Christianity. Whatever virtues or merit the heathen might have were only human and therefore fallible and inadequate to the attainment of genuine spiritual life. The idea that Christianity, too, was a natural religion seemed to destroy its significance as a soul-saving power and to suggest that it might also be infested with imperfections of doctrine and practice. If it were limited and imperfect in any respect, how could any of it be valuable?

Not all the divinity students took this course. In fact, most of them regarded philosophy as a dangerous or a useless subject for theological students. They could not, however, escape these problems by remaining strictly within the seminary, for the evolutionary conception of religion was making its way into all departments. Biblical criticism, systematic theology, church history, and other subjects were already showing the influence of the doctrine of evolution and its application to various fields of thought. William Sumner was teaching at Yale in those years and lecturing on folkways with such brilliance and energy that no student on any part of the campus could escape entirely his penetrating wit and revolutionary interpretations of human nature and society.

The divinity students reacted in various ways to this stimulating intellectual life of the university. Some of them were familiar with the new ideas through courses in their college days. The members of my class included graduates of Amherst, Williams, Dartmouth, Yale, and other colleges throughout the country. All the principal denominations were represented. There were a Hindu and an Armenian. All of the men were older than I, and most of them had had some years of experience in the ministry, in teaching, or in business. They had already been in the divinity school two years and during that time had studied the Hebrew language and literature under William Rainey Harper and therefore had had occasion to come to terms with themselves about the new ideas of religion. When I arrived at Yale, Dr. Harper had just left to undertake the organization of the University of Chicago. He had taken with him Alonzo Stagg, a famous athlete, who was a member for two years of the class in the divinity school which I entered in its third year. Stagg had decided, probably with encouragement from President Harper, that he could do more for the building of character as a coach than as a minister.

My own readjustment to the new teachings was not easy, but it was not attended with any great emotional strain. Several things aided in making the transition possible without the distress many experienced. My denominational inheritance was not greatly concerned about the authority of the Old Testament. Alexander Campbell, in his famous sermon on the Law, had insisted that Christians are not under the Old Testament, that the laws of Moses are no longer binding, that the rules about the observance of the Sabbath are no longer significant, and that the Law and the Prophets have been superseded by the teaching of Christ. In general, I had been taught that the Disciples were dissenters from the prevailing doctrines of Protestantism and that they encouraged liberty of opinion on all but a few clearly established essentials. But I had been taught that those essentials were divinely authorized and that the Christian religion was unique and supreme by virtue of its supernatural origin.

Another notion that helped me over difficult places was the ideal of devotion to the truth. Of course one had to be careful that he did not mistake error for the truth, but the truth, in the end, could only do one good. It might be surprising, it might be revolutionary, it might change the course of action, it might be very costly, but wherever the truth appears it must be acknowledged, whatever it commands must be done, whatever it reveals is at last harmonious with the divine mind and will.

Then too, here were the professors themselves who knew all

these modern ideas and yet were religious. They conducted the chapel hour, they often preached in the churches of New Haven, their lives were given to the promotion of religion. Newman Smythe and Theodore T. Munger were famous ministers in the two Congregational churches side by side in the commons directly adjacent to the campus. And there were distinguished visiting ministers on Sundays in Battell Chapel. There and in other pulpits I heard Lyman Abbot, Edward Everett Hale, G. A. Gordon, Phillips Brooks, Henry Van Dyke, and many others. Thus in the world around us religion was a live and going concern, and its practical activity was led by robust, intelligent men who were not ignorant of the problems which we students faced.

Besides, we had some part in religious activities ourselves. On visits to New York and Boston I preached in Disciple churches, and I became quite at home in the Sterling Place Christian Church in Brooklyn, where I supplied the pulpit many times in the interim between pastorates. I have long been convinced that practical participation in religious work is a wholesome influence in keeping one's religion vital in the midst of intellectual perplexities. Such participation emphasizes the deeper springs of the religious life and helps to keep in the foreground the practical values to which in the end all theoretical considerations must yield for their final test. The church in Brooklyn brought me into contact with people and affairs which touched my imagination and revealed new phases of the human world. I was usually entertained in the home of the superintendent of the Brooklyn Bridge, which at that time was a new and famous achievement of engineering skill. He told me many interesting things about the processes and difficulties of its construction and its operation.

On one of my trips I had a chance experience which gave me a new feeling for the city itself and what the loneliness and helplessness of an individual can be in the midst of it. I discovered when I arrived in New York that I had only nine cents in my pocket. The streetcar fare to the Brooklyn Bridge was five cents, and the toll on the bridge was three cents, so that I had only one cent left when I came to the Brooklyn side, and there was another streetcar fare of five cents to be paid. In my situation as a stranger miles distant from my destination, the long streets and the great, cold stone buildings took on a forbidding aspect. Here were people all about me and bright lights in the houses. Everyone else seemed to have his place and to be at ease, but I was an outsider and oppressed by a sense of sheer poverty and inability to cope with the darkness and isolation in which I found myself. In desperation I boarded a streetcar and waited on the rear platform for a chance to explain to the conductor my plight. When he had collected the other fares and came to me, I told him my embarrassing situation, but by that time I had discovered that I had besides the penny a couple of two-cent postage stamps. The conductor was kind enough but said that he could not take the stamps, since he was not working on his own change. He said if I would take the next car I might find a conductor who could accommodate me. So I was put off at the next corner feeling still more that I was not a member of society. The streets looked even longer than before and the houses more forbidding. In my desperation a ray of hope dawned with the realization that while I had waited on the plat-form of the other car and had told my story, the car had taken me several blocks on my way. Then it became evident that by repeating this adventure with conductors a sufficient number of times I might honorably reach the home of my friend. But finally I found the right conductor and came at last to the hospitable door where I was welcomed as if nothing unusual had happened. My host chanced to be the treasurer of the church and, like an impersonation of providence, gave me the next morning, Sunday morning, before we started to church, quite contrary to custom and without knowing what it meant to me, the money I was to receive for the day's appointment. I have always, since that time, been particularly responsive to individuals whose misfortune re-minded me of that Saturday night when I was nearly a penniless stranger in a great city.

It was the custom in the divinity school to appoint several of the members of the senior class to preach sermons or give address-es in the chapel before the whole school. Having been among those selected for this task, I decided to speak on the subject of Christian union and to present that view of it which any well-indoctrinated Disciple would give. My opening sentence was this: "The day for palliating divisions within the church has passed." I proceeded to show that the proper basis for union was the teach-ing of the New Testament, especially with reference to the conditions of membership in the church. It was there clearly specified that there were three basic requirements: faith, repentance, and baptism. All denominations recognized the importance of faith and repentance, but differences had arisen over the form of baptism. Since all scholars admitted that the Greek word for baptism meant immersion, and since all admitted that immersion was the practice of the early church, it would seem an easy and reasonable thing for all churches to return to the scriptural and apostolic practice. The importance of gaining the strength and effectiveness of a united church to promote the spiritual ends of Christianity against the evils of the world surely should be sufficient incentive to persuade all denominations to give up unscriptural and divisive forms of baptism.

Opportunity was given for criticism and discussion of these addresses, and the first man upon his feet after I had spoken was the venerable professor of church history, George Park Fisher. He was the greatest scholar on the faculty and a man whom I particularly respected. I had studied his books before coming to Yale and felt a kind of awe in his presence. I must confess, however, that I was disappointed in him on this occasion. He began by saying that he took exception to my opening sentence, that the time for palliating divisions had passed. He proceeded to argue that the different denominations are like regiments in an army all fighting for the same cause. Or they are like travelers going by various routes to the same destination. The hour ended with a degree of disillusionment on my part with reference to the open-mindedness and responsiveness to the truth of the faculty and students of Yale Divinity School, but I had the satisfaction of soon having my paper published in the leading religious journal of the Disciples, thus assuring my friends at home that I was fearlessly defending the true faith in the seats of the mighty. The full force of the contention of these learned men against my position only became clear to me some time later when I had an argument with a Congregational minister on this same subject of baptism. After I had set forth the claims for immersion, he simply said, "I think you are right, but what of it?" That is the conclusion to which I also was destined to come.

That year at Yale, studying theology, raised more questions for me than it settled, and I became convinced of the truth of the saying of Sir William Hamilton that no questions arise in theology which have not first arisen in philosophy. I was therefore determined to return to Yale or Harvard the next year to discover, if possible, what help philosophy could afford in solving the problems which theological study had developed.

Toward the end of that first year I had the good fortune to be invited to supply the pulpit of the South Broadway Christian Church in Denver for the summer months. Bayard Craig was the pastor, and he was a close friend of Dr. Breeden in Des Moines, for whom I had supplied the previous summer. The church in Denver had a beautiful new stone building, and it had a remarkable janitor. The janitor was Uncle John Sutton, as we affectionately called him. He had given some thirty thousand dollars toward the cost of the building. His wife having died, he now lived in a room in the tower of the church and devoted himself to the care of the property. He was also an ardent Mason, as were several members of the church board. The Knights Templars' conclave was held in Denver that summer, and they wanted an appropriate service in the church on Sunday during the conclave. Uncle John helped me prepare a sermon on "The Cross and Crown" and saw to it that I wove into it many mystic words and much symbolism which the Masons apparently appreciated more than I did. He wanted me to join the order, and I have at times regretted that I did not do so, but the books he gave me to read, setting forth the vows I should have to take, were too much for my still rather literal-minded and puritanical conscience. I had heard many arguments against secret societies as agencies which drew strength from the church, and now that I was assured that I knew the secrets of the order from the books I had been given, the motive of curiosity no longer moved me.

That summer gave me my first sight of the Rocky Mountains. I went up Pikes Peak on the eighteenth day of August, 1892, and had the excitement of a snowstorm at the top. But what remains most vivid in my memory is the distant view of the plains flecked by flying shadows of the clouds and walled about by the vast ranges circling the whole horizon. I know of nothing that more surely awakens in me a religious feeling than the sight of such mountains. They overawe me. They make an impression of agelessness and unshaken strength. The sight of them gives me a sense of kinship with those who in contemplation of them find sublimity and peace. No wonder men throughout the ages, in moments of distraction and futility, have exclaimed, "I will lift up mine eyes unto the hills." Coleridge, in his "Hymn Before Sunrise," sees Mont Blanc at first thrusting its awful form upward and piercing the clouds as with a wedge; "But when I look again," he says,

> I see that the deep air of heaven
> . . . is thine own calm home, thy crystal shrine,
> Thy habitation from eternity!
> A dread and silent Mount! I gazed on thee,
> Till thou, still present to the bodily sense,
> Didst vanish from my thought. Entranced in prayer
> I worshipp'd the Invisible alone.

Thus, in what is for me a memorable year, the year 1891–92, the world suddenly expanded into new dimensions. I moved from the provincialism of small places into the midst of magnificent and populous cities. I emerged from the complacent environment of a denominational college into the throbbing intellectual life of a great university, and I saw my simple religious faith in relation to the broader, expanding spiritual vision of all mankind. It was the experience of a plainsman discovering the mountains and their far horizons.

There is something strangely elusive about one's past. It is not easy to recall and reconstruct. One may have a warmth of feeling for a period or a particular year and yet experience difficulty in recalling the specific experiences upon which that feeling rests. In the three years of graduate study in philosophy which followed my graduation from the Yale Divinity School, I find the chief helps to memory are items entered in my expense account. This day-by-day record of room and board, books, stamps, streetcar and train travel, repairs for shoes, church collections, ball games, concerts, lectures, and an occasional nickel for candy reveals the exactions of poverty in the efforts to manage existence in the midst of the abundance of good things which Yale University and New Haven offered youth in the early nineties.

I had long dreamed of going to Harvard to study philosophy, after completing the divinity course at Yale. With this intention, after supplying the pulpit of the South Broadway Christian Church in Denver in the summer of 1892, I went to Cambridge. The first and major discouragement was in finding that William James was to be absent in Europe for the year. The second disheartening thing was an interview with Josiah Royce. He was cordial enough and his advice was sympathetic and genial, but it did not fit my temper or qualifications. He himself was interested in metaphysics, and he seemed to take it for granted that a theological student would wish to work in that field. For proficiency in it he stressed the need of higher mathematics and familiarity with certain systems of German speculative thought. I was not equipped in either field and had no heart or resources to travel that road even if the great philosopher Royce did think it was the highway to truth. Santayana, then a young instructor, had not risen to fame, and I doubt whether his type of mind would have appealed to my midwestern practicality. It was James I wanted, and, not finding him, I reluctantly turned back to Yale—reluctantly, because I wanted to be in Boston, toward which family associations and legends drew me, and because I realized that Harvard was the great center for graduate work.

I had another reason, too, and that was the nearness of Cambridge to Wellesley, where my fiancee was taking graduate courses that year. As was my custom when faced with difficult decisions, I wrote down in parallel columns all the pros and cons I could think of and tried to estimate which side had the balance in its favor. For Yale was the fact that I was already acquainted there, and its general religious tone was nearer to the mild orthodoxy which I held. Anyhow, all great universities have many essentials in common, such as libraries, the spirit of free inquiry, and scholarly methods. I notice, however, that in the expense account for 1892–93 are entries for occasional trips to Boston, tickets for the Boston symphony concerts, and one to hear Paderewski in Music Hall. On one memorable Sunday I heard Phillips Brooks preach. In New Haven I saw Joe Jefferson in *Rip Van Winkle* and heard Adelina Patti sing.

The courses which made the deepest impression upon me were the seminars of Professor George T. Ladd in different semesters, on William James, Otto Pfleiderer, Immanuel Kant, and Arthur Schopenhauer. James's great revolutionary work, *The Principles of Psychology*, opened new doors to the understanding of the human mind. He himself spoke of it as "psychology without a soul," thereby indicating in startling phrase the fact that he had discarded the old, speculative, metaphysical conceptions and had turned to the living stream of everyday experience. He viewed the mind as functioning within an elaborate physical organism and presented in detail the results of the new studies in experimental laboratory research. His book had profound significance for all further inquiries in philosophy and theology. It directed attention to the concrete nature of the self, to the force of human habits, and to new interpretations of the emotions and the will. In place of the traditional mysteries of man's inner life, it made clear the growth of ideas through the functioning of the sense organs and the brain, in relation to things and events of the environment. The wonders of memory and imagination were put into terms of imagery derived from sense perception and the operation of the laws of the association of ideas. From James's *Psychology* sprang new principles for the work of education and for the cultivation of religious behavior. It afforded, so to speak, definite handles by which to take hold of the task of developing and reconstructing all human idealisms.

Study of Kant's philosophy was a major intellectual operation in every way. It was painful and laborious, it uprooted naïve ideas of the customary common-sense view, it refuted the familiar arguments for the existence of God and immortality and for miracles. By making a cleavage between the physical and the spiritual realms, it left science free to pursue its quantative, evolutionary hypotheses and opened an independent overworld of moral and religious values. Above the levels of scientific demonstration it put the objects of faith and the realities discerned by intuition. To many scientists and theologians this seemed a very welcome solution, and not a few sincere individuals felt that in this way they could be genuine scientists and at the same time devout believers in the claims of religion. For great numbers of people who never heard so much as the name of Kant, the popularized statement of his conclusions was accepted as the solution of the long conflict between science and religion. It is still the answer which many distinguished scientists give when called upon to declare their religious faith, although there is scarcely an eminent philosopher today who is willing to agree to this separation of knowledge and faith. My own thought remained for years unsatisfied with this dualism until further explorations in other systems led to quite different interpretations of the nature of human knowledge and religious values. But the experience of following the course of Kant's profound critical and reverent thought was of inestimable worth.

The study of Schopenhauer, the arch pessimist, was almost equally exciting and releasing, but in quite different ways. He not only challenged all my traditional beliefs but attacked the very foundations of all moral and religious values. To him science only served to show more clearly than ordinary experience that the world is evil and life itself tragic and futile. He denied that it is a rational world and cited a surprising amount of evidence in support of his dark thought. Dreams of happiness and of ideal hopes are illusions. Nature lures us on in our innocent and trusting youth by promises which she never fulfils. By the powerful impulse she implants within us, she drives us to endless labor and sacrifice, only to disappoint us in the end. Just a little reflection shows what dupes we are, for we never really possess our lives. We cannot catch any experience. Either it hovers beyond us in the future, or, when we try to seize it, it has become a thing of the past. Men are never satisfied, their hungers are never satiated, and time engulfs their finest achievements. Every person is beset by inordinate ambition, by unfathomable selfishness, and by fears of illness, misfortune, and death. War is the natural state of human beings and of all the lesser orders of life. One species of animal preys upon others for its food, and men fight with one another not merely to gain power or goods but for the joy of battle itself. The deepest character of the world is not reason or intelligence but will, restless, capricious will. The human heart is a bottomless abyss of desire and longing, and these are expressions of the blind will. Reason is like the little lamp which miners wear on their caps to light the depths in which they work. The lamp throws only flickering rays about in the darkness but makes nothing clear. If we could see far ahead into life, we would turn from it in horror. So nature illuminates only a few steps at a time, and those very imperfectly and for her own ends. We are compelled to make the greatest decisions of life, as in the choice of mates and vocations, before we are mature enough to judge and while we are swayed by impulse and illusion.

There is no cure for these evils of life, and the greatest possible wisdom is in seeking escape from them. Suicide is not sufficient. It is only a weak way out. The strong man rises above desire and want and refuses to be drawn into ambition for power or wealth or fame. He recognizes only the simple wants necessary to keep him in existence and contents himself with seeing through the sham and with the contemplation of beauty. He will also be led to some practice of sympathy to help his fellow mortals bear their suffering. For Schopenhauer tragedy is the highest form of literature and music is the highest of the arts, for music is embodied will. It moves restlessly in constant digression and deviation from the keynote, expressing the multifarious efforts of the will. Buddhist saints and Christian ascetics have found the best possible adjustment to this world. They are no longer intrigued by it, and they ask of it as little as possible.

I have always been grateful for that course in Schopenhauer. I am not sure but that every theological student should be required to study him. It has become a deepening conviction with me that the only serious enemy of religion is pessimism, for when a man turns completely sour on life there is no chance to get any leverage on his will or conduct. As I see the religion of Jesus, it makes the love of life central. The problem is to live in such a way that life is good and satisfying in spite of all its pain and defeat. A sane attitude recognizes the imperfections and the trage-dies of our existence, but it also believes that there are satisfactions and fulfilments. Christianity itself has sometimes been too pessi-mistic. It has accepted evils as judgments from heaven when they were only the results of human folly or of events in nature. Or it has meekly submitted to evil conditions, such as the wars and depressions which now afflict the world, without any determined effort to abolish them. Religious faith does not require us to be-lieve that the world is wholly good, but it does, it seems to me, require that we recognize that there are values in life and that they can be increased. Schopenhauer put salt into my optimism. He fla-vored it with a bitter and gritty quality which it is now popular to call realistic. It is a useful quality to supply hardness to the bones and endurance to the moral fibers. I also think he was right in saying that the will as he conceived it is deeper than the intel-lect, if such a contrast can be made. He included in the will the impulses, desires, choices, and sentiments. But he held the will to be capricious, utterly irrational, and fundamentally at war with itself. Hence his pessimism. Psychology has developed in the direction of his voluntarism, not in the direction of his despair.

In the summer of 1893 I visited the World's Fair. That was a kind of answer in my thought to Schopenhauer. Against many adverse conditions, including a business depression, the young city of Chicago had created a dream city of such scope and beauty that it brought the world to its gates and displayed the marvels of a new age of invention, of arts and of communication. The old Field Museum in Jackson Park (later the Museum of Science and Industry), which was the fine arts building of the fair, is an impressive illustration of the architectural grandeur that filled the hundreds of acres along the lake. I also have a peculiar fondness for the pavilion which stood opposite the museum, for there was the Iowa building at the eastern end of the long curving line of the buildings dedicated to the different states of the union.

Richard Watson Gilder did not exaggerate when he wrote of the fair:

> Oh, never as here in the eternal years
>   Hath burst to bloom man's free and soaring spirit,
> Joyous, untrammeled, all untouched by tears
>   And the dark weight of woe it doth inherit.
> Never so swift the mind's imaginings
>   Caught sculptured form, and color. Never before
>
> . . . .
>
>   . . . was such enchanted shore
> Jeweled with ivory palaces like these:
>   By day a miracle, a dream by night;
> Yet real as beauty is, and as the seas.[1]

My promised bride joined me there. We watched the illumination and the fireworks along the lake front and talked about getting married in the fall. When she and her mother went back to Iowa, I lingered with Frank Morgan. He and I had been close since editing the Drake paper together. We "did" the fair more thoroughly, even riding a camel on the Midway Plaisance. But in a few days I had had enough, and something else was on my mind. I wrote *her* on the third of July, setting forth a plan for getting married on the sixth. The morning of the sixth Frank and I arrived at Van Meter. Taking a carriage, we reached the Brick House by noon, and I held a council with my mother-in-law-to-be. Though the matter was very sudden and no preparation had been made, we decided to have the wedding at 8 P.M. With my almost-sister-in-law I drove to the county seat at Adel for the license, and Frank performed the ceremony in the presence of the family. The bride wore her graduating dress, and I my Prince Albert suit. In the house built by her father in pioneering days, where

[1] Richard Watson Gilder, "The Vanishing City," *Five Books of Song* (Boston: Houghton Mifflin Co., 1903), p. 201.

she was born, across the road from his mill and dam, it was the sixth anniversary of the day I had met her there, after three years of college courtship and three more of being engaged.

We left that evening for Des Moines and went the next day to St. Paul. We returned to the Brick House for a summer of relaxation, fishing, and playing tennis with my brothers-in-law (after making a court out of the old hog lot). We addressed a considerable number of invitations for a reception at the house. Friends were entitled to an occasion after missing the wedding of the belle of the countryside. When I went back for one more year of philosophy at Yale (1893–94), I did not go alone.

In the summer of 1894 I was offered a fellowship in philosophy in the University of Chicago, by President Harper, whom I had met through my uncle, Sanford Scribner, who was a member of the board of trustees of the divinity school of the university. The fellowship and the associations this involved had a determining influence on my future. I had begun a Doctor's thesis at Yale which I now finished during the year 1894–95 at Chicago. With Professors James H. Tufts, George H. Mead, and Addison W. Moore (and John Dewey a bit later), I entered another new world of thought, through which I made my way to what has been to me a more satisfying and inspiring view of the world, man, and religion. They did not accept the dualism of Kant or the pessimism of Schopenhauer. They were developing an American school of thought generally known as "pragmatism." But their thought did not lightly conform to any label. It was also known as "radical empiricism" and might have been named "practical idealism." Each of us specialized in a particular field, and it was my good fortune eventually to work in the psychology and philosophy of religion.

During the year 1894–95 in a seminar with Professor Tufts I carefully studied the writings of John Locke, the founder of British empiricism and the fountainhead of many streams of thought. His influence, working through David Hume, woke Kant from his "dogmatic slumber" and elicited Kant's critical answer. But the empiricism of Locke, much modified and developed, to be sure, thrust beyond the criticism of Kant and went on through John Stuart Mill and others to William James and John Dewey.

It was in the study of Locke that I made what was for me a

momentous discovery. As I read the pages of his *Essay on the Human Understanding*, I felt at once a strange sense of something already familiar, and, when I came to his ideas about religion, I saw that they were the ideas taught by Alexander Campbell early in the nineteenth century. There was the idea of the reasonableness of Christianity; there was the doctrine that Christianity magnifies only one article of faith—faith in Jesus as the Messiah, and that a practical faith in his attitude and way of life; there also was the rejection of speculative theological metaphysics, of the doctrine of innate human depravity, and of emotionalism as essential in conversion. Everything was brought to the test of the dry light of reason, but with the broadest tolerance and with an earnest and devout appeal for a vital and practical religion.

I felt a new sense of importance and of historical justification for the faith that was in me from childhood. Here were its main ideas in a great and powerful tradition which had affected every phase of American life. Locke's ideas of democracy shaped the political ideas of Thomas Jefferson; his educational views were practiced by Horace Mann; and his religious ideas were basic in American Unitarianism. Today Locke is recognized as the father of liberalism in all these fields. His significance does not lie in any finished and formulated system of philosophy or of religion. It consists rather in his practical, experimental, and common-sense attitude on all questions which he discussed. It was above all a method, a method of patient and reverent inquiry, and a courageous dismissal of old traditions and superstitions which could not justify themselves in the light of practical reason.

From those days I have seen my work as a teacher and minister of religion in a new and brighter light. It gave me greater confidence in trying to promote religion without creeds, in cultivating a simple, practical kind of faith, with the broadest tolerance, and in experimenting gradually with all matters of organization, of interpretation, of forms of worship, and of methods of religious education. Most of all, it convinced me of the possibility of realizing in many new and fruitful ways the century-old plea of the Disciples for Christian union both in the local congregation and with all religious people of every faith and name.

Chapter v | Chicago, 1896-97

My first real contact with John Dewey was on a very hot September afternoon in 1895 when I faced him, James Rowland Angell, and other professors to take the oral examination for the Ph.D. degree in philosophy. Professor Dewey was just entering upon his engagement as head of the department of philosophy. He was then thirty-five. He had been on vacation in Europe for a year before beginning his work at Chicago. He was of medium height and weight, with heavy brown hair and mustache, and he wore glasses. His manner was deliberate, kindly, and marked by a thoughtful, conversational, questioning attitude. This questioning attitude has always seemed to me an interesting characteristic. Even when lecturing, he was still inquiring, as if weighing his words and ready to make any qualifications which the current of his thought might suggest. This is a provocative and encouraging trait, for it at once elicits intellectual co-operation on the part of the hearers and invites a sense of participation in reflection upon the problem under consideration.

There were no catch questions in the examination, but it was searching enough! My training had been in a very different type of philosophy, the idealism of George T. Ladd at Yale, and I had not then become acquainted with Dewey's point of view. My thesis was "The History of Agnosticism," and, as I later realized, agnosticism and the implied theory of knowledge had little favorable consideration in his thought. It made as little appeal to him as the subject of pessimism. These two subjects never seemed fruitful to him. Matters were made worse for us both by the fact that Professor James H. Tufts, with whom most of my work had been done in my one year at Chicago, was absent. But I had the good fortune to stay on at Chicago as an assistant in the department and thus to have the opportunity to become acquainted with Dewey's thought, although never a student in his classes. But in association with him and other members of the developing "Chicago school" of pragmatism, I found a point of view and a method of thinking which transformed my thought and made philosophy a living, practical way of life.

In Dewey's view, philosophy was not an exercise in abstractions or the pursuit of intellectual luxuries but a method of analysis and criticism for the understanding of real problems and of guidance in their solution. The mind of man is not something apart from his common experience but an aspect of endeavor to control and direct activity to fruitful and significant ends. The subtlest thought and the finest imagination never escape the web of actual life or the patterns of its materials and processes. Dewey made effective application of his ideas in the fields of education and ethics and logic with a freshness and originality that created a new outlook in all these fields. It was a long time before the full force of this philosophy became clear to me, especially in the interpretation of the religious life, for he said little about this subject. That was a field so difficult of access to his empirical method that it must wait until the method had been applied and tested in subjects more open to criticism and reflective reconstruction. Highly emotionalized interests, like religion, become so enveloped in prejudices and conventions that they are less accessible to critical, objective treatment.

My own readjustment in the direction of Dewey's thought was greatly facilitated by teaching elementary courses in psychology in which William James's *Psychology* was the basis of readings and discussions. One of my first classes in the University of Chicago, in the winter of 1896, when I had the beginner's title of *privat docent*, followed that stimulating work. Even my own lack of teaching experience and consequent timidity could not prevent the lively, colorful insights and vivid phrases of that text from making their own impression on the undergraduates. It was not difficult to get up vigorous class discussions over the "stream of consciousness," the nature of the "self," and the novel doctrine of the emotions illustrated by the claim that we are afraid because we run away from the bear, we are sad because we weep, gay because we laugh, angry because we fight. The most worn and abstruse topics, like conception and reasoning, came to life under the magic touch of James's lively style and homely illustrations.

In the same winter quarter, beginning in January, 1896, I taught a class for the Disciples Divinity House, in the divinity school of the university, on the theology of Alexander Campbell. This enabled me to work over again the relation of his thought to that of John Locke, which had so much interested me while I was working on my thesis the previous year. With a class of eight graduate students it was possible to have reports and discussions on various problems. Our excitement ran high, for the "discovery" of the relation between Campbell and Locke gave new meaning to Disciple history and placed it in a stream of thought that was influencing modern science and philosophy with what Locke himself called "a new way of ideas." It was the empirical and pragmatic temper applied in religious matters. This meant not only a lessened emphasis upon traditional theology and speculative metaphysics but a rejection of their assumptions and methods. Like Locke, Campbell also rejected the "inner light" and "enthusiasm" as grounds for religious assurance. Both held to the possibility of revelation, but both insisted that any alleged revelation must be brought to the test of reason. Locke had said, "Whatever God hath revealed is certainly true . . . but whether it be a *divine* revelation or no, reason must judge . . . . So that he that takes away reason to make way for revelation, puts out the light of both . . . . God when he makes the prophet does not unmake the man. He leaves all his faculties in the natural state, to enable him to judge of his inspirations, whether they be of *divine* original or no."[1]

This practical, common-sense, non-theological approach to religion was carried through in the discussion of all doctrines, miracles, the resurrection, the nature of the soul, sin, salvation, and the rest. The central doctrine of the New Testament teaching was the messiahship of Jesus, and the one article of faith was the practical acceptance of that teaching. Such practical faith meant an attitude of loyalty and not a metaphysical, trinitarian dogma. For both Campbell and Locke, Christianity was a layman's faith and

[1] John Locke, *Essay Concerning Human Understanding*, ed. A. C. Fraser (Oxford, 1894), II, 425, 431, 438 (Bk. IV, chap. xviii, § 10; chap. xix, §§ 4, 14).

was not dependent upon ecclesiastical authority. It was democratic, reasonable, tolerant, and subject to revision and reinterpretation. Both accepted and employed the principles of biblical interpretation which have come to be known as higher criticism.

My connection with the Disciples Divinity House involved me in the arduous task of raising ten thousand dollars for the purchase of land near the university and money to pay salaries and current expenses. It was hoped also that funds might be secured for a building and for endowment. The idea of the house seemed important and practicable. The plan was to provide through this institution a center in which Disciple graduates desiring to study for the ministry could be associated while they were pursuing their courses in the divinity school of the university, and one in which they could receive special instruction to fit them for understanding and contributing to the work of the Disciples. At that time the Disciples had no graduate institutions for the training of their ministers, and there was an increasing number of men seeking such training. To found a theological school, or seminary, would require a great amount of money and scholars of recognized distinction. Neither the money nor the scholars were available.

The plan of the house offered a solution, for here at the four-year-old University of Chicago were the faculty, library, and buildings of a divinity school which sought to serve ministerial students of all denominations in a genuinely undenominational spirit. Most of the subjects taught were presented as objectively and as free from theological bias as mathematics or biology. Hebrew, Greek, history, and homiletics could safely enough be learned from Baptist, Presbyterian, or Methodist instructors. Genuine scholarship in all these fields ignored sectarian bias and partisan interests. Students from all denominations sat together in the same classes and received the same instruction. That in itself was an important experience, especially for those interested in the development of a common body of knowledge and an acquaintance with men of various religious backgrounds. Such acquaintance was one requisite for the realization of any vital understanding and real union among men identified with different churches.

The economy of the plan for a house co-operating with the university divinity school was evident. A building serviceable as a dormitory and student center would be sufficient, and therefore a few hundreds of thousands of dollars would enable any denomination to afford its students all the opportunities and facilities which the university had provided at a cost of millions of dollars. President Harper had proposed such a plan for any religious body that desired to undertake it. The Disciples were so situated as to benefit more than other large denominations because they had large numbers of students needing ministerial training, and there were scarcely any Disciple institutions equipped to offer genuine graduate training.

The experience of trying to raise money for this enterprise remains vivid and illuminating after these many years have passed. In the enthusiasm of youth it seemed like a very attractive plan for which people would be glad to contribute the relatively small amount needed. It was as if the Disciples were here offered an investment which would yield a thousand dollars of value for every dollar put into it. A real estate venture or a gold mine in Alaska that offered such returns would be easy to promote. But subscriptions were in very small amounts. Ten or twenty-five dollars was sometimes received where gifts might have been in thousands. There were two or three businessmen in Chicago's Loop who could have done generous things. I said to one of these after an exhausting interview, "Well, I feel sure you could make a gift of several thousands if you would." His frank reply was, "Yes, I'd have the money, if I had the will."

I learned that much big business operates on credit and therefore is continually in debt. This makes a convenient foil against solicitors. One member of a famous State Street firm talked to me with such apparent frankness about the condition of his business, and with so much concern about the uncertainty of its future, that in my youthful innocence I felt impelled to give back his hundred dollars to help save his store from ruin! I am still amazed when walking past that place to see that it continues to operate and to allure the public by its elaborate window displays. But we remain friends and perhaps secretly wonder, when we meet, whether either of us properly understood and sympathized with the big, but so different, venture to which one of us had given measureless anxiety and labor. Here was a slight suggestion of the problem which President Harper faced when he undertook to "catch the imagination" of this great city for the founding of a vast institution of learning.

Chicago was bent upon trade and mighty industrial ventures. The pace was swift. Men would risk money in all kinds of enterprises to make more money, but how could they be expected to appreciate the need for a great university pursuing the intangible ends of science and spiritual interests? One great financier is reported to have said that, when Chicago gets round to it, "She will make culture hum!" That may have meant that the men who are immediately absorbed in business cannot be expected to give their wealth for higher educational and religious causes but will do so, if at all, only when they have retired or died. More plausibly, it might mean that those who have inherited wealth and have leisure are more likely to endow the "higher" life. Certain it is that only a pittance of what might be given is really given for schools and churches. In most cases these causes get just the crumbs, and most of these crumbs are from the *poor* man's table! At least, so it seemed then. Subsequently, men of wealth have been more generous toward churches.

Sometimes persons took pity on me for my devotion to the task of trying to raise funds. One man offered me a remunerative job as a salesman for a publishing house. Some real friendships grew out of this work. One was with Mr. Henry H. Honore, the father of Mrs. Potter Palmer. He was then an old man, but he held his gay and buoyant spirit and maintained the gracious courtesy and fastidious dress of his more prosperous years. He was a Disciple from the days of his youth in Kentucky, and he kept his religious loyalty through all the changes of fortune. He introduced me to many of his friends and helped to arrange luncheons and meetings on behalf of the project. The last time I met him was on Michigan Avenue, near Monroe Street, where he had lived in an elegant home before the great Chicago fire. He recounted incidents of our associations and of his early Chicago days when he was interested in many enterprises of the booming city. He was then over ninety. With a wave of his hand and a hearty chuckle, he said, "Oh well, I've made three fortunes and lost 'em." I never saw him depressed in spirit or bitter against the world. His cheerfulness was a good tonic for all who knew him, and his pleasure in the success of other people was much the same as if it had been his own.

Mr. John Gunzenhauser was another friend whom I made by trying to get him to give money for the Disciples Divinity House. He came from a very different background. He had come to Chicago as an immigrant from Germany when he was a boy. He loved to tell how he had begun as a day laborer on the streets, receiving a dollar a day for work with his pick and shovel, and how he always saved a little from his wages. From his savings he was able to buy a little land. This he sold in a short time at a profit and then was able to make a larger investment. This process he kept up in the rapidly growing young city until he counted himself among the millionaires. He was greatly devoted to the new religious faith he had found in America among the Disciples. He talked most entertainingly, in his broken English, of the "plea" they had taught him, and he was a faithful attendant upon the services of the local church in Batavia, Illinois. He could argue the "plea" with zest and shrewdness, but he never persuaded himself by his ready talk into any generous financial support of his convictions. On one occasion, at a luncheon in the interest of the House, when he had spoken about it with great enthusiasm and had raised our hopes that he would start a wave of giving by making a donation of some thousands of dollars, he concluded his stirring speech with a subscription of fifty dollars!

Mr. Gunzenhauser owned much of the land on which the city of Gary was built when the United States Steel Corporation located its huge plant there. He greatly needed the help of his friend, Mr. D. M. Hillis, a lawyer, in clearing title to the land. Mr. Hillis was the only person who knew the history of the case and could give the necessary evidence. When Mr. Gunzenhauser asked for the amount of his fee, Mr. Hillis said he would not take a fee but suggested that he would be glad if Mr. Gunzenhauser would make a gift to the House, of which Mr. Hillis was a trustee. Mr. Gunzenhauser then gave two hundred dollars.

Mr. Hillis showed himself a friend in another instance when he advised a client to make a will leaving half his estate to the Chicago Y.M.C.A. and half to the Disciples Divinity House. This the client did, and the sum expected to come to the house was about sixty thousand dollars. The Y.M.C.A. was beneficiary to the same amount, but neither institution received anything because of the dissipation of the estate. That was one of my first great disappointments in financial matters. The prospect of something substantial toward establishing the house seemed so well assured that its complete failure was a hard blow. With the hope that Disciples in other cities might have more money and more generosity toward our educational enterprise, which was really national in its scope, I went to churches in different states and finally to New York City. There for several weeks I supplied the pulpit of the Central Church, where Dr. B. B. Tyler had just completed a long pastorate.

In this year of my first teaching and of strenuous efforts to raise money for the Disciples Divinity House, I also went on Sundays to preach for a mission church in Evanston, Illinois. Evanston was an old and well-settled suburban city, the seat of Northwestern University and a stronghold of Methodism. There were also well-established Presbyterian, Congregational, and Baptist churches. A nucleus of Disciples, however, desired a church of their own. An evangelistic meeting was held in this old, wealthy suburb, and thirty or forty persons were brought together by it. Naturally, most of the settled residents interested in religion were already identified with one or another of the large, attractive churches of the older denominations. The mission therefore gathered its converts from the less organized and relatively underprivileged people on the edge of town and "across the tracks." They represented a great variety of human beings and came from very diverse religious backgrounds. Few of them had been acquainted with one another before, and they lacked common doctrines and ideas of church organization and procedure. Of course we met in a hall, on the second floor, above a store on the main street. The hall was heated by one large coal stove, and the seats were kitchen chairs. Kerosene lamps hung from the ceiling. The pulpit was a plain reading desk on a high stage at one end of the room. It was difficult, under these conditions, to develop much feeling of intimacy between the pulpit and the pew! My records show that I delivered sermons on "Perfection," on "The Importance of Small Things," and, on a Sunday in June, "The Voices of Flowers"; but also there were sermons on Christian union and on various phases of the social gospel.

As the year went on, new people came and joined the church. A spirit of loyalty and devotion grew, until there came to be, even in that bare, unattractive hall, something of a religious atmosphere and fellowship that warmed our hearts and strengthened our religious faith. There were skeptics and doubters within and without the church as to the wisdom of its beginning and as to the possibility of its maintenance and growth. Many Disciples passed it by because it was on the wrong side of town or because it did not have the appeal of numbers and wealth. By their standards it was a failure from the start, but it has never seemed to me so easy to determine the success or failure of a church by those standards. Certainly that little church touched many lives, and it gave opportunity for self-expression and leadership in a worthy cause to some who would have had no such experience in a large and flourishing church.

I could have stayed on in Chicago, teaching, raising money, and preaching for the mission, but the remuneration from all three kinds of work was very small and some of it quite uncertain. The greatest disadvantage, however, was the distraction of doing three kinds of things in lines so different. One or two offers of pastorates came to me and were given careful consideration, but when Butler College gave me an opportunity to teach, with no other responsibilities, its attractiveness outweighed all others. Just after my acceptance of the chair of philosophy at Butler, I learned that President Harper had been trying to reach me, when I was out of the city, with an offer of a more permanent and more remunerative appointment in the University of Chicago.

When I next saw him, he told me of the plan he had for me but said a friend of mine, with whom he had talked a few days previously, had told him that I had already accepted the Butler position. It was one of those interesting situations in which a very slight circumstance might have changed the course of my life. A delay of one day in wiring acceptance of the Butler offer might have led to my remaining in Chicago, and if my work had gone on in Chicago at that time it would have been in philosophy and a minor administrative post.

More than once the shifts of fortune have made me wonder what the outcome "might have been" under other circumstances than those which obtained. The possibilities are often plainly numerous, and the course actually followed appears as but one of many. It is out of such situations that the idea of fate or providence or luck or choice arises. Sometimes the "decision" seems voluntary and rationally determined; sometimes it seems to issue from conditions beyond conscious control. Fortunately for me, the choice made was no cause for regret. One great advantage was to have the responsibility of just one job, and to have it in the line of philosophy for which my interest was keen. It had already become clear that teaching a subject to others is one of the best ways of clarifying it for oneself. Both sides of the desk have their peculiar intellectual stimulus and opportunity. The teacher's side takes one through a field of study in a more active and better-organized manner than is generally the case with the student's side.

Chapter vi | Teaching at Butler

Butler College was situated in the beautiful suburb of Irvington, just east of Indianapolis. The community had grown up around the college and was notable for its atmosphere of educational and religious interests. But it was near enough to the city to secure urban advantages without the distractions of living in the midst of the noise and pressure of a crowded center. It was a good place to find oneself, to try out—through reading, writing, and class discussions—the various schools of philosophy, and to review with young, inquiring minds the problems raised by psychology, ethics, logic, and the history of philosophy. It would be a new experience to feel responsible for only one role to play, and that the role of a teacher of philosophy; to be able to go to church and sit in a pew; and to let other persons think about the financial cares of the educational and religious institutions. There might even be a novel and refreshing experience in meeting different kinds of people without trying either to save their souls or to get them to give their money for a cause. It was with real enthusiasm that I joined the faculty of Butler College.

In the autumn of 1897 I began teaching there as professor of philosophy and education. Education had been combined with philosophy by my predecessor, and therefore the same combination of subjects fell to me. This situation illustrates one of the difficulties of the small college. The student body was too small and the resources of the college too limited to justify full professorships in both fields, though salaries in those days were not large. I received twelve hundred and fifty dollars per year, which had to suffice for the family of two, and later for a family of three.

Butler College was founded by the Disciples of Christ in 1850, and began instruction in 1855. Its charter provided for coeducation, which at that time was something of a novelty in American colleges. The institution was organized on the plan of a stock company as a means of inaugurating it, and many persons took shares of the stock, hoping that the investment would ultimately yield some financial return. This fact throws light on the limited views of the work of a college in the early days of this country, but it also reveals the conviction, or at least the hope, that the desire for higher education would be so great and so widespread that the tuition would more than pay expenses. It was nearly fifty years before the stock company was dissolved and the college reorganized.

I was one of several young and more or less inexperienced teachers who joined the faculty in 1897. We found a very hearty welcome on the part of the older professors, some of whom had been with the college almost from its beginning. They were mostly men of the classical tradition, teaching ancient and modern languages, literature, history, and mathematics. They had high standards of scholarship for themselves and for the college. Indianapolis was a city with a taste for culture. Its public schools were rated among the finest in the country and supplied an excellent body of college students each year.

The other source of students was the church of the Disciples, numerically strong in the state of Indiana. Shortly before 1897 the churches had been disturbed by the religious instruction in the college. Professor Garvin was the center of the storm. He had ventured upon doctrines conflicting with the historical views of the Disciples. The college held to freedom of thought and teaching for its professor but was finally led to allow him to retire, though many of his students withdrew from the college and from the denomination. Dr. Jabez Hall, a man of culture and irenic spirit who had for many years been pastor of a church in Cleveland, was called to the chair of religious instruction and exerted a unifying influence between the college and the church constituency.

My own first taste of charges of heresy came almost at once

upon my entrance into the faculty, though it came from outside the college and the state. I had published in the *Christian Quarterly* an article entitled "A New Epoch among the Disciples," in which I had set forth the significance of higher criticism and the doctrine of evolution for the teaching and work of the Disciples. A veteran professor in Bethany College published long articles in the widely circulated orthodox paper of the denomination, the *Christian Standard,* charging me with infidelity and pantheism and disloyalty to the cause. But for some reason, perhaps because I was a mere professor of philosophy or because the college and the churches in Indiana were weary of controversies, no disturbance occurred in my relations. The incident, however, made a lasting impression upon me. It impressed me with the marked difference between having the freedom of a tolerant academic position, teaching a subject like philosophy, as compared with teaching or preaching religion under the constraints of a conservative constituency.

My work in the field of education drew me into contact with teachers' institutes and other public meetings where I appeared simply in the role of a teacher and where no religious questions arose. I remember vividly the elation I felt on the occasion of a lecture I gave to the teachers of a neighboring county-seat town. I felt that we were there in a common, public interest which was not limited by any religious differences or conservatism, that we were all open-minded and perfectly free to find out facts and to consider methods of work, new or old, in terms of their reasonableness and practical value. The journey home on the train that night was strangely happy. I felt that I had found my way into an open world where we were dealing with vitally important human problems simply in the light of the best knowledge and experience available. We were not conscious of any censors spying on us; there was no body of sacrosanct tradition or authoritative word to which we had to defer. We might be mistaken about many things, but in an enterprise like that of education we had a right to make mistakes if they were made in efforts to find better ideas and systems of work, and if we were willing to recognize the mistakes when found and to do what we could to correct them. This attitude brought the zest and incentive of genuine responsibility. Whatever his task, an individual is in an entirely different frame of mind when he to some extent makes his own plans for a task and executes those plans with a watchful and serious eye as to their value and further possibilities.

This experience was one of those arresting and fruitful events that sometimes occur in the depths of a man's inner life and give direction to his future in surprising ways. It gave me a clear feeling of the contrast between the two worlds with which I had been most engaged, the religious world as a preacher sees it and the secular world of philosophy and education as a philosopher sees it. Perhaps I should say as he *feels* the contrast, for I am trying to give an account of two worlds as they appeared to me from the inside. The minister's world had always seemed to me more or less prescribed. The truths he should know were largely *given*, given in revelation and weighted with divine and unquestionable authority. He was expected to be deferential and receptive to this body of truth, not because he could judge of its value for himself or because it was to be measured by its fruits. Whenever he ventured to question customary ideas and practices, he was likely to be met with uplifted hands of surprise, or fear, on the part of those accustomed to accede to established forms and beliefs. As a minister, it was also incumbent upon him to be careful of his example and influence regarding other people, especially the young. If he were not ever so careful, the smallest deviation from conventional ways might become license and wild revolt among the young and the weak. This burden of correctness and propriety was heavy upon my youthful soul and for a long time prevented me from deciding to be a minister at all.

The other world in which I had begun to live, especially through the study of philosophy and psychology, was a natural and free world, where all things could be looked at and inquired about and in some sense made to justify themselves to the mind of man. Here were free winds of doctrine, open spaces of adventure, the trails of pioneers of thought and action over the mountains of fear and discouragement, into fertile valleys. Such philosophy had been nourished by the rapidly developing sciences, which were gaining power and courage through their own achievements.

William James was the first great, free, courageous, scientific mind I had encountered. His breath-taking, innovating assertions and assumptions filled me with amazement. The force of many of the questions he put up for discussion, or put down in his books with an air of assurance, may have now lost something of their force through familiarity, but they are still startling enough for most people, especially those people who are not addicted to scientific research and philosophical speculations. Some of his phrases and titles were: "Psychology without a Soul," "Does Consciousness Exist?" "A Finite God," "A Pluralistic Universe," "The Will To Believe," "We do not weep because we are sorry, but we are sorry because we weep," "Moral Equivalent for War," "The Varieties of Religious Experience."

The impact of such an original and daring thinker upon a questing and susceptible youth was at once alarming and reassuring. It was alarming in so far as it unsettled with rapid shocks the traditional conception of the soul of man, the common idea of God, and the ordinarily accepted conception of human nature as ruled by a rigid determinism. It was reassuring because it was a view of the world and man which threw off the claims of any external authority, looked at the facts of everyday experience and respected them, and gave a simple account of truths which could be easily verified.

If a man got lost in the woods and then began to form a plan about finding his way home, how could he know whether his idea, his plan, was true? He might examine the idea itself for a long time as to its consistency within itself, or he might try to remember how it conformed to what he had been taught about the geography of his location; but after he had estimated directions by noticing on which side of the trees the moss grew, or the direction of the prevailing wind and the water current in the stream at his feet, there would always remain just one final and conclusive test of the truth of his idea. That would be to act on it, and to move in the direction which it suggested. If he arrived home, he would know the idea was right. If he did not, he would know the idea was wrong.

It was a pragmatic philosophy. It led James to believe that many ideas received from the past are simply useless and superfluous. Men have been imposed upon by them and have wasted energy and patience in argument about them. Unfounded ideas may have been so long accepted that they inhibit us from even testing them.

They are so widely believed and so honored that few have the courage to question them. Such ideas may beget dark fears or generate fantastic fantasies that unnerve the mind for action or fill it with impractical dreams and delusions.

James's doctrine of the self was a helpful means to enable me to understand my own experience. One self in me had been formed in childhood on the pattern of the society to which I had belonged. It had been shaped to a rather reasonable kind of piety, but this self was too sheltered in the traditional ideas. It was too docile, too timid, too respectful toward the past and toward religious authority. It was a ministerial self of great wishes and emotions, but too much inclined to believe that it was more important to preach and exemplify the proffered message of religion than to examine, test, translate, and experiment to see whether it would work effectively in making religion a really useful and powerful agency in conquering the world, the flesh, and the devil.

The other self in me was a newer acquisition, largely developed after graduation from the divinity school. It was the result of studies in new fields of science, in a new environment, and in contacts with exceptional, stimulating scholars and books. This self looked out upon a different scene. It was the scene of an evolving human race endeavoring through adventures and experiments in all directions to find its way into better conditions and fuller understanding of the meaning and destiny of its life. Here the highest wisdom was the recorded deeds and reflections of individuals and societies who had invented tools, refined language, fought wars of conquest, sailed the seas, penetrated the wilderness, sung songs of love and heroism and beauty, and celebrated the longings, atonements, and aspirations of the blundering yet ever renewed and outreaching human heart. That was a thrilling scene. There were confusion and tragedy enough, but there was no general and complete surrender or despair. Nature patiently sent forth new recruits into the front lines, suffered delay by disasters, rebellion, indifference, selfishness, stupidity, and treachery, but continually renewed the attack with a dauntless will to live. Such was the story of history, of religion, of science, and of art.

Out of this realization of two selves brought face to face there emerged the idea of the possibility of bringing them together in mutual understanding. Why should not the free, experimenting self of the scientific and philosophical bent frankly join with the religious self and apply intelligence, criticism, and experimentation to the interpretation and furtherance of religion? And why should not the idealistic, aspiring self of religious faith, hope, and love make a friendly alliance with common sense and the most refined knowledge? If it was so stirring an experience to stand out on the common ground of the natural process of education and to search in the work of ordinary teachers and pupils for means and methods of improvement, might it not also be possible to get below the surface claims of religion and work there also by native intelligence and by growing skill and insight? Why should not the genuine values of religion as well as of education be taken for what they are and dealt with in the same spirit and with the same gradual fruitfulness?

It might be a difficult thing to maintain the attitude and the procedure of naturalness in religion, where it was so customary to assume that a minister must feel that he was divinely called to his office, that he had the advantage of using an inspired body of literature, and that he might constantly have recourse to prayer for direction and encouragement. But if he could look upon himself as the teacher looks upon himself, then perhaps he would also be looked upon by others as engaged in a normal and reasonable enterprise for which he did not claim or desire some mysterious, exceptional gift of power. At least the ministerial self could thus come to understanding with itself and have a certain inner consistency with itself, no matter what judgments of pity or patronizing sympathy or disdain the worldly wise and enlightened people might cherish.

The position of professor of philosophy and education in the college for three years gave this new self opportunity to become somewhat formed and seasoned. A happy and valuable experience during this period of teaching was that of doing some work in the biological laboratory. I am convinced that it would be advantageous to many college professors to take a course every year with some colleague in another department. I was drawn to biology by problems arising in psychology, and also by questions growing out of the conception of evolution. I was fortunate in being encouraged by Professor Bruner, who had recently received his Ph.D. degree at Freiburg, Germany, in biology and had been called to the department of biology in Butler College. He arranged for me to have time at my convenience in his laboratory, and helped me learn to manipulate a complicated microscope and to recognize some of the numerous and marvelous things in a drop of drinking water or of water taken from a stagnant pond.

I found the amoeba one of the most interesting inhabitants of this microscopic world, partly because it is so relatively simple in its structure and functions. It is a cell of protoplasm, with no shell around it and with no limbs or sense organs. Floating in the water, it lives what appears to be the most hazardous existence. Its body is about one one-hundredth of an inch in diameter. When it comes in contact with some tiny substance, it either accepts or rejects it. If agreeable, the amoeba thrusts out its body in what are called "false feet" in an effort to surround and inclose the object within itself. If successful, it assimilates its prey and absorbs it into itself. Other one-celled animals, protozoa like the paramecium, show a slightly higher organization, having a rudimentary nervous organization, their delicate fibrils acting as conductors of stimuli to a common center through which movements of the organism are co-ordinated.

In these amateurish, elementary observations I caught little glimpses of an amazing microscopic world in which an endless variety of forms appear with their ceaseless processes of searching for food, escaping enemies, and reproducing their kind. The amazement and delight of being introduced to these marvels of the common things all around us, in every drop of water and every grain of dust, were accompanied by equal astonishment at the ingenuity and patience of the scientists themselves who had discovered and interpreted these wonders. Not less exciting was the growing realization of the relation in which these minute, simple forms stand to the ascending animal series, including man. What a pity, it seemed to me, that so many students go on, one college generation after another, spending all or most of their time on the so-called classical subjects, without the slightest awareness of these interesting and illuminating fields of the natural sciences.

For myself there arose a hope of finding some day the time and opportunity to pursue these studies further. Who has not made resolutions toward a favorable future day when he would satisfy some awakened hunger to know more about flowers, birds, fishes, crystals, atoms, or stars? What a pity that we have not always had survey courses for all students! Nowhere more than in college may one realize the unavoidable limitations of the individual's ability to be informed about all the important things of life. Yet he might have at least the wider vision. Already in the free and energetic days of youth he must follow a selected path out of the innumerable paths which open around him. It is perhaps a kindly compensation that each one is likely soon to be convinced that his own chosen subject is the most important, at least for him, and it is also a lesson which should be learned in youth that each person must accept the fact that he plays a small role in the total drama of nature and of society, yet that these little parts together do make the larger drama.

The college had chapel exercises every day, and there was something about this assembly of faculty and students, uniting daily in songs, readings, prayers, and short talks, that built morale and college spirit. Perhaps there was more enthusiasm in these assemblies when athletic teams were to be pepped up or when they returned as victors from the games, but the sight of the student body on any day as we teachers looked upon it from the platform symbolized one of the most important and heartening scenes to be found in human life. Here were hundreds of youths trying to catch up with the learning which the long history of the race had achieved, so that they might get a start on their own careers with the advantage of knowledge of the past. Here were plastic, formative lives, responsive to the best their instructors offered, the tools and the history of culture, and the morals and ideals slowly shaped through centuries of experience and criticism.

At one of these chapel hours when the academic year drew toward its close, the professor of mathematics was introduced to make a farewell talk to his students and colleagues. He had been on the faculty thirty-five years. The teaching of mathematics is not conducive to oratory, but I have remembered clearly the main thing he said, speaking simply out of his own experience. He said that what had impressed him most in all his lifetime in the college was the fact that every year a new group of students entered in the freshman class seeking an education. He might have said it was like successive waves of humanity moving up to the training camp of life. Nothing can give a more vivid sense of the inexhaustible resources of the human race than these thousands, even hundreds of thousands, of youth in the colleges over the earth, marching on in the cause of truth, of useful work, and in appreciation of unfathomed possibilities. They come with the natural optimism of youth, with eagerness and unworn interest, with lofty idealism and eager confidence that they may gain the best that life affords.

Chapter vii | The Hyde Park Church

For the summer of 1900 I was invited to give some courses in philosophy in the University of Chicago, and thus I renewed my old associations. There was no thought of anything more than that one term. During the summer, however, the Hyde Park Church of the Disciples of Christ found itself without a pastor and invited me to the position. It was a complete surprise to me and at first seemed quite impossible. I had enjoyed the life and work at Butler College for three years. I had begun to think of myself as a teacher, concentrating on the subjects of my special interest with students, and on further studies of my own. As I have indicated, freedom in the selection of courses to be given, of problems to be searched out for oneself, and the privilege of speaking a little more as an independent person, if only before classes of susceptible students in a sequestered classroom, bring genuine and legitimate satisfactions to a young college instructor.

But the ministry was not far afield from my interest. In the ten years that had passed since graduation from college, I had been more or less a minister, filling short pastorates, supplying pulpits, and teaching in a church college. Evidently I had not come to be thought of as entirely outside the ministry, or the Hyde Park Church would not have invited me to become its pastor.

When I accepted the invitation I had no idea that there would ever be any opportunity or encouragement for me to teach philosophy in the University of Chicago. I emphasize this because the course of events has been such that it is natural for those who do not know the facts and my reasons for coming to the pastorate to assume that it was the university which primarily attracted me.

It would be only human to interpret the situation that way. The university was very large, and the church was very small. Teaching philosophy in a great institution like this would be something to excite the ambition of a young man out of all proportion to any appeal a pastorate could make under the most favorable circumstances.

And when the church was practically still a mission, belonging to a denomination little known to the city or to its immediate neighborhood, it would be almost inevitable to assume that the university and not the church was the first consideration. That the truth was otherwise happens to be one of those things which is clear and weighty in a man's own knowledge and feeling about himself and difficult, if not impossible, for other people to believe. Subsequent events make it all the harder for people to believe, since, as a matter of fact, so much of my life has been bound up from that very first year with the teaching of philosophy.

My colleagues at Butler experienced the same perplexity and I fear shared the same misunderstanding. They imagined that I felt some dissatisfaction with the college or with the administration, but that was not the case. I had three reasons for making the change. I had always liked the city of Chicago. From childhood I had been familiar with it through frequent visits when I came with my mother to see her sister and her three brothers who lived on the west side in the neighborhood of Ashland Avenue and Jackson Boulevard. The Scribners and the Vaughans lived comfortably, were good Baptists, and had a hearty way of making their small-town relatives enjoy the warmth of genuine hospitality. They showed us the sights of the city, the great stores, the parks with polar bears and monkeys in them, and the endlessly fascinating Lake Michigan, mainly significant to a small boy as an opportunity for excursions. This appeal of the city of Chicago never has diminished but has grown with the growth of the city.

The second reason for coming was the associations already formed in the church and the community during the three years from 1894 to 1897 when I was a graduate student and a teacher, and a promoter of the Disciples Divinity House. I was a charter member of this church and was present at its first services. Dr. Herbert L. Willett and Professor W. D. MacClintock were the moving spirits in initiating the organization. Dr. Willett was the minister, and Professor MacClintock had been on the faculty of the university from its beginning in 1892. No church could have been more fortunate in such leadership. Their friendship and assured co-operation were guarantees of the necessary wisdom and the spiritual qualities for a free and vital church in such a community. They were patient in listening to my sermons, which had neither the grace nor the substance of the preaching each of them could do, and they taught me many lessons and afforded me no end of encouragement. There were also many other old friends in the circle, with the same loyalty and devotion, whose invitation indicated real possibilities for a church, though the total number was small and the community already well churched as these matters are judged today.

The third reason for accepting this urgent call was the conviction on the part of many that here was an opportunity to carry forward the development of a Disciple church in the larger tradition of the Disciples, with awareness of the need for interpreting religion in keeping with the spirit of a new age of thought, and in recognition of the outlook and manner of life in a great and rising city. This third incentive may have been the deepest and the most fruitful for a long term of years, as it would probably have been thought the least significant by many people. The force of this appeal in my own thinking was based upon the religious influence of my father and family and upon studies in philosophy while preparing a thesis for the Doctorate.

As a boy in a minister's home, I received the impression that the Disciples constituted a new and very important religious movement which would appeal to all right-minded persons if they could only know about it and try it out. As I became acquainted with a wider circle of Disciple ministers, teachers, and laymen, I continued to hear this conviction asserted. The claims for this "plea" were then in terms of its conformity to the teaching of the New Testament. The chief stress fell on the conditions of salvation, and it was uniformly pointed out that there were three or four steps involved in the conversions recorded in the New Testament. "Faith, repentance, confession, and baptism," were the steps into the church and into the kingdom of heaven. It was said to be important that baptism be by immersion. When outsiders inquired what were the distinctive teachings of the Disciples, the ready

answer everywhere was: baptism by immersion, the weekly observance of the communion, the absence of any creed of the traditional sort, and emphasis upon personal devotion to Christ rather
than any theological interpretation of his nature—and all this as a
possible basis for the union of Protestants in one grand fellowship.
This dream of Christian union was the one big motivating cause,
for it was felt that if the churches were really united upon a
simple scriptural basis Christianity would rapidly convert and
save the whole world. Obviously no one denomination was strong
enough to accomplish so vast a task, and not all the churches could
compass it so long as they were divided and quarreling among
themselves.

After several years at Yale, where Disciples were scarcely
known by name and very seldom seen in the flesh, something had
begun to happen to my childhood view of religion in general and
of my own in particular. If these ideas, so familiar and so divinely
authoritative to me, were unknown to the learned professors and
unconvincing to them when stated, were they really so important
and so demonstrable as I had been led to think? The criticisms of
Professor George Park Fisher on my paper at Yale concerning
Christian union grew upon me with further studies and contacts
with other teachers and students. I could not doubt their sincerity
or their scholarship. Having been told as a boy, especially by my
older brother, that I was a "stubborn fellow," I began to wonder
whether I was just holding on to certain ideas because they had
been my own convictions and because it was hard to change them
and particularly to admit the change. I sometimes felt that I was
regarded by classmates as a rather naïve protagonist of a provincial
sect. But I was not ready to give up easily the position set forth
in my advocacy of union. The doubt thus awakened grew under
various influences of the university life, until it was superseded by
other convictions with deeper foundations and more constructive
implications. There emerged some tokens of greater maturity as it
became apparent that students were encouraged to investigate subjects for themselves and to reach their own conclusions, whether
agreeing with the professors or not. It finally became clear to me
at Yale that theological and other professors were to be respect-
fully heard but their opinions weighed, for even they were not infallible or immune from criticism in their most settled doctrines.

For several years after Yale I went along in my old religious affiliations, while ranging as widely as I could in psychology and philosophy and watching the varied religious scene with genuine but somewhat detached interest. Then at length I made what was for me the eventful discovery to which I have alluded, the discovery that there was back of the body of ideas and attitudes of the Disciples a very important and respectable philosophical interpretation of man and religion. It was a protest against the old ways of thought that underlie scholasticism and all the creeds of Protestantism. It was the philosophy of empiricism which began to emerge with the Renaissance and developed into a very influential modern school of thought. It was that philosophy which gave me a new interest in religion and attracted me to accept the Chicago pastorate, where the conditions seemed favorable to make the experiment of applying in the most concrete and intimate way this larger conception of the religious faith of the Disciples of Christ. The very conception of religion involved in this new way of ideas offered a release from the old creeds and the sectarian divisions which they supported. It gave promise of genuine union for local churches within themselves and in their relation to churches of other names.

The six-year-old congregation of the Hyde Park Church, with less than a hundred members, already conscious of a broader outlook than was characteristic of the average Disciple church and in the freer air of its community, offered an inviting field for a long-time practical test of the faith that was in me. The location of the little brick building, through the co-operation of the Disciples Divinity House, which owned the land, made it conspicuous. Any success here would be far-reaching; any failure would be pathetic and perhaps ridiculous. Those who saw only the exterior of that diminutive, queer-shaped structure, so near the great halls of the university, were often amused. They called it many odd names, perhaps sometimes in derision but more often in surprise and perplexity. They called it the "'cheese box," the "mousetrap," the "'Frank Lloyd Wright Chapel" (for one of his architect-imitators had designed it). The interior was better than the outside promised. Though equipped with opera chairs, it had a warmth and attractiveness greatly appreciated by the small congregation. There were three little side rooms which lent themselves to a marvelous variety of uses as classrooms, or as dressing rooms for baptisms or dramatics. One was also a kitchen, and the larger one at the back, shut off on occasion by folding doors, was the library, committee room, and meeting place for the women's societies, the Society of Christian Endeavor, and the mid-week prayer meeting. But most suprising of all was the way in which the main part of the church could be transformed for church dinners, bazaars, and parties. The chairs were piled high in the wings, and for dinners the long, plain board tables were brought out of storage from the basement, their homeliness covered up with borrowed tablecloths and flowers. The whole procedure made occasion for friendly co-operation, especially the use of the opera chairs at dinners. The art of sitting straight up to a table in a chair that slants back is something in itself, but there was also fun in getting several persons to learn to adjust themselves in a row of such chairs fastened firmly together. If one person wanted to get in or out of his seat, all the others had to move with him, and if anyone wanted to hitch up closer to the table, all the others had to do the same. These things were conducive to democracy and to good fellowship. Rich and poor, wise and simple, met on a common level on weekday occasions as well as on Sunday morning. Of course some people couldn't "take it," and therefore that building, as well as the preaching, had a selective function and was a real test of devotion and loyalty to the cause. The church was better on the inside than on the outside, but some people never quite see or feel the inside of things.

Of course the church had a debt on its building. That was a kind of orthodox thing which we had to plan to outgrow as soon as possible. It sometimes seems as if the debts of churches are in direct proportion to their orthodoxy! It was partly the grueling experience with that debt on the building that kept up our determination not to have any debt on the new building and to balance all budgets each year. The financial strength of the church was very limited, and it was a generous undertaking to pay a salary of eighteen hundred dollars. This amount was paid by the end of the first year only by my accepting at face value a note for three hundred dollars from a mining promoter who was never able to pay it, though the note did "save face" for all of us. At that time there was no indication that the church ever would have much financial strength.

One of the first enterprises after my accepting the pastorate in October, 1900, was the printing of a weekly calendar for the church. It began with the first Sunday in 1901. On the first page were the names of the officers. Charles R. Wakeley was one of the deacons, and he is the only one of the whole number who is still living and a member of the church. Dr. Willett was one of the four elders. Mrs. Wakeley was the church clerk and reported 132 members, of whom 25 were absent. Since there were no funds to bear the cost of the calendar, an advertisement was secured for the back page from a laundry on Lake Park Avenue. This was justified on the ground that it covered the expense and also among ourselves by the saying that cleanliness is next to godliness! Professor MacClintock, who was one of the elders, gave lectures on Wednesday evenings for which an admission fee was charged, for the benefit of the church. Each week there were news items and comments. One of the comments was on the question raised by some journal as to whether the churches would survive through this twentieth century. Perhaps religion would be "a spiritual force working through literature and art, but without the familiar institutional forms." In any case it was predicted that religion would be more rational, more united, and more Christian.

We were all impressed by the fact that we were at the beginning of a new century. The *Christian Century*, at that time a Disciple paper, had changed its name from the *Christian Oracle*. In the third issue of the calendar was a quotation from William DeWitt Hyde, president of Bowdoin College, on "New Century Ideals."[1] Some of the ideals were:

To weigh the material in the scales of the personal, and measure life by the standard of love; to prize health as contagious happiness, wealth as potential service, reputation as latent influence, learning for the light it can shed, power for the help it can give; to choose in each case what is best as a whole, and accept cheerfully incidental evils involved; to crowd out fear by devotion to duty, and see present and future as one.

The first poem to appear in the calendar was by Dr. J. H. Garrison, entitled "What We Stand For." It was used for many years

[1] Taken from *Outlook*, January 5, 1901.

at the masthead of the *Christian Evangelist,* of which he was the editor. Two of the stanzas are as follows:

> For the Christ of Galilee,
> For the truth which makes men free,
> For the bond of unity
> Which makes God's children one.
>
> For the faith against tradition,
> For the truth 'gainst superstition,
> For the hope whose glad fruition
> Our waiting eyes shall see.

From its beginning the church contributed generously to foreign missions. The presence of missionaries on furlough to study in the university gave personal contacts which helped to clarify the understanding of modern missions of the educational and practical type. It has always seemed to me that a missionary spirit is as natural to religion as it is to education, to politics, and to business. All these interests advertise themselves and press their values into the farthest corners of the earth. Religion deals with the sharable goods of life, and it is a genuine, human impulse to offer to others what one has found good for oneself, especially when sharing it with others increases his share and theirs. Wisdom, beauty, and goodwill grow as they are diffused. Mr. H. H. Guy, from Japan, was one of the first missionaries to bring to the church the idea that missionary work, rightly interpreted, is an exchange of world cultures, in which Christians may learn from Buddhists as well as Buddhists from Christians.

It was difficult to develop an entirely satisfactory order of service in the circumstances in which we had to work in that little building. We had an old-fashioned reed organ, but we usually had an organist sufficiently superior to the instrument to compensate greatly. The names of the singers in the mixed quartet changed often in the first years, but they were always the best we could get. For a period we had a vesper service at 5:30 on Sunday and had the good fortune to secure the services of Albert E. Boroff, bass soloist of Sinai Temple.

The sermon subjects did not begin to appear in the printed announcements until several months after the order of service was given, but when the subjects began to be included they were indicative of the minister's interest in the nature of religion. The first subject was "Personal Religion," then "The Creed for To-day," then "How We Use the Bible"; the next was "The Minister's Message," followed by, "What Is Salvation?" The sermons were undoubtedly of more importance to the minister himself than to anyone else, for they were attempts to formulate his ideas and convictions about religion into a working set of principles to guide his own thought and work. There were two reasons why so much theological and philosophical preaching did not do the church more harm. One reason was that, however important the sermons are to the preacher himself, he is likely to exaggerate their value for the life of the church. The great historic churches give little prominence to sermons. They develop and maintain their religion by dramatic, ritualistic services, by music and symbolism, and by the human associations and idealisms that envelop all religious institutions. In a small Protestant church the same larger and deeper currents of life are active in the unadorned services and especially in the friendships, practical enterprises, education of children, and contact of personalities. Probably sermons are not much better followed by the average person than are lectures on politics or science. The sermon contributes to the religious feeling if it is a message vital to the minister. Something of his conviction and emotion radiates to his hearers, and it is important that he have ideas which carry conviction and emotion. He must be prepared to have someone notice his ideas, but for the most part his hearers will not be too exacting.

The Disciples of Christ organized their first church in Chicago in 1849, and in 1900 twenty-two churches and six missions were represented in the Chicago Christian Missionary Society. The local congregations were known as Christian churches or Churches of Christ, and they were all quite of the traditional, orthodox Disciple pattern. They were not equipped with buildings or leadership suited to the city, and their ministers, coming from smaller cities and towns, were, with one or two exceptions, soon discouraged by the church problems of the city and withdrew to more congenial fields.

Other denominations in Hyde Park were represented by ministers who rose to eminence in their communions. Frank Crane was minister of the Hyde Park Methodist Church, Bishop Page was at

St. Paul's Episcopal Church, Dr. Jackson at the Hyde Park Baptist Church, Dr. Vance at the Presbyterian church, F. E. Dewhurst at the Congregational church, Dr. Fenn at the Unitarian church for a short time before he was called to a professorship at Harvard University. Dr. Gunsaulus was preaching in the Auditorium Theater downtown. The Christian Scientists had no church in the city, and Alexander Dowie was just beginning to build his Zion. The University of Chicago was still in its first decade, with perhaps half a dozen buildings but with President Harper projecting his miracle of modern educational enterprise.

The experience of going to the Hyde Park Church of the Disciples of Christ, under the circumstances which I have related, was a decisive event in my life. I have never had any regrets about it. On the contrary, I have been deeply grateful, and especially grateful for the comradeships and satisfactions that have followed from it. The thought of it gives me a profound sense of reverence for the ways we have been led. It gives new meaning to that old hymn:

> O God, our help in ages past,
> Our hope for years to come,
> Our shelter from the stormy blast,
> And our eternal home.

Chapter viii | Liberating Religion

        The habit of deciding on a topic for the sermon ten days in advance of its delivery, for announcement in the calendar, was cultivated as much for the minister as for the people. I had often found that, unless a subject was decided upon and definitely announced, there was a danger of spending more time in selecting a theme than in preparing the sermon. It was surprising to discover that subjects could be formulated a week before the sermons were to be delivered much more easily than two or three days before. There was much less worry and anxiety in choosing subjects when their discussion was not too imminent. And it was interesting to find that a better sermon would come from a poor text thought about for days than from a good text hastily treated. When the theme was once in print for all to see, it became a kind of magnet in the mind which drew to itself related ideas from reading, from conversation, and from reverie and reflection.

        I do not believe in a subconscious mind, but I do think something goes on in the fringes of the main stream of consciousness and in moments of relaxed attention. Involuntary mental activities often carry on the patterns and the interests of the periods of concentration. Probably no one gets the most out of his mind except in moments of intense, conscious effort. Such moments need to be supplemented by others of relative detachment. Sometimes the most original and fruitful association of ideas comes when the censor is off duty. One should not be too tense in the game of thinking any more than in playing golf. Those who do creative

work of any kind, however much they may labor to gather information and to order their thoughts, find that their best insights
and discoveries are likely to come when the mind is receptive and
seemingly passive. If one is ever to be inspired, it is apparently at
such times, providing only that serious and competent work has
already been done.

I came to the Hyde Park Church with the conviction that religion should be intelligent and that it was important to have ideas
about important religious matters which could be clearly stated
and circulated. Some years of teaching philosophy would partly
account for this conviction, but it was also partly due to the influence of a transition period when religion was subjected to
searching criticism, and the old doctrines were being shaken to
their depths. If the word "ideology" for a system of ideas had
been in vogue, I would say I was seeking a religious ideology for
myself and for any who would think with me. I did not want a
theology. I disliked the word, and my religious training had
taught me that theology was not necessary and might be dangerous, because it suggested dogmas that churches required people to
believe whether the dogmas made sense or not. But an ideology—
a body of ideas concerning important matters—that was another
matter. To my outlook upon religion it was desirable to have
ideas, but to keep them subject to revision and not to impose them
upon others. I was willing enough that other people should know
what these ideas were. In fact, I had a genuine missionary zeal
about them and therefore proceeded very soon to print sermons
as a means of offering these ideas for consideration to anyone who
might be interested.

My first printed sermon was "A Personal Confession of Faith,"
in June, 1902. It emphasized the standpoint from which I proposed to work as a minister. It particularly stressed the desire not
to be thought to represent a "devitalized orthodoxy." Then, too,
I wanted it to be understood that this would be a free pulpit, that
the denomination to which I belonged had discarded creeds, encouraged individual liberty, and taught that characteristic religious experiences, like conversion, are capable of rational statement and have their true significance in ethical and practical life.

I was excited about the doctrine of evolution. I said the religion
of the Hebrews, like that of other peoples, began in nature wor-

ship. The Scriptures contain the records of their religious evolution. These records are not faultless or infallible. I said I believed that the process of evolution continues in the church today and that Christians are inspired in the same way, whatever the degree, as were the men of old. Salvation is the conscious participation by thought and deed in this boundless, holy life, rather than the escape from the consequences of original sin and the fall of man. It is won as the soul ripens in knowledge of the sciences, in appreciation of the arts, but above all in faithfulness to the elemental and instinctive relationships of life. Salvation is ethical. It means developed character. It is a life process and signifies the realization of the natural powers of the soul. I believe that heaven is this participation in the divine life and that it may be enjoyed here and now. I believe that hell is the failure to attain this realization of one's powers. No one believes any longer in a hell of literal fire, but everyone has seen men suffering the tortures of hell through perverted desires or ignorance or wasted opportunities or stupid selfishness. I believe that there are two essential conditions of salvation, faith and repentance. Faith is the recognition of the ideal; repentance is the adjustment to it. I believe that Jesus Christ is the proper object of faith because his words and example inspire men to the highest spiritual life.

I confess that for myself I take little interest in the doctrines of the trinity, the pre-existence of Christ, the virgin birth, the miracles, the substitutionary atonement. My faith in Christ does not depend upon these things, nor do I feel obliged to accept them because I accept him. His life and words stand on their own merits without the need of artificial supports. I believe that there are two lines of evidence for the supremacy of Christ in religion which do appeal to modern minds. One is the portrait of him as a teacher and inspirer of men, given in the gospels. The other is the influence which he has exerted on a large part of the race for two thousand years. I believe that the church is essential to the salvation of the world, but not because it was founded by Christ. The redemption of men is a social as well as a religious problem, and it therefore requires a social institution. All the great, persistent interests of humanity embody themselves in social organizations. The church is a natural product of the religious life. It is only a means to an end. The same principle applies to the ordinances.

Many people are saved without them, and many people are lost in spite of having observed them.

I believe that all churches are essentially Christian and that people are being saved in all of them, though the environment may be more favorable in some than in others. I believe in the work of world-wide missions. It is the duty of every man who possesses spiritual truth to give his neighbor the opportunity to share it. I believe that the church should everywhere ally itself with other social institutions, such as the public school, organized charities, social reforms, and the various instruments of culture. The church still suffers from its long association with ascetic ideals and does not yet quite know how to make itself at home on the earth and in the present life.

The conclusion of that sermon was this: Finally, I believe that Christianity is entering upon the profoundest transformation it has experienced since it came in contact with Greek thought in the second century of its history. No one who grasps the meaning of these tendencies can doubt that the outcome will be advantageous to religion. It will be freed from many encumbrances, purified from practices no longer beneficial, and enabled to exalt with unparalleled energy the spiritual and ethical ideals of Christ. The watchword of the future church will be that of the prophet Micah: "What doth the Lord require of thee, but to do justly, and to love mercy, and to walk humbly with thy God?" (Mic. 6:8). Its supreme command will be that of Christ: "Thou shalt love the Lord thy God with all thy heart, and with all thy soul, and with all thy mind, and with all thy strength. . . . Thou shalt love thy neighbor as thyself" (Mark 12:30–31).

I have given these excerpts from that personal confession of faith proclaimed in June, 1902, because it was a kind of declaration of the platform on which I intended my ministry to proceed. It was also an attempt to let the congregation know what to expect and doubtless was partly motivated by the hope that it would attract to the church persons of like views. It was this sermon, or one of the same kind, which astonished a visitor so much that she exclaimed to one of the members afterward: "Well, what do you think of that?" The member replied, "Oh, I don't know. It doesn't hurt me, and it does him so much good to say it!" A deacon, who had been worrying about the outcome from the moment he saw the subject announced, said to me, "It wasn't as bad as I feared it would be." Another said: "That was not new to me. I thought things out that way when I was a boy plowing corn on the farm down in Indiana."

These remarks give some indication of the tolerance with which such views were received and perhaps suggest some lack of excitement in the pews over what was so keenly exciting to the pulpit. Strangely enough, this attitude of patience, intimating at times a degree of indifference to such doctrinal sermons, had a more restraining effect upon the minister than outright opposition would have had. In this instance at least, a pacifist spirit, whatever its cause, had the effect of tempering the aggressiveness and belligerence of the minister.

I dislike to think to what extremes the minister might have been irritated by conservative elders and deacons. I gratefully remember the understanding sympathy, if not always complete intellectual agreement, which was accorded me by the leaders of the congregation, W. D. MacClintock, Herbert L. Willett, and Oliver W. Stewart. They knew that good Disciple churches never required theological commitments from their ministers but stressed freedom of interpretation for all members on all theological matters. Their one most significant loyalty was to the spirit and teaching of Jesus.

In that confession of faith I had touched lightly upon a subject which was to become the focus of attention both in the local church and in the denomination at large. That was the subject of immersion. Was it essential to the Christian life and to church membership? I had said, "I believe that the various denominations are nearer together than they themselves realize and that they should heartily recognize the Christian character of every other and seek a closer fellowship, and they would immeasurably further the kingdom of God by ignoring their differences and fraternizing with each other by giving and receiving (church) letters."

Six months later I preached and printed another sermon, "Christian Union and the Disciples." I reviewed the long advocacy of union by the Disciples and pointed out many influences in modern society that strengthen their claims for the need and the possibility of union. We were experiencing a new social consciousness which was modifying the old religious individualism. A new interpretation of the Bible under the influence of modern biblical scholarship had removed the legalistic and authoritarian text proofs upon which immersionists had relied, and the beginning of church federation was offering a practical plan of action.

Conservative Disciples were sharply challenged by the federation movement. To hold aloof from it contradicted their plea for union, but to participate in federation with other religious bodies would be a recognition of the Christian status of those bodies. The liberal leaders of the Disciples worked for federation movements on the ground that no denomination was called upon to do more than to participate in such practical activities as all approved. But conservatives and liberals alike saw that church federation meant the recognition that members of other churches were Christians and that for Disciples to engage wholeheartedly in federation meant a breaking down of exclusiveness and ultimately the facing of the question of the importance of baptism and the form of its administration.

I had long been convinced that the Disciples were destined to modify their insistence upon immersion as a condition of membership in the local church. In my college days I had asked a veteran editor of a religious journal how he reconciled insistence upon such scrupulous care about the ordinance of baptism and such freedom about the ordinance of the communion, for the Disciples had always practiced open communion. His reply surprised me, for I knew he was conservative and regarded as a very "safe" man. He said, "That is a question the Disciples will have to face."

Before 1900 there had been at least two instances of Disciple churches receiving persons into fellowship without immersion. One was the Cedar Avenue Church in Cleveland, of which Harry Cooley was the minister and Mayor Tom Johnson a member. The other was a church in New York City of which James M. Philputt was minister. Those instances passed away with a change of ministers and left only a memory. But they will continue to be cherished as evidence that, before a century of Disciple history had elapsed, new possibilities were at hand for the fulfilment of the dream of practical Christian union within the local congregations of the body which had had the will and the courage to go beyond

Protestantism and its divisions to the free faith wherein all could unite.

The practice of making baptism by immersion optional with those who wished to join the church was not adopted in the Hyde Park Church at once. It was undertaken first as an experiment, a social and religious experiment. The idea of experimentation in matters of religion was something of a novelty itself. The prevailing idea in Protestantism had been that the important items of organization and procedure in the church had been prescribed either by the Scriptures or by decrees of councils. Even churches of the congregational type, such as the Baptist and Congregationalist, usually deferred to custom or to the action of associations.

The Disciples carried the independence of the local church still further and conceived it to have final authority in practical matters like employing ministers and paying salaries, in church architecture, and in methods of missionary work. They already allowed the utmost freedom of opinion to individual members. There were pronounced differences among ministers as well as among laymen on doctrines, including miracles, the atonement, the manner of inspiration, future punishment, and the trinity. Some held unitarian views, but since practical loyalty to Christ was the basic bond of fellowship it was not essential that persons should be brought to conformity to any speculative dogma about the trinity, and there was a general disposition to consider co-operation and fellowship more important than any intellectual formulation of belief.

For the first time in the history of the controversy between Arians and Athanasians, unitarians and trinitarians, the whole discussion was minimized and other solutions of the problem proposed. It was seen that there was the possibility of loyalty to Christ without becoming entangled in the old dilemma. It was as if at last Christian people had begun to say, "We will not try to solve our religious difficulties by mathematics, choosing between one and three. We will cultivate another kind of relationship, one that belongs to the quality of love and affection. We will say that it is important to see the person and work of Christ in terms of the greatest possible devotion."

But what is it that awakens the fullest human devotion? Is it the idea that a supernatural being comes into the human world and is protected by an inherent immunity from the sin and evil of the world? Or is it more appealing to think that a genuine mortal, tempted in all points like the rest, succeeded in living a life that awakens the admiration and devotion of the best men in all the ages? This is the moral measure of greatness, and it requires no such metaphysical presuppositions as traditional theology has taught.

Let me quote what I was to write later:

> My experience as a student and as a teacher of philosophy had brought me to regard religion as a natural growth in human life, and as subject generally to slow and unconscious changes in the prevailing culture. The success of the physical sciences through the use of experiment and the consequent modification of their ideas and procedure was being duplicated in the biological sciences, and the suggestion naturally followed that the social sciences might utilize the method of experiment in various institutions. Experiments were being made in education, such as Dewey's Laboratory School in our neighborhood; in social settlements, as in Hull-House under Jane Addams; in politics and industry and in the arts. Why not in religion?[1]

Here then was a vital experiment, an experiment to determine whether fruitful efforts could be made in modification of the most sensitive doctrines without breaking the bonds of peace and fellowship. Certain groups had made different creeds the basis of communion, but no group had ever before endeavored to comprehend persons of all creeds within the fellowship of local congregations. But this experiment contemplated also the introduction of a system which would gain the values that come from the comprehension of differences, not by suppression but by free expression.

Every denomination tends to become partial and highly specialized: the Methodist too emotional, the Quaker too quietistic, the Episcopalian too ritualistic, the Presbyterian too theological, the Congregationalist too tolerant, the Baptist too legalistic, the Disciple too textual or too formless. All the older denominations continue traits inherited from the Old World. Many of them were

[1] "Theory in Practice," in *Contemporary American Theology: Theological Autobiographies* (2d ser.), ed. Vergilius Ferm (New York: Round Table Press, 1933), p. 5.

crowded in the soil where they first grew and were warped by their environment. Some were state churches and still bear the marks of aristocratic and governmental alliance. Some were products of protest and persecution.

In America there has been no restraint upon their growth and the cultivation of their characteristic traits, except the influence of the New World itself and of the interaction of these groups among themselves. Here in America, for the first time, Christianity has come under the influence of a democratic society. In a land of free elections and of frequently changing administrations, all kinds of authority and power are more often subjected to criticism and modification. Government is empirical and open to revision, and the same comes to be true of religion. Certainly it is true that nowhere so much as in America have the results of critical studies of the Scriptures, of science, and of church history been so promptly and vigorously brought to bear upon old conceptions of religion. Ministerial education in the seminaries and religious education in the churches are striking illustrations of this fact.

The experiment of receiving unimmersed persons into our church was carried through several stages. The first year it was called "associate membership"; for several years it was designated as "membership in the congregation"; and it was sixteen years before the final action was taken to abolish all such distinctions and welcome all persons into full membership upon their own terms, providing only they were in sympathy with the church and ready to co-operate in its work. A person could join our church with a letter from any denomination or simply by "confession of faith," which meant believing in the ideal of Jesus and wanting to follow his way of life—with or without baptism. That was left to preference.

Here seemed to be the basis for a union of all churches. It might be called union by declaration. It would overcome the splitting up of Christendom which has resulted from the claims of various bodies to have the only beliefs and rites leading to salvation. What is needed is an interpretation and practice of religion to bring all religious people together, not only tolerating differences but using them to vitalize religious life. A free church can have no exclusive creed and no limitation as to who can join it among any who sincerely want to belong to it and work with it. That there never has been uniformity of belief on all points in any creed is well known, and such agreement is psychologically impossible.

In our church the experiment of open membership has proved successful. It has brought people into its fellowship. It has elicited generous financial support. Most important of all, it has given the minister and the members a sense of integrity and peace within themselves. In this local church there is felt to be a living demonstration of Christian union, not in the sense of having converted all the members to one view of Christianity but rather in the sense of enabling men and women of different backgrounds, temperament, taste, and needs to associate together in the finest good will and devotion. The experiment has been a success also in the fact that the congregation has held its place within the Disciples of Christ. It has participated in missionary and educational enterprises and has received all the recognition and responsibility in denominational affairs that could be desired. By this very fact of its acceptance in the denomination the experiment in terms of its membership becomes more than a local matter. Other congregations were soon stimulated to make the same venture into the actual practice of Christian union, and the influence of the idea began to be really established.

Interestingly enough, this radical innovation never created any tension or division in our congregation. Very little talk about it was heard among ourselves. The principles were so clear and so in accordance with any reasonable issue of Disciple history that the plan commended itself without argument or opposition. Criticism from outside had no disturbing effect inside but did help to make known the idea.

In other denominations the lack of interest at the beginning of this century in the cause of baptism is sufficient indication that here is not what Christian union depends on. All Protestant churches, except the Baptist, would receive persons by any mode of baptism. Yet these churches had their rivalries and their conflicts, and they lacked any urgent desire to be united or any sense of religious duty to promote union. But the awakening social conscience and the realization that churches could scarcely cope with their common problems even if they were all united led to the federation movement, which has slowly gathered momentum and effective methods of work.

I wonder sometimes, as I look back upon it, why I was so interested and so absorbed in the work of a little congregation in the big and uncaring city. There were about eighty active members when I came in 1900. Money was not abundant. There seemed no reasonable hope that in a lifetime much could be accomplished. I could have given my time to teaching, and apparently no one would have blamed me or much regretted it. No one will ever be able to prove that I did the best thing or that something else might have been better. That is an interesting but rather fruitless reflection upon the past. When you face the future, there are always numerous possibilities, but, when you look back, you really see only the way you have come. Your fancy may build out others of those possibilities into marvelous achievements, but you probably do not see all the developments any one of the other possibilities would have had. You do not feel the worries, the anxieties, the temptations, the burdens of any other than the way you took. When the going is hard, there is a tendency for the roads you did not take to be lighted by fancy and smoothed down into rosy paths.

But there is also a lovely work of the mind going on concerning the experiences actually had. The mind forgets much. I do not mean simply that it cannot retain all the details of the days with their cares and discouragements. I mean also that the wholesome mind, with a kind of instinct to cherish the pleasing and the refreshing memories, turns away from the drab and the painful aspects and holds on to the things from which may be derived some feeling of achievement or some material for humor or some lessons on life itself. Often, with Paul, I have realized the foolishness of preaching, but also with him I have felt a strange impending woe if I did not carry on. At least rare joy and comfort have come to me as a minister in the sense of having some part in cultivating a reasonable faith that binds the members of one church together.

It has been a real joy to see this church grow from its very beginnings. There has always been a wonderful co-operation from Disciples who believed the Disciples were meant for liberal and progressive religion, but my greatest gratitude has been for those from many denominations who have responded to the liberal ideas of this pulpit and have entered into and exemplified so generously the effort to achieve a visible demonstration of real Christian union, in spirit and in fact. Others have come into the church without previous church membership. They have entered into its fellowship with earnestness and devotion. Thus, from many directions and from many types of experience, the members have here entered into the intimate relationships of religion and have dedicated themselves to the highest and the loveliest things in life.

without previous church membership. They have entered into its
entered into the intimate relationships of religion and have dedicated themselves to the highest and the loveliest things in life.

Chapter ix | The Psychology of Religion

As I have said, I came to the pastorate of the
Hyde Park Church in 1900 without any plan or purpose to teach
in the university. But almost immediately the needs of the department of philosophy made it convenient to ask me to teach some
of the elementary courses, as I had done before going to Butler
College. I taught mainly sections in ethics and psychology at first,
and with no definite appointment beyond one quarter at a time.
It was not long, however, until an appointment was offered me as
instructor in philosophy, to give two-thirds of the amount of
work done by regular instructors. The teaching was to my liking;
the older men in the department, Professors John Dewey and
J. H. Tufts, were friendly and encouraging; and the remuneration, though nominal, was important to me. Just how we survived
the first years with the expenses of a household with four infant
children, some severe illnesses and operations, and all the rest, is
one of those factual mysteries which scarcely seem possible even
after living through them!

At that time the department of philosophy included psychology
and education, and I gave every year one or more beginning
courses in psychology. I generally followed the lines of the *Psychology* of William James and continued to appreciate how he
brought psychology alive, both by his fresh material and by his
fascinating style. It was truly said that he made psychology as
interesting as fiction; yet he stuck to the facts of familiar experience and of scientific method. Even now, after more than forty
years since it was published, there is no better way for the novice
to get into the subject than by reading his *Briefer Course*.

When the three departments of philosophy, psychology, and education branched off in their organization, I continued for some years to teach psychology, but in 1905 I offered for the first time a course in the psychology of religion. This was an academic innovation, not only in the University of Chicago. Psychologists were occupied with what they called "pure" psychology, and their interests were more in the new fields of physiological and experimental psychology. They were then shy even of social psychology and were quite content to have that left to the department of philosophy, where Professor George H. Mead carried it to famous results. The subject of religion has always been pretty exclusively left to theological schools, and they have not often had the resources or the inclination to treat it from the standpoint of the sciences. The scientists, on their side, have let religion quite alone, as something sacrosanct to theologians or too vague and intangible for scientific treatment. It was probably the work of William James in his Gifford Lectures at Edinburgh, *The Varieties of Religious Experience*, in 1902, which gave academic respectability to the psychology of religion. The subtitle of that work was *A Study in Human Nature*.

My own enthusiasm in this direction was greatly deepened by new books just then appearing which threw light not only on the early stages of the Greeks and Hebrews but upon the aborigines of Australia, Africa, America, and islands of the sea like Borneo. I have said of my book:

> *The Psychology of Religious Experience* was the outcome of several years' work influenced by the new studies of Hall, Starbuck and Coe, dealing with conversion, and the illuminating studies in social psychology by Mead and Thomas among my associates, and by such social psychologists as Durkheim, Lévy-Bruhl, and their followers. Rich materials were becoming available from anthropological studies by men like Spencer and Gillen, Howitt and Rivers, and from investigations of primitive religion by Frazer, Robertson Smith, Marett, Crawley, Cornford, Jane Harrison, and others.[1]

It became apparent that religion had undergone change and evolution along with all other aspects of life and that some valid principles could be seen throughout the varied cultures of the

[1] "Theory in Practice," in *Contemporary American Theology: Theological Autobiographies* (2d ser.), ed. Vergilius Ferm (New York: Round Table Press, 1933), pp. 4-5.

world. One of these principles was that the objects with which religions were most concerned were objects that held, or had held, places of highest importance in the life of the people. Often these objects were of economic importance, as in the case of cattle for the Greeks and of sheep for the Hebrews, but sometimes they were objects which became important through association and consequent symbolism. It is possible to see religious value or sacredness accruing to wheat and wine as the Hebrews gave up their nomadic life and became tillers of the soil and keepers of vineyards.

Another principle throughout the religions of mankind is the enactment of ceremonials at the times and occasions when the sacred objects are most in attention, as at seedtime and harvest, at birth and death. Then men celebrate and perform ceremonials which not only are symbolic and dramatic but also are felt to have effects in controlling nature and in satisfying human needs. These ceremonials are largely magical; that is, they do not depend upon any clear conception of natural causes which produce the desired effects, but depend rather upon routine performances which are customary and traditional. For example, the prayers employed in the ceremonials are usually expressions of simple wishes in forms of words which are believed to have power in themselves to compel compliance. Such naïve belief in mysterious words and gestures is superstitious because it is not based upon verified knowledge or upon sufficiently tested experience. Magic and superstition may often be seen also in so-called civilized communities. To direct a thought against another person with the desire to injure him, and with no other means of influencing him, is an attempt at magic. To believe that the star under which a man is born determines his history and career is superstition. Magic and superstition persist in the higher religions to an amazing extent, and they persist even more stubbornly in the world of sports and in common life.

It is more important to see that the psychological principles mentioned may be exemplified in sane and practical forms of religion. The ceremonial celebration of the life and teaching of Jesus at Christmastime is religious for every one who considers his words and spirit worthy of being cherished as a cure for the social ills and unhappiness of the world. To use Christian ideas and atti-

tudes against selfishness and war is not magic if they are embodied
in laws and institutions and educational procedures. Nor are they
superstitious when they have been tested in many instances. In
both primitive and civilized religion there is devotion to something regarded as vitally important. In the higher religions the
sacred things are the human values to which the good life is devoted, such as love, intelligence, and practical techniques. So far
as these are really cultivated, magic and superstition are outgrown.
Love and wisdom may be presented in beautiful celebrations
which move the imagination, release the emotions, and impel
people to make them powerful in life. To see the qualities of love
and wisdom embodied in symbolic personalities like Jesus gives
them greater appeal for many people and makes them more effective against the evils of life.

One may also see in this account of religions among all peoples
of the world, savage and civilized, the meaning of the idea of
God. The gods are the objects upon which life seems to depend.
Among the Egyptians the river Nile was God because from its
waters came life for the soil and sustenance for animals and men.
Each great God had lesser gods or spirits about him which were
revered and celebrated for the particular functions they performed. In many countries, as in Greece, the mighty power was
identified with an animal such as the bull or the ram. In the course
of time the sacred animal became partially human, and the god
was transformed. He then appeared with the body of a man wear-
ing the skin and head of the sacred beast. Even when the god was
quite completely humanized in appearance, the animal traits and
names were still applied to him. The sheep was deified by the
early Hebrews, and their great feast of the Passover has continued
for ages in partaking of the paschal lamb and the appropiation of
his divine powers. The same continuity of symbols appears in the
Christian religion, which exalts the Lamb of God, or, to make the
meaning clearer, what might be called the Lamb-God.

There is an interesting problem in psychology in this development and transformation of the Christian deity. Devout Christians
cherish the imagery of the sheepfold, of the gentle lamb, and of
the ceremony of the symbolic eating of the flesh and drinking of
the blood of the Lamb of God in the Holy Communion, but they
shrink from frankly facing the humble origin and the historic

continuity of the symbolism. One task which religious people may find in the history and psychology of their religion is that of developing a generous understanding of the fact that ideas and values of the highest importance may be wrought from the humblest and simplest patterns of experience. Many refined persons cannot endure participation in the communion, because their attention is arrested at the level of the idea of the literal act of eating flesh and drinking blood.

How do enlightened people manage to do such a thing? They must know the history of the ceremony and its unbroken continuity from primitive practice. The answer is that they have carried on the transformation to the inner and spiritual meaning which Jesus himself stated. Many of the difficulties in the spread of Christianity arise from the crude orthodox use of terms in their literal and materialistic sense. Jesus wanted to lift his followers to appreciation of reverencing God in "spirit and in truth." He did not deny the old sacrificial usages or their value in their time. He recognized their place and function in the cruder stages, but he sought to attain a higher level. Many who see that the spirit and truth of the personality of Jesus belong to his mind and heart still insist upon wrapping that mind and heart in a mantle of the old animal form. Otherwise there would be no meaning in their contention about the virgin birth or the physical resurrection. In this surviving conception of Jesus from the material, bodily standpoint arises also the insistence upon the importance of considering him to be entirely unique and the exclusive channel of truth and moral wisdom. But in so far as he represents the spirit and the truth which are essential to the good life, he shares with all other spiritual and wise men those attitudes and ideas which are of supreme importance.

Of course it was not my concern to make practical applications like this in the classroom. I scrupulously avoided doing so. But it was necessary in my own mind to remember the bearings of these studies upon the practice of religion, for every week I had to come back to the pulpit and speak to understanding people. Here was needed something more than classroom analysis and academic generalizations. A minister has to face facts if anyone does. He has to answer questions of people who want to know the answers for very real reasons. Parents want to know what to tell their children. Those in bereavement want to know what comfort there is for their broken hearts. Young men, pressed in the hard competitions of life, are anxious to learn how they may work at their jobs and be Christians. Sick folks want to know why a lingering illness comes upon them or upon their families. Is it because God is angry with them? Why do they seem to be singled out for such suffering when some mean and immoral people bear no apparent punishment for their sins?

I had a rare opportunity one day to realize how puzzling my double life of teaching and preaching could be for some people. Miss Elena Landázuri, a musician and artistic soul whose home had been from birth in Mexico City, came into my class in the psychology of religion. One day she waited after class to speak to me. Her mother was a Roman Catholic, and her father, whose views she favored, was a free thinker. In her somewhat hesitant English she said, "They tell me you are the minister of a church in this neighborhood." "Yes," I said. Thinking for a moment of what she had been hearing in class and trying at the same time to think what a minister's mind is supposed to be like, she said, "And so you are a minister. Well then, I may become a nun!" Perhaps it is also a real part of this story that she later joined my church and afterward, upon her return to Mexico, entered the Catholic church, which she has served very faithfully ever since.

The study of the psychology of religion, especially with the help of social psychology, threw light upon the state of religion in the United States. Here some two hundred denominations and cults subject individuals to a confusing variety of faiths. In isolated primitive cultures a person seldom escapes the patterns of his group. He accepts without question the customs and the faith of his ancestors. But in a free society like ours he may be confronted with widely varying faiths, each one making its appeal for his co-operation. The demand to understand and weigh their doctrines and claims is no easy thing, and often results in the individual's giving up his inherited faith without finding another to which he can commit himself. Ancestral beliefs never were a matter of reasoned and critical conviction but were childhood and adolescent emotional fixations. So new teachings tend to lack power of persuasion and depth of appeal, even for Americans reared in a Protestant group. Their scientific training and social contacts carry them away from familiar dogmas, yet supply nothing commanding in their place.

It has become a conviction with me that psychology may in the long run do much to change the conception of the fundamental nature of the religious life, which, on the whole, is now too generally made a matter of doctrine. It is too intellectual. At the doors of most churches one is met by required beliefs in a particular conception of God, in a speculative theory about the divinity of Christ, definite ideas concerning sin and salvation, the efficacy of ordinances, and the claims of supernatural revelation. What people are really seeking is access to refreshing fountains of life, sources of strength and guidance. They crave association with people and institutions which may convey to them a sense of what is most worthwhile in life and what may furnish impulsion toward real and enduring values. They know pretty well what those values are when allowed to let their own deepest desires express themselves. They want health, security, friendship, knowledge, justice, beauty, homes and happy children, work and its fair rewards, and the promise of a better society for the generations to come. Appreciation of these values and the willingness to work for them, against whatever obstacles, are sufficient tokens of the religious life. Wholehearted devotion to them is the acceptable service of God. Reverence for such values is the essence of piety. Each man's station in life and his relations to other people set the frame of his duties and opportunities. By his faithfulness to these his character is measured and his satisfactions wrought out.

Religious ceremonials have an important part in the religious life. They unite a group, whether a kinship tribe or a voluntary congregation. Sitting together in council, marching in processionals, eating a feast or a symbolic meal, facing the same ordeals and trials, experiencing the common joys and ecstasies of life, the members of a group share experiences, have the same hopes and vision, and undergo kindred emotions. The movements and fortunes of the group are the substance of the individual lives. The language they speak together, the signs and gestures they exchange, weld them into a living whole. The faces in the circle around the fire or around the table provide conditions through which each one feels the currents of a pervasive life. Without such a group, whether large or small, the individual feels himself cut off and lost. Expulsion from his group is the heaviest penalty that can be imposed. Ostracism from all human associations is the description of hell; it is the outer darkness where there is wailing and gnashing of teeth. Despair over the loss of one's social status is the index as to how important that status is for the normal self-feeling of a person. This interrelation of a man's inner world of the self and of the enveloping world of people and things is a key to the understanding of the religious life. The ceremonials gather all members into a united body and pervade them with a common spirit.

Here is a very real meaning of God. He is that other and larger self in which each little self lives and moves and has its being. That larger being which is God comes close in upon a man through the immediate circle of family or friends with which he is so thoroughly bound up that he is not fully conscious of it until the bond is disrupted and broken. And that encompassing life reaches out into wider circles through neighbors and fellow human beings, through ancestors and through countless persons who make up the world of people, living and dead, whose deeds and spirit constitute the deep soil from which his own soul has been molded and enriched. Not to be aware, however vaguely, of that great cloud of spirits through whom one has his language, moral judgments, and the profoundest incentives is to lack an essential condition of being a real human being. The ceremonials carry the magnitudes of the ages and quicken the sense of the vast life which sustains every soul.

Even the so-called physical environment enters into the reality of the self. Just as a person comes to depend, strangely enough, upon the familiar objects of his house, the scenes of the street where he lives and the city where he dwells, so also the stars above him and the seasons of nature make an order of the world through which he feels himself at home and integrated in life. Even the weather affects the personality. Few people feel as comfortable in themselves through a stretch of cloudy, stormy days as in sunshine and in warmth. In such reflections as these psychology discovers the real living self and its relation to that indescribably great other self with which each individual is bound up. It is a deadly mistake to think of these psychological experiences as merely subjective and without meaning for the universe or for some understanding of God himself. God is more often lost to our understanding and appreciation by setting him off from ourselves in another order of reality than he is by sensing him as the encompassing relations of our immediately intimate self and of the farthest ranges of perceived and imagined existence involved in our own reality and activity.

It is upon such lines of thought that I have answered for myself many of the puzzling questions that appear in the experiences of the mystics. All religions from the lowest to the highest are mystical in the sense of being full of the sense of mystery and wonder. But instead of being unusual and exceptional, mystical qualities are characteristic and common. The elation we feel in meeting old friends after long absence or the thrill and awe that may sweep through us any day at sight of the sunset or of the stars still holding their ancient places in the depths of space are mystical. The smile of recognition on a baby's face or the morning greeting of a friend may move us to tenderness and patience for a whole day. The mystics cultivate such moods. They read the deeper meanings and linger with them, where other mortals hurry along and wait for no illumination. It is strange how matter-of-fact and unseeing many people can be in the midst of unending marvels of beauty and mystery about their feet; the expanse of the lake, the lights of the Outer Drive, the skyline of the city's tall towers, the colorful shop windows, the Salvation Army lassies and Santa Claus on the crowded streets days and nights before Christmas. Not only are the colorful, sensuous effects arresting, but still more so are the thoughts these familiar things may awaken. The lake is kept clean and clear by its ceaseless motion; the lights belong to the triumph of man against the old night of darkness; the tall towers existed first in some dreaming minds; the Salvation Army lassies are here because General William Booth once had a mighty impulse to make the religion of Jesus Christ effective in the most needy places of the world, such as Whitechapel in London, where you see his monument. It marks his challenge to the crime and misery of the slums of all the cities of the world.

Religion tends to make a man's mind work like that. It sensitizes him to the mystery and strangeness of ordinary things, invites him to look beneath their surface, and habituates him to the poetry in the plain facts of life. It is somewhat disconcerting that religion does not more often develop this normal, rewarding mystical experience. It might well be cultivated in place of many hard doctrinal arguments and fervid moralizations. Most of the sayings of Jesus have this mystical quality, and their meaning is doubtless frequently missed because his interpreters do not sense it. We should listen for the overtones in his words, as when he says, "Consider the lilies of the field, how they grow. . . . If God so clothe the grass of the field, which today is, and tomorrow is cast into the oven, shall he not much more clothe you?" (Matt. 6:28, 30). He saw the sower and the seed in a new light. His imagination played over the poorest and most sinful people he encountered, and he dreamed of halos on their heads.

Many other religious problems became more understandable and meaningful to me when they were viewed psychologically. One of these was prayer. Under a study of prayers in different ages and cultures, prayers began to appear as conversations, or rather as one side of conversations. We often carry on one-sided conversations. Byron wrote a poem in which he talked to the ocean, and Coleridge addressed a hymn to Mont Blanc. "Prayer is the heart's desire, unuttered or expressed." It no more implies some one, definite, consistent idea of God than talking to a human being presupposes some metaphysical theory of his personality. It is the habit of people to talk. Thoughts overflow in words even when we are alone. It is refreshing and releasing to express ourselves. We can scarcely avoid it.

A second reason why we pray is that our own ideas get clarified by uttering them, and the wiser and more sympathetic we imagine the one addressed to be, the better we formulate our words. Frequently the framing of a question to ask a person suggests a helpful answer. Having some idea of his mind, we begin to see how the question would appear him, and the question is partly answered in a more careful statement of it. Prayer is in part a matter of putting the case up for another to see, for God to see. In that way our prayers sometimes bring their own answer. Doubtless millions of people pray best when they kneel before the image of the gentle Buddha or the compassionate Christ.

Fortunately, not all our prayers are answered, some of them never, and some of them only after long delay and when we may have forgotten them ourselves. Many prayers are answered in strange and unexpected ways, and many would be answered if we had the courage and the importunity to offer them. Prayers are sometimes too petty to get a hearing; they may be too selfish or too thoughtless or too difficult even for God. Considerate prayers include the proviso, "if it be in accordance with Thy will," or "not my will but Thine be done."

The prayers most likely to get real response are those which are carried over from words into action. A farmer who genuinely prays for good crops will plow and cultivate and care for the growing grain. Perhaps what cannot be worked for in some intelligent and definite way ought not to be prayed for. Jesus cautioned his disciples to be careful about their prayers, not to make them too long, repetitious, vain, or mandatory.

It seems to me a piece of rare good fortune that I, a minister, had the opportunity to pursue scientific studies of religion and to share them with hundreds of young students in the university. The church was a kind of laboratory for cultivation and observation of the living processes of religion, while the university was a place for their systematic study. This did not subordinate the church. There I had the active attitude of the participant, in the classroom that of the observer. It is one thing to pray and another thing to psychologize and philosophize about prayer. God for the religious man in the religious mood is not felt as the idea of God is considered in the analytical attitude. Yet it has been my conviction and experience that reflection helps religious practice to be sane and precious, showing its true function and importance. There is no conflict or contradiction when it is realized that two dimensions are involved, both belonging to a full life which would be impoverished without either. Psychology and philosophy of religion renew religion. A religion without their benefit will not satisfy a modern critical mind. The fact remains that knowing about religion does not take the place of religion. Frequently I meet some man or woman now grown to maturity who expresses deep appreciation and gratitude for the classroom hours we had together. Not a few of them have been members of my church who found their way back to religion through the study of it.

It is a satisfaction also to know that the first book I wrote, *The Psychology of Religious Experience* (1910), which embodied the research of several years, has been much used as a textbook in colleges and theological seminaries and has held its place for thirty years in the literature of the psychology of religion. Even if in many hands it chiefly presents a view which needs to be criticized and "answered," yet even there it bears its witness. Now and then some incident reveals the distance to which a man's work may radiate from the little place where it began. It made an impression on me to have a report from a colleague within two months of the publication of that book that he had the first sight of it in the window of a book shop in Berlin. It was another thrill to receive a copy of the book translated into Japanese.

These experiences are little suggestions of what I have referred to as the great enveloping life of the world in which we have our place. We have reason to believe that the vast whole of which we are a part is responsive to what we do. From that fact we may draw comfort and courage and some discipline of prudence about the deeds we do, the words we speak, and the very thoughts we think.

Chapter x | A New Type of Missionary

Our local church was born of the missionary spirit. It was through the American Christian Missionary Society, which was the "home missionary society" of the Disciples, that the little group of Disciples in and around the University of Chicago received funds to assist them in securing Dr. Herbert L. Willett as their first minister in 1894. He was then a graduate student in the department of Old Testament language and literature, under President Harper, and was nearing the completion of his work for the Doctor's degree. From the first, contributions were made out of the small resources of the congregation for foreign as well as for home missions. Frequent reminders of these obligations appeared in the church calendar and annual reports of the early years. Every year the financial statements showed some increase in missionary gifts in fair proportion to the expenditures for current expenses. Even when debts and special demands were difficult to meet, the missionary funds were never allowed to fail. This policy has become the spirit and habit of the church.

It has been a deep conviction that the Christian religion involves in its very genius this out-reaching, expansive attitude and that a self-centered church defeats itself. It is not only religion which manifests this tendency to project itself. Every vital human concern seeks to push out into the world and share its good things. All cultural interests offer themselves to others. Commerce and trade, education, science, and art seek new fields and converts. Whenever a man or a woman discovers some satisfying and rewarding idea or invention, the natural impulse is to tell others about it and to encourage them to adopt it.

This is especially true among civilized peoples and with reference to the most important things of life. Christianity has made its way around the world not simply because of a command of its Founder but most of all by the inherent dynamic desire of those who experienced it to enable others to benefit by it. As each church is made up of those who have felt its power, so they in turn endeavor to reach other individuals and help them to create organizations which may cultivate the religious life for themselves, in widening circles. To fail in this process of growth and development is evidence of having missed the primary spirit of the religion of Jesus Christ.

It was at the beginning of the year 1910 that our church began to think of sending missionaries to the Orient, to either Japan or China. Two conditions prepared the way. One was the general missionary spirit of the local church, and the other was the fact that in the membership were two students, Mr. and Mrs. Guy W. Sarvis, who desired to do work in one of these countries. Another influential fact was the rising enthusiasm for educational missions, especially in old lands where learning had been honored for centuries.

In China the prevailing respect for the wise man offered an atmosphere in which modern Christian education was receiving enthusiastic attention. The Boxer uprising of 1900 caused the death of 135 missionaries and 1,600 Chinese Christians. The rebellion was put down by the united action of French, German, British, and American forces, and China was made to pay a huge indemnity. The United States relinquished a large part of its share in this indemnity to provide Chinese students with opportunity to study in American colleges.

A new China was born from these events, and an extensive modern system of public instruction was inaugurated, including provisions for universities, colleges, and lower schools. The young Chinese turned their faces toward the West and its culture. The University of Nanking sprang from that period, a "union institution," consolidating Methodist, Disciple, and Presbyterian schools previously established. It was to this new union university that Mr. and Mrs. Sarvis were to go in 1911, he to teach sociology and she to conduct work in domestic science in a girls' school.

It required one thousand two hundred dollars a year to provide their support. To raise this amount among the members of the little church of two hundred members whose total budget that year was less than three thousand dollars seemed a visionary project. But a letter was sent to all members suggesting that one thousand two hundred dollars could be secured if there were forty-eight subscriptions at twenty-five dollars each. That letter said: "The most vital missionary work of the future is certain to be that of the educator. The Orient desires the full measure of Western civilization, and the best medium for conveying this is the school."

In a statement to the church Mr. Sarvis presented his own idea of the importance of going out to China. He said: "Such an experience inevitably means the breaking down of provincialisms in our thought life, the ability to look upon the world and its processes with a truer and more adequate breadth of vision. It means the opportunity of seeing life through the eyes of the East as well as through the eyes of the West." Mr. Sarvis already knew something of this interaction of cultures, for, although a young man, he had been for two years a secretary of the Y.M.C.A. in Calcutta, India, and afterward had traveled across the continent of Africa as companion and secretary to William Edgar Geil.

Mr. and Mrs. Sarvis were graduates of Drake, a Disciple university. They looked forward to this missionary opportunity with more than ordinary understanding, from both the religious and cultural point of view. They felt the need of religious work at home particularly, Mr. Sarvis said, as he went up and down the streets of Chicago, but he was also convinced that,

so far as human judgment can determine, there is no place in the world where a given investment will produce greater results than in the Orient, and there is no agency in existence besides the church which is willing to invest men and money there for any but selfish reasons. . . . I do not say that the church succeeds much better than others in living up to its ideal, but unless she succeeds she will be superseded. The church is the great idealistic force in our civilization. She attempts experiments and tasks that to the hardheaded seem visionary and impractical.

He felt also that the recent educational reforms in China were opening the doors to what was called "secular scientific education" and that it was important that a great union Christian university, such as the University of Nanking planned to be, should radiate the spirit of religion along with secular culture. Through her long history China's scholars had been her rulers. In the new day opening, her modern scholars should be men of the broadest intelligence and deepest religious spirit. One observer said, "She was formerly able to sit in the splendid isolation of her great valleys, self-contained and self-sustained . . . but now she had started on the road to progress."

Our friends arrived in Shanghai just as the revolution against the Manchus occurred, and for months Nanking was unsettled and uncertain as to what the outcome would be. Finally the republic prevailed, with Sun Yat-sen as president and Nanking as the capital. In October, 1912, Mr. Sarvis wrote that they were celebrating in honor of the founding of the new government under the democratic name of the Chinese People's Country. The foreigners in the city, including the missionaries of the various churches, gave a reception for the president. Mrs. Sarvis wrote of that occasion: "We all shook hands with the George Washington of China, and some of us talked to him. He is a most modest, unassuming, unpretentious man, and we all think he is one of the greatest patriots that ever lived. . . . He was with us an hour and a half, and so charming to everyone."

The letters of these missionaries came to many members of our congregation with interesting accounts of the country, the people, and their customs; of the summer home of all the missionaries at Kuling; and of the pestilence, famine, and varied life of the very rich and the very poor Chinese. Professor W. D. MacClintock, the leading layman of our church, visited the Sarvises that first year, and a few months later Dr. and Mrs. Willett were also able to be there. These visits and the constant exchange of letters with our members contributed to an unusually close and intelligent appreciation of this foreign field and its problems. Mr. Sarvis wrote of his teaching, saying that he had classes in economics and in the history of western Europe. It was difficult work because of lack of adequate use of Chinese by the teacher and of English on the part of the students. He also had charge of Sunday night meetings in the middle school and helped in athletics on the playground, which also called for quick answers and directions in the new vocabulary. There were about four hundred students in the university, and six different denominations were united in its work.

A church or an individual never knows quite what will develop out of a great venture such as this mission was. Our missionaries went to China under appointment by the Foreign Missionary Society of the Disciples, and our church became what was called a "living link" by supplying the financial support. Conservative Disciple papers and individuals began to lift their eyebrows as soon as this living-link plan was announced. Was not Mr. Sarvis a member of the church in Hyde Park? Would he not be tainted with the unsound ideas and practices of this church? Did not the Missionary Society become involved with these questionable things by accepting this arrangement? The ground of the objections was that the church practiced "open membership," that is, received unimmersed people into its fellowship. For some years this practice had been under fire but with no power on the part of critics to change the policy, since each Disciple congregation is independent and free to order its own affairs. But now that the Missionary Society had made an alliance with the church, the matter took on new proportions and threatened greater dangers. The society depended upon contributions from churches all over the country, most of which would oppose any compromise in the matter of receiving members without baptism by immersion. The opposition saw their opportunity to put the society and all concerned in an embarrassing position. The *Christian Standard* of Cincinnati published pages of editorials, correspondence, and discussion to thwart the evil thing.

Editorially they said:

Of course Mr. Ames would like to have his congregation a living link to the Foreign Society. Of course he would have a man ready, trained, coached and tried out, in disseminating the divisive and destructive views he holds. Of course the field chosen would be China, and the work teaching in a Methodist-Baptist-Presbyterian-Disciple college, where opportunity is given to influence all the mission work of the region. . . . The whole thing looks a good deal like a preconcerted and carefully worked out scheme. . . . The Foreign Christian Missionary Society, by sending Mr. Sarvis to the field under pay of the Hyde Park Church, becomes party to the Hyde Park anomaly. They have no right thus to betray the trust reposed in them.

These objections were carried into the National Convention of Disciples which met in Louisville, Kentucky, in October, 1911. The Rev. J. B. Briney arose and moved that the Sarvises be recalled from China because of their living-link relation with the Chicago church. To show further cause for this action, he told the convention of another false doctrine that the minister of that church had recently published in a book entitled *The Divinity of Christ* (1911). He read the following passage from that book which he found in the chapter entitled "The Empirical View of Jesus":

Miracles and wonders were familiar to the Hebrew mind, as to all primitive minds, and consequently this teacher and leader [Jesus] was accredited with miracles and wonders. It was commonly believed that the gods took the women of the human race for wives, and it was inevitable that as Jesus came to be regarded as a great personage this half divine, half human parentage should be ascribed to him also. That these miracles and this birth should still be regarded by informed men of the present day as actual, literal facts is striking evidence of how much of the primitive age of child wonder and savage credulity still survive in the world.

There were many orders for the book after that session.

Mr. Briney's motion was ruled out of order by the president of the convention on the ground that the convention was not competent to deal with doctrinal matters, that the convention was created and conducted for the promotion of practical missionary work and not to exercise authority in beliefs. An appeal was made from this ruling by those who favored the motion, but not enough votes could be secured to support the appeal. The tension was at a high pitch. Everyone recognized that it would be unprecedented for the convention to act upon such doctrinal questions as open membership and the theological dogma of the divinity of Christ; yet it was clear that the agitation by the conservatives against the missionary work might seriously affect its financial support and have other disturbing effects. I was persuaded by these apprehensions to go before the convention after Mr. Briney's motion had been ruled out of order and make the following statement:

I rise to a question of special privilege. I am the pastor of the church in Hyde Park, Chicago. I wish to say a word concerning our living-link relation with Mr. and Mrs. Sarvis. I shall not presume upon your time to speak of the sacrifices of the church in creating this living link or of the deep personal relations involved. I shall trust your minds and hearts to understand the following statement: "In order to show that there has been no sinister motive in its living-link relation with Mr. and

Mrs. Guy W. Sarvis, to promote harmony, and to advance the great missionary work of the Disciples, as its pastor I will urge the church in Hyde Park to relinquish its living-link relation with Mr. and Mrs. Sarvis."

This statement was received with great applause, and several conservative leaders at once declared to the convention their satisfaction. It was explained in the church papers the following week that this did not involve the recall of Mr. Sarvis from the mission field, nor did it prevent the church from contributing to the society. In the course of a few weeks, however, the reactionary *Standard* took the position that another sinister victory had been won by the Hyde Park Church, since the only change, after all the excitement, was the elimination of the words "living link." The church continued to send its money to the general treasury, and the missionaries remained on the field.

Mr. Sarvis' role in China often took him out of academic work to attend also to the effects of some great catastrophe, such as famine, pestilence, or war. In 1912 he went to Wuhu, where famine had followed the great floods due to the breaking of the dikes on the Yangtze River. A million acres of rich rice lands were flooded, which normally would yield five hundred pounds of rice to the acre. Seven thousand people lost their lives in the floods, and other thousands died from starvation and disease. The situation was one in which a missionary trained in sociology was particularly useful. Mr. Sarvis made reports at the request of the government and in subsequent years in similar crises came to have a very effective influence. He studied the effect of floods and famine on the morale of the people and found that it deprived them of the stimulus to thrift and destroyed their hope. There was also scandalous grafting from relief funds by Chinese officials, according to an ancient custom of "squeeze" in handling public funds. The missionary sometimes showed up this system by administering relief in one area and comparing the results with a neighboring area administered by the Chinese.

The idea of maintaining missionaries in educational work was appreciated by the Chicago church, in spite of the task of raising the funds and enduring misunderstanding and misrepresentation. Evidence of this is the fact that in 1914 Mr. Clarence H. Hamilton was also appointed by the Foreign Missionary Society of the

Disciples to go to the University of Nanking. He went to teach philosophy. He had done his college work at the University of Chicago and had also received his Doctor's degree in philosophy. For one year he had taught in Bethany College. He had become well known in our congregation, for he was the regular pianist of the church during a considerable period of his student days among us. His training in philosophy and music, his youthfulness and charm, made him a rather unusual "foreign missionary." But the character and standing of the University of Nanking really made his work there not very different from that of a Christian teacher of philosophy in any similar institution at home. Our church added his salary to its budget and paid it through the Foreign Christian Missionary Society without any question about the living-link relation.

Mr. Sarvis and Mr. Hamilton continued at the University of Nanking until the civil strife and anti-foreign agitation of 1927–28. Mr. Hamilton had married a missionary in Nanking, and both families, each with four children, had established themselves in many helpful relationships in the university community and in the foreign colony. Changes were coming upon mission fields at the time, especially in China and Japan. Large numbers of young people from both countries had been studying in the United States, England, and Europe and were returning home to teach. The missionaries themselves favored the trend toward making both religion and education as much as possible the responsibility of the people themselves. This naturally affected higher education more than the mission churches, but there it did lead to the appointment of too many inadequately trained pastors. The kind of men who went out from our church may be appreciated in their coming back to teaching on American campuses which are among the best.

Mr. Lewis Smythe, another member of our church, was on the faculty of the University of Nanking at the time of the Japanese invasion and World War II, when it was necessary to move the universities to the far west. He made a study of co-operatives, especially in the weaving industry, and was commissioned by Madame Chang Kai-shek to develop this industry as rapidly as possible for the needs of the Chinese soldiers.

Earlier missionaries were primarily evangelists, seeking converts by the quickest method. The poor were the most accessible to this approach, in their physical need, and the missions naturally gathered most recruits from among them. Their poverty stimulated the missionaries to bring the resources of the West to bear. The consequence was the development of medical missions with hospitals, doctors, and nurses; agricultural and horticulural missions; and more educational missions. Whatever concerned the welfare of human beings came into the program: the status of women, the political system, international relations, the use of machinery.

Our church never relaxed support of the missionary cause. We continued to have a special interest in mission schools and colleges. But we came to realize that, with the new dimensions of the missionary effort, a seasoned civilization like that of China had much of value to give the missionaries and the countries they represented. Not only could Christian ideals be conveyed by appeal to Chinese poetry and philosophy, but it had to be recognized that in some ways the Chinese surpassed Westerners, as in respect for the aged. To many Americans who had no familiarity with Chinese culture the books of Lin Yutang made impressive the wholesome idealism and life-wisdom of the Chinese. At the same time the Chinese themselves were gaining appreciation of the contribution of modern science to better living. The philosopher Hu Shih (in an essay in *Whither Mankind*, edited by Charles A. Beard in 1928) contended that tools make the main difference between East and West. The East did produce epoch-making tools but had not kept up. Hu Shih saw no glory in poverty and said it was more spiritual to have machines do heavy and dirty work than to break the backs of men and women. He would put a new science-reliance in place of medieval defeatism.

The thought of Hu Shih, influenced by John Dewey as well as by the sages of China, is in the direction of the development in Christianity toward the idea that whatever helps men to have a better life has religious value. The new type of missionary exemplifies this conception of religion as taking seriously the welfare of human beings, physically and psychologically, striving to release them from meaner and lesser things, for those things like knowledge and social order which are basic for an intelligent meaning of the "spiritual" life. The new type of missionary is supported by a new kind of church and by a new and more vital religious faith. This kind of missionary and this kind of religion have received a cordial welcome among the leaders of foreign countries, for it is more and more evident that education and science and a religion which fosters these work for the common interests of mankind around the whole world. Christianity in all its forms tends to go beyond the bounds of race and country, and in its more enlightened forms overleaps all barriers of nationalisms, languages, and cultures. And in all cultures it works not by imposing its will but by spreading like leaven in the minds and hearts of men.

Chapter xi | The Social Gospel

My book-lined study, with a leafy view of
Kimbark Avenue toward the Midway, within earshot of the
chimes of Rockefeller Chapel, has photographs of family and
friends. I cherish the volumes of the church calendar, which I have
from the beginning. My son printed it during his high school and
university years, using a hand press in the third floor "print shop"
next to my study. Often it was late Saturday night before the
thudding of the press could stop. Until the new printer was pro-
ficient, I used very brief quotations on the back page of the little
sheet which was folded once to make four pages. When he left
home, his sister Adelaide took over his job for some years.

Around 1905 (before it became a family enterprise) the calendar often carried on the back page a five-hundred-word outline of
the sermon from the preceding Sunday. The monthly *Messenger*
frequently printed sermons in full. For several years the *Messenger* was printed by a commercial concern which solicited adver-
tisements in the neighborhood, printed all the copy we sent in,
and supplied the church, without cost, all the copies it could use.
Nearly forty complete sermons were published in this way in the
ten years after 1905. It is possible to see from the subjects of the
sermons what were the lines of emphasis in the thought and work
of the church.

Much attention was given to the theological questions concerning God, prayer, salvation, the divinity of Christ, the religious
nature of man, the perplexities of faith. In that period the question
of open membership in relation to the plea of the Disciples for
Christian union was given much thought. Besides, there were al-

ways difficult financial problems, even though they were on a relatively small scale. A little church budget, if unbalanced, may be as disastrous as a large budget which does not make ends meet. Among these interests and the ever present pastoral cares, it is gratifying to note that the social gospel was a prominent concern. My own philosophy and religious thinking naturally led to a social emphasis.

Even when the subjects, as one reads them over, suggest a decidedly theological sermon, as a matter of fact the treatment of the subject was designed to find newer and more vital interpretations than traditional theology afforded. For example, it was pointed out in the sermon on God that the growth of the idea of God is often based upon the character of the environment and is also connected with the development of the social organization. I said: "When the mother was the head of the family, the deities were goddesses. Later, when the father became the recognized head of the family and tribe, the deity became masculine and took on the attributes and characteristics of paternal authority." Also:

The conception of God appears everywhere bound up inextricably with the actual conditions of life. . . . The idea of God has its place fundamentally with reference to conduct and not with reference to abstract thought. . . . Faith in the justice of God means a readiness to labor and sacrifice for the establishment of justice on the earth. All indifference to human sin and to the outrages of selfishness, brutal power, and bigotry is infidelity and atheism.

In this practical manner of conceiving religious ideas is revealed the reason why this pulpit was sympathetic to the social gospel from its beginning, though the expression "social gospel" is not the happiest designation. It was my contention that Christianity is essentially social, that love of neighbor and fair dealing with him were the heart of the gospel of Christ.

The occasion for a new social emphasis was the emergence of the modern industrial revolution, which put distance between the employer and his men, between different classes of people, and vastly extended what we call impersonal relations. The loss of the old face-to-face relations of small groups opened the way for new forms of exploitation which revealed their unethical implications only with long experience and studied criticism. This put new demands upon the imagination if the Christian principle of brotherly love was to operate effectively between individuals who had no direct personal contact. Too often, through impersonal procedures great corporations could seek their own ends without due consideration of the consequences to labor or to customers. Industrial and business enterprises could attain power over politicians and courts; this worked hardship upon great numbers of persons in the general public. These tendencies sometimes became so unfair as to elicit laws against monopolies and against unjust discrimination in railroad rebates and labor relations.

Although business and politics were gradually forced to modify their practices, through the influence of competition itself and through political pressure, it was difficult to arouse religious leadership to a sense of responsibility in such matters. The force of habit and the danger of offending rich businessmen and powerful executives tended to intimidate and silence the spokesmen of religion. They were told not to concern themselves with business and politics but to confine themselves to religion. This usually meant to devote themselves to personal religion and to avoid discussion of social problems.

But there were men within the church who realized that religion could not escape concern with social problems. Her scholars and ministers pointed out the social implications of the teachings of Jesus. Around the beginning of the twentieth century an extensive literature appeared with the social emphasis. Francis G. Peabody of Harvard University published a book, *Jesus Christ and the Social Question;* Shailer Mathews of the University of Chicago wrote *The Social Teachings of Jesus* and *The Church and the Changing Social Order*. Walter Rauschenbusch dealt with *Christianity and the Social Crisis*, and Washington Gladden with *Social Salvation*. E. A. Ross, professor of sociology in the University of Wisconsin, stated the issue forcefully in his book, *Sin and Society*. He stressed the fact that people's sins are no longer their own alone, that evil things do not pertain so much to personal habits as to methods of business, to wage systems, to tenement housing, which belong to collective responsibility.

Quotations from these men appear in the church calendar in the first decade of this century. There were also sermons on social religion. In 1906 a sermon on "The Great Doctrine of Jesus" said he taught the value of human life and its capacity for development. He taught the innocence and the significance of childhood. He put the second commandment upon a level with the first and thus introduced an entirely new emphasis upon love to one's neighbor. The practical application of this central message of Christ may be seen in the new concern for public health, in the enfranchisement of women, the care and education of children, and in other humanitarian and social reforms.

Among the hindrances to the practice of this religion of Jesus were mentioned competition in business, class distinctions, and race prejudice.

This interest in the social gospel was represented not only by sermons of those years but also by the organization of practical agencies in the church. One of these, called the "Chicago Fund," was for aiding various charitable and civic enterprises, such as the Bureau of Charities, the Chicago Law and Order League, the Citizens' Association, the South Park Improvement Association, the Jackson Park Sanitarium, the American Home-finding Association, and a social settlement. This fund was designed to relate the work of the church more closely to the great philanthropic, humanitarian, and civic enterprises of the city and to afford practical expression for the growing sentiment in the church on behalf of such concrete activities. Several hundred dollars were immediately subscribed for this fund, and the announcement of this at the close of the year 1907 was accompanied by the statement that "the pastor considers this one of the most important and vital things ever undertaken by this church."

Two years later, other agencies were added to the beneficiaries of this fund, including the John Hamline School Extension Work, whose purpose was to develop the use of school buildings as social centers, the Illinois Children's Home and Aid Society, the Chicago Boys' Club, the Chicago Society of Social Hygiene, the Visiting Nurse Association, the Chicago Tuberculosis Institute, the Municipal Voter's League, and the University of Chicago Settlement. Alexander M. Wilson, then the superintendent of the Chicago Bureau of Charities, and Charles T. Hallinan were appointed from the church members as a permanent committee to look after the fund and to enlist other members in active participation in these social causes. The committee had the advice of Professors Charles R. Henderson and Graham Taylor.

Mr. S. M. Singleton, secretary of the Citizen's Association, writing a letter acknowledging a remittance from the church for his organization, said: "Permit me to say that the association will be proud to have your church organization as a member. Yours is the first church that has ever applied for membership in the association. . . . The association will be glad to have suggestions from you and your people at any time as to matters which, in your opinion, should receive its attention." That was the kind of reception the church met from all the organizations with which it co-operated, and for more than thirty years financial and personal co-operation with such enterprises have been continued through the benevolence budget of the church and through its social service council.

There has always been a problem of keeping agencies of this kind sufficiently in the attention of the members of the church, and of making the members appreciative of the underlying nature and purpose of the social idealism of our view of religion. One method used was the publication of information concerning the work of the organizations to which the church contributed. Another was the report of money given and of the replies of representatives of the organizations, like Mr. Singleton. An important factor was the church library, which was dedicated to Lillian White Grant, a devoted member taken from us. The books represented the current literature of philosophy and religion, biblical study, the history of Christianity, science and nature, great biography, education, anthropology, and sociology. In this last section were books by Jane Addams on *Newer Ideals of Peace* and *Democracy and Social Ethics; The Bitter Cry of the Children,* by John Spargo; *The Spirit of Labor,* by Hapgood; *Problems of Poverty,* by J. A. Hobson; *Tuskegee and Its People,* by Booker T. Washington; *The New Womanhood,* by J. C. Fernald; *The New Internationalism,* by Harold Bolce; *Social Unrest,* by J. G. Brooks; *The Country Town* by W. L. Anderson; *The City,* by F. C. Howe; *The Shame of the Cities,* by Lincoln Steffens. Sometimes we were able to have such authors come and speak to us. Among them were Jane Addams, Hamilton Holt, Vachel Lindsay (who for a time gave addresses for the temperance cause), Mary McDowell, and various professors from the University of Chicago.

Occasionally we were able to show that social work at home

was in spirit very much the same as the work of missionaries in foreign countries. Dr. Macklin of China told of his medical work in Nanking; David Rioch gave a thrilling story of his orphanage, which cared for hundreds of boys after one of the great famines in India; Ellsworth Faris told us of heroic adventures in opening a mission in the Congo in Africa. Dr. Williams, afterward a martyr in the Boxer Rebellion in China, gave an account of agricultural and technological educational work in China, and for many years after 1911 we had continuous information about educational and sociological missions from Mr. and Mrs. Sarvis and others who went from our church and served in China.

It was always surprising to me that so few people seemed able to see the social gospel aspect of foreign missions even when they had some appreciation of this kind of religious work at home. The word "missions" has suffered the fate of words which have become identified with some distasteful associations. It is meaningless to some minds to speak of "educational missions" or "medical missions" or "technological missions." At least so far as this church is concerned, its missionary enterprises were carried on in the same spirit as its social service work through its "Chicago Fund" and other agencies. It had the same motivation of humanitarian religion at home and abroad.

A further means of cultivating the social interpretation grew out of the Chicago Fund. Seven years after its organization, the chairman of the church committee on the Chicago Fund extended this committee into what has since been known as the Social Service Council. This chairman was Mr. W. T. Cross, the secretary of the National Conference of Charities and Correction and a member of the church. In 1915, under his direction, the Social Service Council planned an exhibit to make a graphic display of its activities and the causes it represented. That "Social Service Week," as it was called, remains a vivid memory to all who participated in it or visited the exhibits. Booths were constructed all around the interior of our little brick church, and in the booths were charts, maps, and statistical displays of the work of many welfare agencies of the city and nation. The exhibit was open every afternoon and evening, and talks were given by professional social workers.

On two evenings of the week a play was given by the dramatic club of the church. The play was *Lyngaard and Company* and was directed by Mrs. Margaret Allen from the Little Theatre. In the public announcements the following statement was made:

The purpose of the week is to emphasize the religious character of social work and the social interests of religion. This reciprocal relation, recognized by most churches today, is here graphically represented with reference to this local church. The causes are those with which our members happen to be connected. There are many others equally important. It is the spirit and principle involved in making this an affair of the church which are particularly significant.

Much of the success of this enterprise was due to the tireless planning and labor of Mr. Dwight Sanderson, then a graduate student in sociology and later professor of rural sociology in Cornell University.

In 1911 I read a paper on "Religion and Social Consciousness" at the Disciples' National Congress. I began with a reference to the fact that the churches had an increasing interest in missionary enterprises and that this was true because missionary activity was not primarily theological or evangelistic in the traditional sense but humanitarian and cultural. I spoke of the growing realization that it is necessary to build up the whole social order on Christian principles and said:

It has been discovered that it is folly to segregate men into churches and prevail upon them to repent of their sins in business and in politics, without endeavoring to change also the business system and the political methods into which they must return. . . . We no longer feel secure about our individual health, no matter how robust and clean we ourselves may be, if we are compelled to walk through foul streets, breathe impure air, and use polluted water. Therefore religious people are becoming zealous about politics, child labor, intemperance, tuberculosis, woman's suffrage, better housing, sanitary shops, public education, white slavery, the race problem, prison reform, immigration, public playgrounds, labor legislation, and the conservation in every way of the sources and functions of human life.

When appointed on the board of preachers at Harvard University in 1913, my first sermon in Appleton Chapel was on Christianity and social service. The sermon noted that successive periods in the history of the church had emphasized different ideals of the Christian life:

The first century was the age of the martyrs. In the fourth century asceticism withdrew men from the world into solitude. In the twelfth century the typical figure was the crusader-knight. The mystic of the fourteenth century sought direct access to God without intervention of priest or institution, and in the sixteenth century the theologians, formulators of the creeds of Christendom, were the great Christians. And now in the twentieth century the Christian ideal is undergoing another transformation. The theological saint is losing prestige. His creeds are discredited by greater knowledge and broader vision. As the image of the theologian dissolves and fades from view, there is emerging the ideal of the social worker.

The reasons given for the influence of this practical, social Christianity were that it is the most biblical of all the historic forms. The Good Samaritan was a more typical New Testament Christian than the martyr or the monk, the crusader or the expounder of creeds. Second, not only do modern welfare movements constitute the fruits, the good works which Christianity requires as the test of genuine religion, they also beget that inner disposition of the heart which has been magnified by evangelical Christianity. Third, by social idealism Christianity is gaining a new apologetic—an apologetic which the plain man in the street may quickly comprehend. We are no longer acutely convinced and persuaded by arguments concerning the fundamentals of the older theology—miracles, inspiration, future punishment, and the rest—but we are sensitive and responsive to a religion which opens schools in India, hospitals in China, and neighborhood centers along the coast of Labrador, a religion which creates institutions of learning, of health, of comradeship, and of hope in all the dark places of the earth.

Moreover, the layman is able to appreciate the service which he can render in religion so applied. This new direction of effort has made secular talents sacred by devoting them to noble ends. All labor which improves society, lessens injustice, increases happiness and refinement, is thereby sanctified. In this larger service of man, the lawyer, the teacher, the mechanic, finds his task idealized and spiritualized. This ideal of social service is an ideal full of practical deeds and of sweet reasonableness, and full also of the romance and mystery of the infinite life manifesting itself in the will and purposes of men.

That sermon was optimistic, and it represented an optimism

more or less characteristic of the two or three decades previous to the war of 1914. But it was not an optimism which ignored the evils and sufferings of mankind. No age ever had a clearer or more poignant realization of the tragedies and horrors existing in the world. That period was notable for its understanding of the long and pathetic struggle through which the race has come. It did not delude itself with the picture of a golden age in the past, which by some miracle might be recovered. It rewrote the story of man's place in the order of nature and in the animal kingdom. For the first time in history it became evident what an inheritance of animality man carries and how numerous and powerful are his enemies—disease germs, insects, and the fathomless passions of the human heart.

It also was becoming apparent that, if the great hope of mankind were to be found in religion, it would have to be a religion that was more than sentiment and ignorant fear. An intelligent religion, swept clean of superstition and magic, motivated by a conviction of the potentialities for good in developed human nature, was the only kind of religion that could sustain a reasonable faith in the future of man. The new emphasis upon social religion brought the problems of life within reach of understanding and possible control and made it conceivable that the evils of life could be effectively attacked. But the men who believed most in a religion of social service did not assume that its ideals could be easily and surely attained. They felt about social problems much as they did about matters of health. Scientists knew that they possessed a method of research which might hope to discover the secret of any disease, but they were prepared to pursue their researches for an indefinite time and by ways yet to be found.

The idea that progress is always upward and onward has never been characteristic of the wisest man of this modern age. They have been inured to disappointment and uncertainty in their most cherished inquiries. No one knows better than they how devious and arduous is the way that leads to discoveries and advancement in knowledge. It has more often been the theologians who were overly optimistic, for they held to the doctrine of final perfectibility, though they could give no reasonable grounds for their faith except the inscrutable will of a God who moved in a mysterious way his wonders to perform.

One of the greatest obstacles that the religion of the social gospel encountered was the difficulty of getting religious people to believe in themselves, to throw off the long-standing idea that man is evil and that he has a deep-seated natural disposition to choose the worse rather than the better part. Another obstacle was the doctrine that the outward conditions of life had no relation to the inner and spiritual realities of religion. So many "saints" have lived in dirt and discomfort that it is hard to see how they could have been better if they had been accustomed to baths and good food. But it is possible that there might have been more and better saints if pious people generally had lived with more appreciation of the laws of health and of the conditions of efficiency in this present world.

Our church never surrendered its emphasis upon the social and practical aspects of the Christian religion. Its Social Service Council has been constituted by those members who are professionally engaged in social work and by others vitally interested in it. Among them we have continued to have teachers of sociology, workers in social settlements, in the Y.M.C.A. and the Y.W.C.A., in the city park and recreation system, in public relief, in the public schools, in civic organizations, and in other welfare agencies. The church contributes money to some forty different causes, amounting to several thousand dollars each year, and the money raised for these causes comes regularly and more painlessly than any other funds. This is an indication of interest and conviction about this phase of religion, but it continues to be difficult to disseminate and sustain a maximum of understanding and enthusiasm for it throughout the whole membership. It is not always easy to make social workers themselves aware of the larger program of social work. Like other human beings, they tend to be absorbed in the special interest for which they are responsible and to fall unconsciously into a kind of atomistic competition on behalf of their own special cause.

One-sided devotion has affected in recent years the whole idea of the social gospel in the churches and, together with a resurgence of the old theological tradition in Protestantism, has tended to influence church people to feel that after all there is something secular and too humanistic in the social emphasis. It is therefore important to remember how many-sided religion is at its best. It is essential to have regard for sound teaching in doctrinal matters, to cultivate sane and satisfying forms of worship, to promote religious education of young and old, to keep the business life of the church sound, to enhance the social and joyful side of religion, and to elevate and cleanse the individual souls of men by great spiritual insights and visions. The social gospel is not the whole gospel, but it is a deeply significant and fruitful phase of religion which has added richness and vitality to the growing life of the Christian faith. Our age demands a non-theological, practical faith which is earnestly loyal to the spirit of Jesus Christ, a faith which labors for the welfare of all mankind with the very love and ardor of Christ, a faith which is scientifically intelligent and experimentally adventurous in dealing with social problems.

Chapter xii | World War

Upon the peaceful world I had known all my life a world war came as something unreal and unbelievable, in spite of its tragic actuality. An American born after the Civil War grew into mature manhood with the feeling that war was a thing of the past, and with some reason, in his immediate environment, that it would not be a thing of the future. The war between Japan and China in 1894–95, the Boer War in 1899, and even the Spanish-American War and the Russo-Japanese War seemed remote and of such short duration that they did not destroy the feeling of an essentially settled peace. The United States was a peaceful nation. Its developments in the arts and sciences, in industries, education, and social reforms, absorbed its energies. It was a common belief that the forces of civilization had come to the beginning of a new era and that the evolution of mankind had attained a new level of law and order. New light had been thrown upon the history of the race, and the stages of savagery and barbarism appeared outgrown. Life was still tragic enough in the slums of the cities and in the less progressive lands of the earth, but education, missions, and social idealism were on their way to uplift all people everywhere.

When I was a boy, the Fourth of July parades of the veterans of the Civil War, led by brass bands and by fife and drum corps, made a stirring scene for me, but they were reminiscent of something far past. The uniforms, the muskets, the bayonets, and the cannon were aging and out of use except for gala occasions celebrating the heroism of other days. America had united her states and had set about the common enterprises of utilizing her vast resources and absorbing millions of immigrants. The territory was so immense and the opportunities so inviting that peaceful pursuits engaged all classes and all individuals. At least here, between the oceans, was a land secure from aggression and blessed with freedom to follow in ways of peace the ideals of life, liberty, and the pursuit of happiness. The hopes of Washington and Jefferson, of Franklin and Madison, were attaining fulfilment, and the faith of the Pilgrim fathers was being justified.

Suddenly Germany threw herself against the iron ring of her encircling enemies and broke through upon Belgium. This action was much more deliberate than it appeared at a distance. Students and travelers returning from Germany had reported for years the vast military preparations that country had been making. The Kaiser had clanked his sword and threatened destruction upon those who hemmed him in. This brief and sudden war was to be the prelude to the world-wide spread of German *Kultur*. But France, Italy, Britain, and their allies could not see beyond the deadly onslaught of the beginning.

With amazement and bewilderment we in America saw the fateful drama unfold and engulf the nations, until our souls were made to feel that we must decide whether we could ourselves escape her domination if Germany conquered Europe. Here we were with enormous manpower and measureless riches standing by, while England and France were bleeding to death. In May, 1915, the "Lusitania" was sunk without warning by a German submarine, with a loss of 1,153 lives, of which 114 were American citizens. That was practically the end of the considerable sympathy for Germany which had previously existed in America, and strong pressure was immediately put upon President Wilson for a declaration of war. From that moment every intelligent American began to realize the possibility that this country was on the verge of war, and a deep searching of heart stirred the nation as to whether such a step could be justified. The question came home with force to ministers.

Gradually the high idealism and the fine phrases of the President gathered force in religious as well as political circles. If we entered the war, it would be with the purpose of "making war to end war." It would be "a war to make the world safe for democracy." Like many others, I was slow to face the situation. It still

seemed unbelievable that we could be forced to abandon the long
era of peace, perhaps the longest the world had ever known. I
even went so far as to think and to say:

What if Germany should conquer the world and put her officers in
charge of every state and city of this country? They would be a relatively small force in comparison with the total population, and the
genius of the American people would yet cling to their democratic
ideals and to their long-cherished faith in freedom and love of peace.
Such an overhead rule might lie upon the surface of the national life but
would scarcely reach the soul of the people. There had been such a history in China, where the Manchus had conquered the land but never
completely changed the depths of that ancient culture. After two hundred and fifty years the rule of the Manchus was overthrown, and China
emerged into a new era of freedom and self-government.

But at last the provocations, the propaganda of hate, and the
threatened submergence of our British cousins and the friendly
people of France, the ally of our early struggle for freedom and
democracy, brought us to the bitter conviction that it was our
moral and religious duty to go to the help of liberty and justice.

A thought that influenced me to sympathize with this grim
decision was that, after all, the world is young. In point of time
we are not far removed from the ages of barbarism and slavery.
We are still easily moved by passion and by childish ideas. Memories of the horrors of old wars are easily forgotten. We are readily
imposed upon by the oft-repeated fallacy that human nature does
not change and that under the veneer of our apparent civilization
and religious idealism still lives the beast in us, not really tamed or
subdued. Pugnacity, they say, is an uneradicated instinct, and it
will inevitably burst forth and overwhelm us, when the provoca-
tion arises. There was abundant evidence that men and women,
too, could easily rationalize their belligerent attitudes and elevate
themselves to a righteous frenzy on behalf of a defensive war pic-
tured as being fought for noblest ends.

There was also the argument that to assent to this war was not
to commit oneself to the justification of war in general. A war of
defense was something different from a war of aggression. A war
for territory or for power was more vicious and damnable than a
war to preserve freedom and oportunity for human growth and
peace. To achieve the ideals of democracy is an immense undertaking, and the means to that accomplishment have to be forged

out of long experience, suffering, and struggle. If we feel forced into battle today, it may simply mean that our race is not so far along the road of high human hopes and dreams as we had thought. But the future before us is long, and better and steadier wisdom beckons us on against every loss and defeat.

There was in my heart and my mind a kind of stubborn optimism against all the dread and tragedy of any development the war might attain. Had not Europe seen a Hundred Years' War between England and France and a Thirty Years' War involving all European countries? The latter war lasted from 1618 to 1648, and in it the German peasantry suffered incredibly. It is estimated that a quarter of the population was killed and more than a third of the cultivated lands desolated into wilderness. Education disappeared. Yet in two hundred years Germany recovered and attained a place of world leadership in the sciences, the arts, and philosophy. Probably no greater disaster is possible today, and the resources of civilization are more widely scattered over the earth and conceivably might more rapidly be recovered. In Australia or Africa or some islands of the sea, the records and instruments of our culture might be kept for another new day of constructive peace. The argument was that if the catastrophes of past centuries have not completely destroyed the treasures of a significant civilization, it is not likely that war madness can do so now.

Instead of believing that universal peace could be achieved by spreading absolute pacifism throughout the world by exhortation and martyr heroism, it became my faith that peace was more likely to be increased by understanding more thoroughly the causes of war, and by more systematically organizing and motivating human society with a view to peace. William James wrote an arresting paper (in 1910), "The Moral Equivalent of War," in which he suggested that the heroisms of war, which undoubtedly appeal to youth, might be abundantly supplied by drafting youth into heroic patriotic enterprises:

To coal and iron mines, to freight trains, to fishing fleets in December, to dishwashing, clothes-washing, and window-washing, to road-building and tunnel-making, to foundries, and stoke-holes, and to the frames of skyscrapers, would our gilded youths be drafted off, according to their choice, to get the childishness knocked out of them, and to come back into society with healthier sympathies and soberer ideas. They would have paid their blood-tax, done their own part in the immemorial human warfare against nature; they would tread the earth more proudly, the women would value them more highly, they would be better fathers and teachers of the following generation.

James further said:

The martial type of character can be bred without war. Strenuous honor and disinterestedness abound elsewhere. Priests and medical men are in a fashion educated to it, and we should all feel some degree of it imperative if we were conscious of our work as an obligatory service to the state. We should be *owned*, as soldiers are by the army, and our pride would rise accordingly. We could be poor, then, without humiliation, as army officers now are. The only thing needed henceforward is to inflame the civic temper as past history has inflamed the military temper.[1]

These words of Professor James were written years before World War I. They were the reflections of a great pacifist, but he knew that the military spirit had brought hardihood, discipline, and marvelous elation and excitement. "The horrors make the fascination. War is the strong life. . . . History is a bath of blood." This essay of James was a great resource for my spirit when we Americans realized that Europe was engulfed in the most terrible war of history and that we ourselves must face the possibility of participating in it. It afforded some explanation of why the war had come, revealed the depths of its irrationality and uselessness, but at the same time made a strong case for the idea that men might in the long future find substitutes which would develop the stern and hardy qualities of vigorous manhood without cruelty and without wanton destruction of human life.

Other writers have stressed the economic causes of war, the power motive, and the part played by the capitalistic and nationalistic systems. All this provided a broader basis for an intelligent and vital pacifism and showed where the evil might be effectively attacked. Such thoughts helped to make it understandable that wars might be inevitable in the present time but not inevitable forever. The time element in the kingdom of heaven is on a scale of a thousand years being but as yesterday, or as a watch in the night. The long-suffering patience of God is difficult for human beings to appreciate, but it is also a genuine ground of hope that

[1] William James, *Memories and Studies* (New York: Longmans, Green, 1911), pp. 291, 292–93.

it may allow years and centuries enough for our little blundering efforts to find the paths of righteousness and peace.

At the eleventh hour the United States went in, set up training camps, speeded up the manufacture of munitions, and began the organization of the nation's resources on a wartime basis. In the midst of it all I had a deep feeling of resentment that it was necessary, but the situation brought a resolution of soul to encourage and comfort those who had to go and those who did their bit at home. It was in the year 1916 that I began to write letters for sermons. I wrote a letter to an American soldier, one to the mother of an American soldier, one to Uncle Sam. On one side of the pulpit hung the flag of our country, and on the other side hung the honor roll bearing the names of all those from the church who were in any form of service. The "Letter to an American Soldier" began:

It is still difficult for me to think of you as a soldier. Just the other day you were here at your regular work, in citizen's clothes, dreaming of the possibilities for your future in business. Now you are about to be on your way to France. In all the history of war, was there ever anything like this marshaling of armies to fight battles so far from home without expectation of plunder or booty? . . . I should like to see you through the rounds of a typical day. You write that you get up at 5:30 and keep going all day for twelve hours and then have instruction in the evening. It would be interesting to see you taking care of your tent, making your own bed, and getting ready for inspection. Nothing would surprise your mother or your sister more than that. When they remember how your room used to look at home until someone came around to straighten it up, they can hardly believe that you really take care of things yourself.

You used to be so particular about your meals, too, and now you have to line up for mess and take your share in a tin plate and your coffee in a tin cup. But you say you are gaining weight and never felt better in your life. Evidently Uncle Sam is taking good care of you. . . . Three things have impressed me as I have read the accounts men have given of the life you are about to experience. One is the marvelous excitement of it. I do not mean the mere agitation and nervousness but rather that strange calm which accompanies the most alert attention in a great crisis. Careless and profane young fellows were possessed by a new spirit when they stood ready any instant to go over the top. With true courage they plunged down the fiery path as if it were the moment for which they had waited. Another thing I feel in all that I read and hear of the war is that we Americans are actuated by as noble and unselfish an interest as ever led men to battle. Not the love of war but the hatred of it has impelled us.

One other thing I want to tell you. There is a star for you in the service flag in the church. It is not a small thing that the symbol of you is put on the wall beside the altar. Here blends the deep and tragic will of the common soldier with the faultless courage of Christ. He, too, went forth on a great adventure of love. He battled for the souls of multitudes and died for his faith in them. In gratitude the world has lifted him up and made his very cross the symbol of the way of life.

In a "Letter to the Mother of an American Soldier," these lines were written:

In the old days soldiering was an occupation which attracted adventurous, reckless men, who frequently gave up all social restraints and moral standards for the frightful business of war. . . . Now we are in a war where women take their part at home. At least, they knit. On trains, in streetcars, at the opera, in my classroom, around the tea table, and even at church one sees the deft, swift gestures of allegiance. . . . The housewife, by saving wheat and meat on her table, has the sense of definitely and vitally aiding in the operations at the front. The other day I found that the elevator boy in an office building where I frequently go had been replaced by a girl. She is a slight little slip and looks like a play figure from the stage in her natty uniform with its braid and buttons. I asked her how she got on with it, and she smilingly said, "Oh, I've been here only two days and I think I shall like it, but my shoulder gets pretty tired pulling these doors back and forth all day." Since then I have noticed her in the little iron cage, and it seemed to me she had settled into the routine with an air of conviction and contentment about her, born perhaps of her determination to do her part in the grim war.

The honor roll of our church carried the names of forty-nine men, four of whom were with the Y.M.C.A. overseas. One of these four, John Roberts, died of influenza November 6, 1918, while in charge of the Y among the English troops in Lucknow, India. He was a graduate of Drake University in 1916 and had come to the University of Chicago that fall to enter upon training for the ministry. He was a man of unusual promise and in India had proved himself so well that at the time of his death he had been chosen by Sherwood Eddy to be his secretary. Mr. Eddy was then at the head of the Y work in the Orient. On his last Sunday before leaving to go into the service, Mr. Roberts made a little farewell talk to the congregation which proved to be his farewell indeed. Mr. James McBurney and Mr. Charles M. Sharpe were also among the Y.M.C.A. men and wrote interesting letters from France which were published in our *Messenger*.

Mr. Harry D. Kitson, instructor in psychology in the university, wrote from a training camp for artillery officers in France: "I am leading a very busy life from 6 A.M. until 6 P.M., with conversational lessons in French in the evening. I am finding France a very agreeable place. Oh, there is enough that is disagreeable, but there is no use talking about it, and one learns over here to adopt the attitude of the French and to endeavor to forget the miseries of the war by as many devices as possible; it's the only way to retain one's sanity."

Wayne Farrar wrote to his uncle Oliver W. Stewart:

The night our company went forward to consolidate the line was one I'll never forget. We started from a recently captured village with our complete machine gun equipment on our backs. We hiked uphill and down. It was raining and the roads were in terrible condition. We slipped and tugged and fell and got up and carried on. The worst was yet to come. When we got to a certain valley, Fritz let loose. Of all the shelling any men ever got, we got it. They lit all about us, gas, high explosives, and everything he had. There we were lying in the mud with our gas masks on, some, I suppose, waiting for the end. One young fellow fell almost on me. I have seen both our men and the enemy lying by dozens dead. I have helped bury both. When we buried the dead Austrian outside our dugout the other day, I made a cross out of two pine boards. I scratched on it, "Austrian. Buried September 16." . . . Even after all, Uncle Ollie, there's something about it that edges a fellow on. The whirring of machine gun bullets, the whizzing of shells, the noise from our own guns, just the excitement of it all, has some sort of fascination. A fellow is glad to get away from it, but going into it again doesn't lower our spirit.

The stained-glass window over the pulpit in the new church was placed there in the summer of 1924 in memory of Fryar Patrick Hutchinson, who was killed in action in the Meuse-Argonne offensive October 8, 1918. He was the son of Dr. and Mrs. E. B. Hutchinson, many years very devoted and active members of the church. Fryar joined the church at twelve years of age in 1912. He graduated from the university high school in 1917. As soon as the United States entered the war, he was anxious to enlist, and on his seventeenth birthday, without consulting his parents, he enlisted in the Marine Corps. His winsome ways and eagerness to get into the war won him friends among the officers, and after training three months on shipboard and at Quantico, Virginia, at his own request, he was sent overseas in June and took part in engagements in August, September, and October.

He was one of the most popular boys of Hyde Park, and the inauguration by friends outside the church of the plan for a memorial window in his honor brought subscriptions from all classes of people. Mr. Charles J. Connick was engaged for the work. A decorative design was chosen for the six windows at the front, with figures of Joan of Arc and St. George for the two middle ones. These figures were chosen partly because they symbolize the relation of France and England with America in the war. The bronze tablet, with an engraving of the old church and the roll of honor of those who went to war, was later removed to the new church and set in the stone wall on the east aisle near the fireplace. On the tablet are the names of the sons of families long identified with the life of this church, Holloway, Howard, Hutchinson, MacClintock, Park, Radley, Sharpe, Ames, Thompson, Bean, Finn, Hallam, Russell, and MacDonald.[2]

In the church library has been placed a set of volumes of war pictures presenting in most vivid detail the ghastly death-dealing work of machine guns, shells, hand grenades, barbed-wire entanglements, and bayonets. The publishers thought those pictures would help to restrain future generations from going to war. Many books were published to depict the sufferings, brutalities, and insanities of the war. *All Quiet on the Western Front,* by Remarque; *Three Soldiers,* by Dos Passos; *Mr. Britling Sees It Through,* by Wells; and many other stories of the war spared the reader none of its horrors. Motion pictures and dramas have been even more realistic in revealing the infernos of battles and hospitals and the long aftermath of disabled, shell-shocked, and ruined humanity.

Scientists, like David Starr Jordan, have shown the disastrous effects of war in biological terms. War draws into soldiers' graves the genius of men unfulfilled in science, art, statesmanship, and religion. People are beginning to believe that wars are matters of economics, in the sense that nations struggle to obtain territory

[2] Facing the chancel, in the west wall, is a memorial window honoring Charles MacClintock, a member who died in World War II.

with natural resources, to develop manpower for armies, and to turn the energies of peacetime into preparation for further war. We have come to regard the very treaty of Versailles not so much as the conclusion of the war but as the cause of more war.

How, then, shall the world be delivered from this continuing cycle of death? Perhaps William James was right. Mankind must be enlisted in other enterprises which will challenge our heroisms, awaken still greater enthusiasms, and set nobler goals for the imaginations of men. In this year 1940 a humble illustration of this great principle is afforded by the changing sentiment about college football. This game, which has grown to a prodigious place in the affections of college men, honorable college presidents, alumni, students, and the general public, has been discarded by the University of Chicago on the ground that it perverts and obscures the proper function of a university. The students voted in a general poll to continue the game by "subsidization," but President Hutchins told them the other day that there is no such thing as legitimate subsidization of football and cited the rules of the Big Ten conference to prove it. He did it so convincingly that these same students approved him with thunderous applause. But his most telling words for my purpose were, "Other sports develop co-operation, team spirit, sportsmanship, and fair play just as well as football." The two striking analogies between this sport and war are that the direction of interest can be changed and that the desirable qualities arising from war may be obtained by other forms of intense co-operation for better ends.

One of these forms of constructive co-operation in our society is science. In spite of wars and the ensuing depression, the scientists have kept on with their patient, enthusiastic collaboration in the search for the truth about many things, great and small, that are of concern to humanity. During 1939, 43,000 patents for inventions were issued in Washington, and that was 4,000 more than in the previous year. The vast majority of the fruits of science are for the advantage of common life, for better and cheaper clothing, for better means of health, for better and safer transportation, for more comfortable beds and better cooking stoves.

The other and still profounder means for the enlistment of our powers and talents is religion, an intelligent but passionate religion that shall enlist us in the great spiritual cause of developing a world-wide society of good will and unselfish ends. It is not enough that religion should be aroused negatively against the evils of war. It is essential that religion create constructive agencies in manifold ways to make the spirit of Jesus Christ, and his kingdom of love and righteousness, a living ideal in the hearts of men, with such intelligence and vividness as to elicit the devotion, the sacrifice, and the heroism necessary to transform the ideals of individuals and the purposes of all social institutions.

Chapter xiii | Pastoral Work

Pastoral work, in the sense of cultivating a close and understanding companionship with the people of the church and the community, seems to me the most important single feature of a minister's task. Nothing else brings such real results, and failure at this point is more certain than at any other to arrest the growth and invite disintegration for the church. Sermons are important enough to require careful and thoughtful attention, but the most brilliant sermons are not sufficient in themselves to build up a congregation. Organization is important, financial sense is a requisite, but pastoral work is indispensable.

By pastoral work is meant conversational contacts with individuals in a variety of ways, and always with genuine interest in them. The individuals are of more concern to the minister than the subjects talked about, whatever these may be. The minister's ear must be attuned and alert to what the other person says. People do not talk with him long without revealing what they think about most and what lies most upon their hearts: their daily work, its difficulties and its satisfactions; their health and happiness; their doubts and longings; their memories and hopes; their beliefs and problems; their family and friends; their achievements and secret ambitions.

Any or all of these come to the surface when people talk with friends and with a friendly, human minister. His very profession often elicits and shapes the subjects of conversation. His presence as a representative of religion sets the sphere of discourse, not always toward particular questions but almost inevitably toward certain aspects of living experience and of vital reflection. No other professional man—lawyer, doctor, teacher, politician, or scientist—invites easily so wide a variety of topics or so intimate an attitude. This is partly because religion is itself so inclusive of all the things that life involves, and because wide and quick sympathy is assumed to motivate the heart of a religious man. If a minister has learned the influence and appeal of what he represents to the minds of unaffected people, he does not need to ask formal questions or propound issues. The questions and the problems flow out to him and offer him abundant opportunities to see the souls of men and to find the depths and heights in them, or the shallows and the transparencies.

One day someone told me about a neighbor who once belonged to the Christian church in a small town and had recently moved into our city. I went to see her. She would have been glad to talk to any friendly soul, for she was desperately lonesome. Her husband was a railroad man, away from home much of the time. When he was gone she shut herself up in their little apartment, locked the doors, and was very cautious about having windows open. She had tried to overcome her fear of the city but seldom could get up the courage to make an excursion downtown. How women she saw passing by had the courage to go out alone and to venture as far as the big stores she could not understand. She could laugh a little about all this when she felt safe within her own walls, but she never adjusted herself to the streets and people of her new surroundings. She had a longing for the church but seldom came except on the rare occasions when her husband could come with her. My visits gave her a chance to talk about her church back home, about the minister, and about the ladies' aid society. It was a great release and gave opportunity to relive those happier days. She joined our little church, but apparently the most she ever got out of it were pastoral visits at long intervals and some calls by women of the church.

Many people are affected in much the same way by moving to the city. A family came here from the South, after living all their lives in a beautiful little city where their church was one of the best and largest and not far from their home. Like many other church people, they rented an apartment first and located the church afterward. The flat was new and shiny, near transportation and a lovely park. They joined the church at once, for they were devoted to the denomination and were genuinely religious. Soon they found they were living far away from the church, too far to walk and with no convenient car line to it. In their home town they had been accustomed to have church people for neighbors and to have them drop in frequently. But here no one seemed to care about them, and they felt that the church and the minister were indifferent. It was extremely hard on their Southern sociability and their religious loyalty, but they held on, later moved closer, made many friends, and finally were able to tell with understanding humor their experiences in getting adjusted to Chicago and to the church.

There is something overpowering and devastating in the isolation which many people feel in the great city. A man I knew sold out his business in the Loop and moved away because his restaurant denied him time for social life with his neighbors and even prevented opportunity to get acquainted with his children. "I have to leave home early in the morning before they are awake, and I get home in the evening after they have gone to sleep again," he said. Living in crowds of people in hotels and apartment buildings without really knowing them, and traveling with crowds on trains and streetcars where you seldom recognize a face, does something to people. It hardens some into insensitivity to others, and all of us city dwellers are compelled to revise our conception of "neighbor." A neighbor has to be something more than a human being living next door. In the old horse-and-buggy days it was the custom to speak to everyone we met on the road. Now we pass others so fast we could not speak if we would, and the familiar gestures of friendliness have disappeared. That partly accounts for the hit-and-run drivers.

"Social distances" make a real opportunity for the church and the pastor. The church is the one institution that provides for all comers hospitality, friendliness, and identification with the most ideal social causes. It offers the individual a place among worthwhile people and opens the way for him to do something real and rewarding in the world's work. The minister symbolizes this friendly institution. He is its voice and its agent. Through him the doors of life open upon many scenes and upon many paths of comradeship and usefulness. The minister is at times too conscious of the importance of his role. He may press his cause too insistently and too directly. His case is good enough to make its own appeal, when he adequately and ingeniously presents it. His own intelligent confidence in it is its best commendation, but this confidence may be betrayed by haste and too great urgency. The common friendliness of any person is enhanced by his station and calling, if these have the support and the quality of a vital and engaging purpose and intention.

The pastoral work I have tried to do is more than ringing doorbells or hopping about the streets to accumulate as large a number of "calls" as possible for the report to the next meeting of the church board, or at the annual meeting of the congregation. What seems to me important is to be at hand when people are sick or bereaved or experiencing some radical change or crisis. It is not always easy to know whether a call from the minister is welcome at such times. Frequently a letter or a telephone conversation with someone in the home is preferable. It is the manifestation of interest and concern that is important.

One day a member of the church said, when I met her on the street, "I have been sick and you didn't call on me." I said, "Oh, I'm very sorry you have been sick. Did the doctor call on you?" "'Certainly he did," she answered. I said, "Why, that was nice of him. How did he find out you were sick?" "Well, I called him and told him I wanted him to come and see me," she replied. I smilingly promised, "The next time you are sick and want to see me I'll come as soon as I can, if you will let me know."

One never knows the courage and fortitude possible to human beings unless he sees them in some extremity. A woman with three children and a shiftless husband called me to come to her home. We sat down to talk and, to my surprise, she seemed more lighthearted than usual. "Well, I have a notice from the store that my payments on the furniture we have are so far behind that they are coming to take it away, and I have a notice from the landlord that the rent is so long overdue that we must give up the flat. Isn't that a coincidence!" she said, with a burst of laughter. She was one of the poorest, bravest, and shrewdest women I have ever known. By some means we fixed up the situation and prevented the double disaster, but, even before she saw a way out, she did not despair or dissolve in tears.

For years she carried on with her needle and her pluck, never quite giving up but never achieving security. The kind of thing she had to endure is illustrated by this scene. One evening all five of the family were at supper when the husband, provoked by some incident, fell into a rage and, gathering up the tablecloth by the four corners, whirled it around his head, dashed everything on the floor, and stormed out of the house! In the course of a few days he returned, and once more she listened to his pleadings and promises until she let him stay. Finally, he was committed to an institution, but there too her concern and devotion followed him till he died. I have never ceased to marvel at her fidelity. I could not justify it on any rational ground, nor can I yet think of it without a sense of wonder at this love in a human heart "so amazing, so divine."

The tragedies I was obliged to witness and to counsel over were not all among the poor and underprivileged. Many people say to me: "You are fortunately situated in a university neighborhood, and the people you deal with are a specially favored class. You can scarcely know from your experience what the average pastor has to deal with." Perhaps so, but through the years things have happened here which I prefer to think cannot be surpassed on the side of suffering and tragedy. There are also the other things, things that touch the heights of love and nobility.

There was a couple, educated, traveled, and well-to-do, who sent for me late one evening to advise them what to do with their domestic wreck. The woman, carefully dressed and having the speech and manner of a cultivated lady, lay on the couch in the living room, while her young husband sat in a chair across the room, bewildered and alarmed. Her brother was present. The woman felt that they had come to the end. She said that her husband was not a success, that they could not have a family, that the uncertainty and worry about their future had shattered her nerves. He, however, wanted to go on and was willing to provide the money from his inheritance. He was submissive and self-effacing, rather too much so. Some show of strength and self-assertion would have helped his case, but they went farther apart, and after some months he gave her all his money, still hoping to soften her heart and win her back. But she took all his fortune and eventually married another man and set out to make a career for herself, though without success. No word of the pastor was able to make the slightest change.

It was like being present beside a deathbed. Unmanageable forces were in control and moved fatefully to one end. Death itself could not be more inevitable, and I had seen the oncoming of death, too. Early in my ministry I had been called into one of our loveliest and most religious homes. The only daughter, after a long, brave fight against tuberculosis, was slipping away. With her last breath she smiled her farewell upon us and peacefully passed away. In the deep, tense silence her father uttered the benediction of resignation and faith: "The Lord gave, and the Lord hath taken away. Blessed be the name of the Lord." Whenever I hear those words, I hear them in his assuring tones.

A pastor, living closely with several hundred people of one church for many years, has life and death come before him in many forms. Even the moments of death are not all terrible. In the great majority of cases the forebodings of death are far more dreadful than the event itself. Sometimes it is very welcome and comes as a desired release from suffering and weariness. A patient in the Home for Incurables knew he could live but a little while and wanted to talk to me. When I asked him how old he was, he said: "I am fifty-five, but I have lived a hundred years. My family is gone, my business is gone, and my strength is almost gone. I have tried to do the best I knew, and I want you to pray for me." I prayed for his peace of mind and for courage in his heart to face the great adventure before him. As I left, he turned his face quietly to the wall and peacefully passed away.

Such experiences have deepened in me the realization that human life runs a natural cycle, and somewhere in the course of years, even though it be ninety or a hundred years, the lifeline ends. This is not a fatalistic view. It is not an acceptance of the theory that "when a man's time comes, he is bound to go." One day, returning from the funeral of a physician who had died in his early forties, the driver of the car spoke of knowing the deceased well and of his own sense of loss in the doctor's death. "But," he said, "I suppose when your time comes, there's nothing can be done about it." "Oh," I said, "I do not believe the exact time is set for each of us to die." We were alone in the car, and he looked around in the greatest surprise. "Well," I said, "what was the doctor himself trying to do for people all the time, if not to carry them through sickness which but for him might have been fatal? You know how through the last ten days or so he has kept at work when he should have been in bed taking care of a cold, as he would have made any of his patients do." "Maybe that is so," he said, "but I've never heard a preacher say that before."

Funerals also make people think about the question of immortality, not in the detached and academic manner of theological discussions but with the hot and desperate longing to know whether there is a life after this life. One of our members was on the faculty of Lewis Institute when he died, after a brief illness, and left his young wife desolate and solitary. She came up to me after the service in their home, drew me to one side while people were still standing about, and said in her deeply thoughtful way, "Now tell me, what do you really think about immortality?" "Well, my dear friend," I said, "I cannot say anything different here from what you have heard me say many times before. I hope for it myself, but I cannot prove it or know it. You know my own conviction is that the best thing to do is to make the most of this life, in a true sense, and trust God for the rest. If there is a future life, he who has lived up to his best, as your husband has done, will be well prepared for it and will share it. And if there is no other life than this, the good man will surely have had the best this present life can give." "That is what I believe too," she said, "but I wanted to have you say it to me right here and now. It is truly a comfort."

A minister friend used to say that he thought one reason ministers were not better understod as normal, fairly happy, and companionable men was that so many people never saw them except at funerals. There, in the nature of the case, they were compelled to be serious and to talk about the sad and most baffling things of life.

I would remind him that ministers are also present at weddings and that at no other time does the atmosphere of happiness and fine sociability more completely encompass our human kind. Then there is feasting and cheer and the radiating joy of love's inmost felicity. Flowers, music, kisses, and radiant beauty symbolize the full bloom of life. It is the high religious celebration, with all that is holiest and highest in human affection and hope.

Youth stands at the threshold of new vistas, and the world opens out upon new possibilities. It is a fitting scene for miracles of wonder like the first miracle of Christ in Cana of Galilee.

I often wish it were possible to gather up into some imperishable form the names and faces of the hundreds of lives which have built into the deep spiritual structure of our local church, so that all who become members of it might really know that whole company of devoted souls. We honor the early leaders like Dr. Herbert L. Willett and Professor William D. MacClintock, whose words and spirit are not likely ever to be forgotten. Mr. W. L. Carr was a resourceful superintendent of the Sunday school, where he led the singing, as he did at parties of the Wranglers, the young people's organization. Mr. Horace Lacey served faithfully as financial secretary, followed by Mr. Edward A. Henry. But many others no longer with us should be remembered.

Mrs. Hutchinson was especially encouraging to me in the early days. Well known in the whole community, she and her husband, Dr. E. B. Hutchinson (who pulled us through the usual children's diseases), identified themselves with the little church in its unpretentious building and gave it their wholehearted enthusiasm and support. They had no Disciple tradition to bring them into our fellowship. She had been an Episcopalian. She told her friends about our church and made social occasions in her home to extend its influence. She brought the spirit of Hull-House to the church and enriched its life by what she had learned as one of the first residents in that famous settlement.

Her love of the church was natural and unaffected, as if she had been born into it and as if it suffered no lack in her esteem because it was the youngest and smallest of the churches in the neighborhood. She brought her children into it, gave her skill and energy to it in many activities, and found comfort in it in the long months of silence and uncertainty when no definite word came from the front, where her son Fryar had been killed in the Argonne. The ardor and affection of her intense Irish nature could not surmount the agony of those tragic months, and she died of a broken heart from the strain of the suspense and sorrow. Such people as Mrs. Hutchinson helped to broaden the spirit and fellowship of the church and to commend it to a larger public than it otherwise could have reached.

The quiet, understanding loyalty of the members themselves has been the most effective pastoral influence in the church. In their conversations and discussions they removed false impressions about the church and upheld its ideas and endeavors. Mrs. Faddis was one of these. She was a widow, in her middle seventies, the mother of many grown children. She was of pioneer stock and had been a devout Disciple many years. On one of my visits to her home she told me how a zealous conservative of the congregation had come to see her, to ask if she would join him in a protest against the minister's teachings and innovations. She said she told him, "Why, my brother, this is the first church to which we ever belonged in which my children have really been happy, and as long as they are interested and happy, I shall do nothing such as you suggest."

Much of the pastoral work of the church was also done by other methods than that of house-to-house calling by the minister. From the first there was much use of the printed page: the weekly calendar, the monthly *Messenger*, form letters, sermons, and tracts. These had the advantage of going to all members whether or not they were able to be present Sunday mornings. Personal items, plans of work, ideas, and reminders of many kinds thus found their way into all the homes and helped to bind together in a common mind and spirit all members and friends. There was therefore never any excuse for anyone to be unaware of the temper and doctrine of the church. Fair notice was given to very conservative people what kind of church it was, and this helped to insure a united and informed congregation.

Sometimes people went elsewhere when they realized what they would be getting into. One very orthodox Disciple couple was much shocked over the practice of open membership. They could not tolerate the idea of a Disciple church receiving into full membership Presbyterians and others without immersion. After some deliberation they registered their feeling about this matter by going to a Presbyterian church and uniting with it!

When the new church and church house were built, new forms of pastoral work became possible, especially by means of dinners and recreation. There might be a talk, some music, a play, or slides, and usually games and dancing. The purpose of the church dinners may be said to have been solely the promotion of acquaintance and sociability. No financial profit was derived from them. When I proposed that we have dinners on Sunday in the church, the main objection was that it could not be done, that people preferred to have Sunday dinners at home. But we said the only way we could certainly know was to make the experiment. When the plan was tried, it was so well supported that no one has ever suggested its discontinuance. Sociability and comradeship have always been strongest among people when they eat together. It is a kind of basic human experience, and, when men and women and children partake of a common meal, they see and feel themselves to be fellow human beings. When they eat together in the church, they may sense the fact that in this simple way there is generated a very appreciable religious fellowship, that is, a fellowship that is enhanced and deepened just because of the place and time and manner of its occurrence.

Thirty years ago I printed a few paragraphs in the *Messenger,* reflecting a not uncommon experience in pastoral work:

I have been out calling this afternoon. I made nine calls. Three of the families were about to move. One had just arrived, the better half of one was leaving town for a visit, and one could not be found at all. Of the other three families, one was cleaning house, one was away from home, and the ninth house was settled and quiet. But in the course of the afternoon I learned that these good people were talking of moving out of the city. I hurried home to make sure that my own family were not moving away! It gives one vertigo to discover so many changes in one afternoon. It is rather difficult to fix the attention of people upon the eternal, immutable realities of religion while they are experiencing so keenly the vicissitudes of this mortal life.

In 1930 that kind of pastoral work came to an end for me. For some weeks I had felt pain in my left knee when walking. One evening in February, after we had been out for dinner, the pain was worse than ever, and the few blocks going home were torture. When the doctor came, he ordered me to the hospital to have the fluid drained from my swollen knee and then discovered other conditions which led him to say that I should keep off my feet as much as possible and that probably I would be under that handicap the rest of my life. That was the end of my thirty years of conventional pastoral work. Fortunately, I had built up other methods—what I may call "pastoral printing" and pastoral dinners. But as the weeks went on, I felt that I should resign from the pastorate, especially since I was trying to carry the work of two other positions.

But the church people did not accept the resignation, and I finally acceded to their persuasion. I had never learned to drive a car, and I began to think I had been very foolish years before when my dear friend, Mrs. Waite, had started a move to raise money among the church members and friends to buy me a car. But I had dissuaded her and the committee from the undertaking when it came to my attention, and the committee had readily agreed, since such an effort might increase the difficulty of raising the regular church budget. Perhaps I have at least lived longer than I would if I had been furnished so dangerous a thing as an automobile. For years I have had to hire taxis for the short trips from my home to the university and to the church, but I have been assured that, after all, it is cheaper to hire cars than to own one.

In any case we went along together in the church, for ten more years, and I had more quiet hours in my study. With the fine co-operation of the leaders and members of the church we were able to maintain a happy and deepening religious life together.

Chapter xiv | Building a New Church

The original name of the church was the Hyde Park Church of Christ, which was changed to the University Church of Disciples of Christ when the permanent location was decided upon in 1921. For six years the church met in halls, the Masonic Hall and Rosalie Hall at the corner of East Fifty-seventh Street and Harper Avenue. They were "upper rooms" on the second floor of the business block. In 1899 space was leased on the ground of the Disciples Divinity House at the corner of Fifty-seventh Street and what is now University Avenue (then Lexington), and a small brick building was erected which was to cost seven thousand dollars. At the beginning of 1900 the congregation had its own house and a debt on it of about half the cost. No debt was ever more resistant to efforts made to annihilate it. A considerable item of it lingered on for ten years against earnest and unabated endeavors to pay it off. That debt, and the decade of difficulties with it, gave the minister and the members a deep-seated fear complex agains debts of any kind. It proved to be a very useful lesson for all future years.

That little building seated about two hundred people, two hundred and fifty and more when occasion compelled. Mr. Samuel MacClintock gave the architecture the descriptive name of "squat gothic." The central part had an almost conical roof, but the walls projected beyond the roof on four sides, which gave the effect of large alcoves on three sides of the interior. But the interior was a pleasant place, with a dome of relatively good height and a floor space convenient for the curving lines of opera chairs running east and west, with a slight convergence before the pulpit and the choir space back of the pulpit. This choir space was made to accommodate the piano or reed organ and the quartet. A screen at the east end hid the small boy who pumped the organ. This small boy who performed this task for some years was my son. One day he called my attention to the names of the musicians printed in the calendar and asked why his name was not there with the rest. I explained that only the names of the singers and organist were given. "Yes," he said, "but they couldn't do anything without me." I have never been sure that he did not have a just claim, but he held on to the job in spite of the discrimination against him!

In March, 1911, there appeared in the *Messenger* this announcement: "If the members and friends of the church will secure an attendance of at least two hundred people at the Sunday morning service for six weeks in succession, beginning April 2, the pastor will undertake the task of securing fifty thousand dollars for a new building." After that period of six weeks, it was found that there had been more than two hundred each Sunday. The average was 247. The minister was surprised but greatly encouraged by this result. In reporting it, he said:

We have made many new friends and have extended acquaintance with the church in many directions. This experiment has proved that we can get good audiences at our present location, and it has shown that the method of getting them is to stir up our own members. Of course we cannot promise a fifty-thousand-dollar building every three months, and it was doubtless the suggestion of a new building which made the attendance possible. But certainly the interest and activity of the members and friends is the important factor in the development and efficiency of the church.

In the same report it was stated that "the work of securing money for the new buildings has begun." The beginning was the sending of a letter to several representative pastors and business men of the brotherhood to elicit their indorsement and encouragement of the enterprise, saying: "It is hoped that some individuals of large means will see the opportunity which our location and work offer. At the present time, however, there are no definite assurances of this kind, and we absolutely have the whole task before us."

The proposal of a building and the hope of receiving help from people outside Chicago had some justification in the reasonable expectation that Disciples throughout the country might be made to appreciate the opportunities in having adequate buildings for the church and the Disciples Divinity House erected adjacent to the University of Chicago. These advantages were set forth in the letter, but without appreciable, visible results. Other letters and announcements were published reiterating these advantages:

The Disciples Divinity House would need a hall and a chapel. The hall would provide offices, lecture rooms, library, parlors, and recreation rooms. The church needed a chapel for its services and a hall for its classes and social activities. The occasions and activities of the two institutions are such that they would not conflict but would very decidely supplement and support each other. . . . It is estimated that this cannot be done for less than one hundred thousand dollars, and that twice this amount could be appropriately expended.

The publication of these plans brought encouraging letters from many leaders among the Disciples in various parts of the country. Charles T. Paul, head of the Missionary Training School, then located in Indianapolis, wrote:

I doubt whether any other building enterprise now before the Disciples of Christ can compare in importance with the proposed joint structure of the Disciples Divinity House and the Hyde Park Church of Chicago. . . . Academic relations with a great seat of learning like the University of Chicago is an opportunity which should be secured and honored by an enduring divinity hall architecturally comportable with the contiguous university structures. Such a building devoted to thorough biblical scholarship and sound Christian training has vast meaning for the future ministerial, missionary, and educational leadership of the church. The whole enterprise is a work of necessity and farsighted vision.

Dr. A. B. Philputt, pastor of the Central Christian Church in Indianapolis, wrote: "It ought to be a proud day, not only with the Chicago Disciples but with us all throughout the Middle West, when a worthy building shall arise on your well-chosen site, facing the great groups of Chicago University structures. Within its hospitable walls our young men will find shelter and companionship and inspiration through all the years."

Pastor C. G. Kindred, of the Englewood Church, Chicago, said in his letter:

Your attempt to erect a building has interested me immensely. It is not much more yours than mine; it will belong to the brotherhood, and as such it will be a part of our history. So don't be discouraged or over-persuaded, but do something worthy of the cause and the location. To me that corner is the finest one of the university, and the Bartlett Gymnasium and the Commons call for more than an ordinary structure. . . . Feeling you will understand me, and, being human, will appreciate any word of encouragement, I write to pledge you my interest and influence.

Dr. E. L. Powell, famous preacher of the First Christian Church, Louisville, Kentucky, sent this word:

I should think that the arrangement with the Hyde Park Church is altogether admirable. It is particularly gratifying to be assured of the organic relation of the Disciples Divinity House with the university. This means much. . . . I do not know of any institution among us which offers just the instruction provided in the courses of the House. As respects the history of our own people and the interpretation of this religious movement in the past century, there is offered an especially fascinating series of studies. Here is provided a great opportunity for someone who has large wealth to consecrate it to the very noblest use. This is a work which will go on in its influence in the coming years.

These letters were written in 1913 and published in the *Messenger*. Four years later the records show that nothing of this plan had been achieved, but they also show that the dream had not vanished. In a very long letter from me to the church in 1917 the first suggestion of attempting to raise a building fund was recalled in these words:

I once asked you to bring your bodily presence here and fill the church every Sunday for six weeks, with the promise that if you did so I would undertake to secure a new building. I have not forgotten that promise. Fortunately there was no time set within which it had to be accomplished. But as I think of that six weeks now, it is eloquent with reference to the latent possibilities in your life.

At the end of that letter I became truly prophetic for once in my life, as subsequent events proved, for I said:

What would it be, O dear readers, if you gathered yourselves into one great holy purpose to fuse these things into definite expression, into facile symbols, and into effective working agencies. Then every member would feel new tides of life here, people would seek a share in such a potent spiritual atmosphere, and as by magic, buildings and money and men would be available for the fulfilment of your dreams.

It was to be yet two years more before the tangible beginning of the fulfilment of that dream occurred. But in 1919, more than eight years after the six weeks' test of attendance, and after the World War had come and gone, it was possible to announce that a friend of the church had promised to give the first twenty-five thousand dollars.

On September 7, 1919, Mrs. George Herbert Jones's name appeared in the calendar among those of new members. The names of Mr. and Mrs. B. Fred Wise were also in that list, and these three people were to play a great part in the fulfilment of the dream of a new church and its activities. Mrs. Jones had attended a series of Wednesday evening talks by the pastor, and Mr. Wise had been in his classes in philosophy in the university. Mrs. Jones had long been in search of a satisfying religious faith. From her earlier Anglican church connection she had received a deep religious spirit, but in later years she had sought in theosophy and other faiths for something more adequate to meet both her practical and her ardently mystical spirit. Within two years she gave one hundred thousand dollars for the new buildings, and finally twenty thousand dollars, which altogether was half their total cost.

Although her husband, Mr. George Herbert Jones, was wealthy, what she gave was from her own fortune, inherited from her father, Elias Colbert. I quote a paragraph about him from my words at her funeral service, reported in the *Messenger* for February, 1929.

Elias Colbert was born in Paris, and grew to young manhood in England. When left a widower, he brought his infant daughter to Chicago (in 1857), and she was his close companion through her childhood and down to the close of his long life. (He died in 1921 at the age of 92.) He was a journalist and a close friend of Joseph Medill, founder of the *Chicago Tribune*. He wrote one of the best histories of the early days of this city. He had strong scientific interests and was connected with the department of astronomy in the old Chicago University. His daughter shared these interests and cherished tenderly his library of books and papers gathered in the pursuit of a wide range of subjects.

Mrs. Jones first came to the church through the influence of a friend of hers, who was also a friend of the church but not a member. To quote again from the remarks at her funeral service:

She seemed to find at once something which her nature craved. She responded to its inquiring thought, its informal spirit, and its aspiring faith. Through all the years of her membership she was present when possible on Sunday morning and usually rode many miles from the home on the north side or from the farm on the south (near Midlothian) to be present, She became a member of the church when the congregation was in the little brick building which was so small that no one could find his way into it except through an earnest and genuine religious quest. How deeply she responded to its ideals and purposes was shown in her magnificent contribution to the new building. She felt a keen satisfaction in the beauty and charm of the architecture and was happy in seeing the work of the congregation enlarged and enhanced by more adequate facilities. Yet she never assumed any other attitude than that of just being one of the many members. . . .

It would not do her justice to say that she ever found answers to all her questions. Her mind still searched for fuller light and more complete satisfaction. She had a great sense of the mystery of life. There was on her mantel a poem, "My Creed," by Howard Arnold Walter, which she greatly cherished. Two of the lines are,

> I would be friend of all—the foe, the friendless;
> I would be giving and forget the gift.

And another expression of her spirit is in these words which she also had constantly before her eyes.

> I shall pass through this world but once.
> Any good I can show to any human being,
> Let me do it now;
> Let me not defer or neglect it,
> For I shall not pass this way again.

She knew much happiness and she lived in the midst of unfailing and watchful love. Hers was a full and ardent life in the midst of the world's greatest age. She had golden keys to unlock many doors and a mind to appreciate the beauty and the marvels which she found.

I have spoken at length of Mrs. Jones, for it was her hand and heart more than any others' which made our dream into stone and ongoing forms of service. Our first real meeting was in my office at the university, where she sought me to talk about some of the things she had heard at the church. Later at the Blackstone Hotel, where the family then lived in the winter, I came to know her better, with her husband and children, in a fine friendship that has continued through the years. I buried her father and her only son and married her only daughter. I cherish with deep gratitude and keen appreciation this little quotation which she gave me as her pastor and friend: "Oh the comfort, the inexpressible comfort, of feeling safe with a person, having neither to weigh thoughts, nor measure words, but pouring them all right out, just as they are:

chaff and grain together, certain that a faithful hand will take and sift them—keep what is worth keeping and with the breath of kindness blow the rest away." In the east aisle of the church, set in the enduring stone of the wall, is a tablet in her memory, with her oft-repeated remark, "I believe in churches." That is the simple expression of her faith, and I hope those words will reverberate in the hearts of all who read them through many years and decades yet to come.

Wartime had increased building costs to twice what they were when we first dreamed the dream of building. Our ideas of what we needed had grown from the first thought of fifty thousand dollars to two hundred thousand, and it was arduous work to bring the subscriptions to that amount. About seventy-five thousand were raised outside the church membership, and practically nothing from Disciples in other churches either in Chicago or elsewhere. The brotherhood did not respond with any material aid, as our correspondents, already quoted, had hoped. But the reasons for this were understood. This local church had adventured on several innovating ideas and practices. It was conscious of radical pioneering, and it was better if it were able to go its way without hampering gifts from conservative people. On New Year's Eve, 1920, Friday evening, the announcement was made of the completion of the fund of two hundred thousand dollars, and joyous celebration was held.

But a larger task was yet to be met than had been anticipated, the task of adjusting the plans and uses of the buildings for the purposes of the church and the Disciples Divinity House. Some members of the boards of both institutions had not expected the minister to complete the building fund so quickly, if at all, and when the fund was actually subscribed the necessary legal arrangements were not ready. These agreements were completed only after more than a year of negotiations. Finally it was decided to the full satisfaction of all parties that the church should purchase the west half of the lot owned by the Disciples Divinity House, one hundred and fifty feet on University Avenue and ninety feet on Fifty-seventh Street, the church to pay twenty-five thousand dollars for this corner. It was felt that the two organizations would work better together if they were completely separate in their ownership of property and in management of their work. The Disciples Divinity House at this time had a small endowment of about eighty-six thousand dollars, and the twenty-five thousand dollars from the sale of half its lot was the beginning of a building fund. More than a year elapsed before the details of the building plans were complete and ready for the contractors' estimates. When the bids came in, it was found that it would require forty thousand dollars more to construct both the church and the church house, and it was at first agreed to proceed with the church proper and take a longer time for the church house. But the spirit of the pastor and the church people finally rose to this last emergency also.

Mr. Howard Van Doren Shaw and Mr. Henry K. Holsman were the architects. Mr. Shaw was primarily responsible for the designing and Mr. Holsman for superintending the construction. Mr. Shaw became greatly interested in the plans and gave them the best of his fine imagination and artistry. At first he recommended a type of extreme English Gothic, with high stone pulpit into which the minister would ascend by several steps. As we looked it over, I remarked that it was very lovely of its kind but was unsuited to the minister and congregation for whom he was preparing plans. In some surprise he asked what I meant, and he listened intently to my idea of what the building should be. The pulpit should be more nearly on the level of the pews, because it was a democratic church; there should be clear windows to let in plenty of light, not stained glass windows at the sides which would make everything dim but not "religious"; there should be a fireplace somewhere in the church proper to symbolize hospitality and the undying fire; and, while we wanted the church solidly on the ground, it should have lift and aspiration such as columns and arches could give it. Instead of being offended or discouraged with me, Mr. Shaw came out to a church service and looked us over, read our literature, including my book *The New Orthodoxy*, and set himself to what he afterward regarded as one of his best achievements.

There are some unusual features in the building, some intentional and some inevitable, like the cracks in the terazza floor. The great bays on the west contrast with the columns and the broad aisle on the east. It was originally intended that the main entrance to the church should be on Fifty-seventh Street in the southeast corner; but, when it was decided to build the church house at once, it was seen that it would be more convenient to have a common entrance to the church and the church house where the narthex is. When the great Gothic window in the south end was not brought down almost to the floor, as first planned, this change made an effect, almost accidental, which resulted in a deep ledge high behind the pulpit, where the stone was built up to the glass. The wall there is five feet thick and the ledge affords appropriate space for the angels in our Christmas pageant! At the opposite end of the building, at the back, on the sill of the little window of the echo organ chamber, is a sinister figure. It is Satan himself, about whom in this place many rationalizations have been made. It may be taken to stand for a motif in traditional Gothic ecclesiastical architecture, which is disposed to have the evil forces of life suggested around the roof and edges of the building by gargoyles, imps, and demons. To my mind this figure expresses my own conviction that the church ought to be open to everyone, to sinners as well as saints, and to the devil himself as well as to the angels.

It was a wonderful day, the first Sunday in October, 1923, when we dedicated the building. We had been twenty-three years in the little old brick structure, and for twelve years we had been dreaming how we could get out of it into something better. I must say it had served well in its day and had become very dear to the hearts of hundreds of us whose souls had been happy and aspiring under its humble roof. The communion service was held in the old church that dedication day. Words written by Dr. W. E. Garrison for the occasion were sung by Mr. Wise, to the music of Schubert's *Ave Maria:*

> Here have we seen Thy face, Father and Friend,
> Here have we heard Thy voice, Comrade and Guide,
> Beneath this roof we have been near Thee,
> Within these walls we feel and hear Thee,
> Here press Thy hand and touch Thy side.
> 'Neath loftier arches be Thou with us still,
> Our Friend, our Comrade and our cheer,
> Thy presence ampler spaces fill,
> And make Thy dwelling there as here.
> There may we hear Thy voice.

We marched to the new building, singing as we went, "The Son of God Goes Forth to War." Dr. Willett preached the dedicatory sermon on "Beauty and Strength." Mrs. Quinney played the organ numbers. The church was dedicated without indebtedness. Under Mr. O. B. Holloway's careful management the building fund had accumulated five thousand dollars in interest on deposits in the bank. President E. D. Burton, of the University of Chicago, gave an address in the afternoon on "The Church and Education." Mr. Lorado Taft, the sculptor, was to have spoken in the evening; but, because the lighting fixtures were not completely installed, his address was given the following Sunday evening.

On June 3, 1928, a Skinner pipe organ was installed at a cost of twenty-seven thousand dollars, and the dedicatory recital was given by Mr. Arthur Dunham. The pulpit, a gift to the church by two of its most staunch members, Mr. O. B. Holloway and Mr. W. I. Schermerhorn, was dedicated September 29, 1929. Mrs. Gary Sutcliffe, then a new member, gave the pulpit chairs and the lovely tapestry on the south wall below the window.

The prayer of dedication of the pulpit expresses the spirit and purpose of the whole building enterprise, extending through so many years and enlisting the generosity and devotion of so many people. Without that spirit and purpose the building would have become merely a heap of stones, if not a vanity and mockery. The closing words of that prayer were these:

May there be winged words spoken here that shall echo far, and touch with power, widening circles of those who grope for the way of life and blessedness. In all that is here spoken may there be the restraining and the quickening spirit of the great teacher, Jesus Christ, to whose cause and service this house of worship is itself dedicated. And bless, we pray Thee, the congregations which listen here for the accent of heavenly words, to nourish and to sustain their spirits. May men and women, youths and little children, find here, according to the measure of their need, the beauty and the wisdom of the kingdom of God in its fulness and redeeming power. May the voice which utters itself here be the voice of the common faith and the aspiration of all hearts. And as, through the years, there are sounded forth the words of life and death, of challenge and instruction, may there also arise deeds of love and devotion which shall make this world a better place and fill it more and more with the peace of heaven. Amen.

Chapter xv | Going Up to Jerusalem

In 1926 the *Christian Century* offered prizes for new subscriptions. The prizes were a tour to the Orient, a sedan automobile, a cruise to the Holy Land, and several lesser prizes. Some women of our church promoted a plan to get enough subscriptions to win a prize for the minister. This was a large undertaking, since churches of various denominations throughout the country entered the contest. There were eleven prize winners, and my name was fourth in the list. My choice was the cruise to the Holy Land, toward the cost of which the prize entitled me to accommodations of the value of one thousand dollars. This tour was conducted by Mr. H. W. Dunning, of Brookline, Massachusetts, a veteran traveler and guide.

My fortune as a prize winner came as a surprise, and in accepting it changes had to be made in other plans. My courses announced for the summer quarter had to be shifted; pulpit supplies for two months had to be secured and family affairs adjusted. If I had foreseen what weddings I would miss, and other events of very great personal importance, I might have decided to forfeit the prize. But life is like that. When you choose to do one thing it generally means that you choose *not* to do other things. Curiously enough, and luckily, we usually are not so much aware of the surrendered lines of action. We tend to be more conscious of the interests to which we are committed, and they absorb our energies. It is unfortunate if, having given allegiance to one set of interests, the imagination keeps wandering off in other directions and makes a waste of emotion and power over "what might have been."

The summer is not the most popular time to make tours of the Near East, but Mr. Dunning had often done so and gave assurance that it could be managed satisfactorily. One piece of work I had agreed to do was to prepare a paper on "'Mysticism" for the Sixth International Congress of Philosophy, meeting at Harvard University in the coming September. I was anxious "to set the world right" on this subject of mysticism and thought I could find time for writing on shipboard or at odd hours in the midst of sightseeing. So I carried along notes and paper and the worry of it. A task like that is never out of mind until it is done, and it can spoil many otherwise free hours by a haunting feeling that it should be receiving attention.

On the third day of July I sailed from New York on the "S.S. Duilio," bound for Naples, where I was to overtake Mr. Dunning's party, which had sailed a week or so before I could be ready to go. On this Italian ship I found a friend, Miss May Rogers, a member of my church, and quickly made new friends who also added to the pleasure of the voyage. Being late in making reservations, I had to take whatever accommodations I could get and found myself in a stateroom with three other men, one a Catholic priest returning to his native Italy to retire from active service, one a Black Shirt Fascist organizer from New York, and the third a roadhouse or tavern proprietor from the vicinity of Philadelphia. We were sufficiently diverse and novel to each other to be mutually interesting.

Mr. Dunning's party arrived in Naples, after a week or two of travel in Europe, and I found a congenial company. The Rev. L. D. Anderson, of the First Christian Church in Fort Worth, Texas, and I were to be roommates for the rest of the journey. The Rev. W. N. Briney and his wife, of the Broadway Christian Church of Louisville, Kentucky, were also in the company. Mr. Briney's father had been one of my severest critics and opponents in the Louisville Convention of 1911, already referred to, but the son and I did not let that mar our comradeship.

Our sightseeing began at once as we looked out over the beautiful Bay of Naples and upon smoking Vesuvius. We made the usual visit to Pompeii, but under strikingly different conditions from those in which I had made my first visit there sixteen years before. Now, by means of better roads, automobiles, and boats, we were able between eight in the morning and eight in the evening to see Pompeii and its fascinating ruins, take the glorious scenic drive to Amalfi, have luncheon at the Capuchin monastery, go shopping in Sorrento, and get back to our hotel in Naples for dinner. That day was a kind of pacemaker for the days to follow, each one so filled with marvels of beauty and historic associations that every day touched a thousand years of events. That sense of condensed history and summarized centuries of human experience increased as our journey extended.

On July 16 we went aboard the "Sphinx" and on the seventeenth were well into the Mediterranean, whose shores were the cradle of civilization and the boundaries of the known world for ages before the rise of modern European peoples. It was thrilling to see with one's own eyes things that had lived in imagination from the schoolday Latin of Horace and Virgil. We passed Stromboli, with its smoking volcano and its home of the god Aeolus, of the Aeolian winds, and safely made our way between the terrible Scylla and Charybdis, the rock and the whirlpool of destruction, looked upon Mount Aetna and sailed out through the Straits of Messina into the storied world of myth and legend.

In two days we were within view of the shores of Greece. We had only one day for Athens. One day in Athens! When I thought of all the days and nights I had spent on the history, literature, philosophy, and art of Athens, it seemed the height of irony to be limited to just one day there. But I determined to make the most of that day. I was on deck at four o'clock in the morning, as we approached Piraeus, and saw the sun rise over the city of Socrates and Plato as they, too, had seen it rise centuries ago. My notes say:

The Bay of Phaleron stretched before us, and in the distance was Mount Hymettus. Along the horizon the mountains were thrust into the sky and threw back their heavy shadows upon a world of unworn wisdom and beauty. It was not easy at first to discern the Acropolis. The goddess Athene no longer stands upon its height to mark for the traveler by sea or land the sacred spot. But at last the glasses found the unmistakable bold lines and revealed in the growing light the grey mass of the Parthenon itself.

We also looked toward the island of Salamis, where the Athenian fleet under Themistocles defeated the Persians in 480 B.C. and thereby sharply determined the course of history, ending the hope of the Persian conquest of Europe. Modern automobiles awaited us at the dock and drove us up a beautiful broad avenue, newly paved, to the Acropolis. Along the way were many survivals of the far past. Under the hot sun the workmen were plying their trades—carpenters, gardeners, potters, brick makers, masons, donkey boys, and merchants with their wares—in a way which made me half expect to see Socrates somewhere questioning the youth, or Alcibiades driving past in splendor.

We were soon at the gate of the Acropolis, guarded now by a high iron fence and a five-dollar tax for each person who entered. The magnificent buildings whose ruins we beheld had been erected under the rule of Pericles in 438 B.C. and the years following. The visitor is stirred to a feeling of deep resentment that the Parthenon, generally regarded as one of the three or four most beautiful buildings ever built by the hand of man, should have been wrecked by man himself after it had withstood the forces of nature and the ravages of many wars for more than two thousand years. It was uninjured until 1687, when it was blown up by the Venetians in their attack upon the city. At that time Athens fell into complete oblivion and was only rediscovered by explorers and scholars of the nineteenth century. But even in their ruins these most beautiful works of antiquity still hold their graceful lines and carry a majesty of repose and strength. To no other feature is this appreciation more in point than to the Erechtheum, with its famous Porch of the Maidens, where four strong and graceful figures take the place of columns to support the roof.

In the Theater of Dionysus we sat in the marble chairs of the front rows, where the dignitaries and priests of the golden age of the city once sat and witnessed the plays of Aeschylus, Sophocles, Euripides, and Aristophanes. The Temple of Jupiter, with its great ground area and its fifteen remaining massive columns, gave me one of my most memorable impressions of grandeur. As I gazed up their great height, Mr. Dunning, noticing my rapt amazement, said, "Oh, just wait until we get to Baalbek." I couldn't imagine at the moment how we could expect to see anything of that kind more impressive. Outside the walls of the city was the ancient burying ground, by the tombs of which were many well-carved monuments. The scenes on those monuments have lingered with me all the years for the new feeling they gave me about death. The deceased was represented as bidding farewell to the family, but there were no surface signs of grief. There was a quiet dignity and composure, as if neither the one departing nor those remaining had anything to fear. There was the air of the accept-ance of fate without despair, the manner of tenderest affection to-gether with strength and peace.

Many other things in that one day in Athens left their indelible impression. There was Mars Hill, where Paul preached his im-mortal sermon to the curious Greeks who gathered round him to hear some new thing, and heard more from him than they were prepared to believe. In the evening a young Greek whom I had engaged as a special guide after the rest of the party had returned to the ship took me for a walk through the ancient Agora, or market place, to the Temple of Theseus, and through many little streets where the houses were built in the style of the ancient city. At nine o'clock we went down to the shore of the Bay of Phaleron for dinner. We sat down at a table in an open-air cafe at the water's edge. The new moon rose over the water of the bay, send-ing its little path of light directly to us. When we had finished our meal and had watched the people gathering in great numbers for their late evening of feasting and music, we made our way back to the ship, and my one day in Athens was over, according to my watch. But in reality the living of that day had only begun when its hours were numbered. It proved to be one of those days that renews itself in memory and reflection without end.

The next day we arrived in Constantinople in the afternoon and had a wonderful view of the terraced city rising from the sea, crowned with palaces, churches, and mosques. In the evening we rode through the Bosporus, past oriental gardens, harems, and the mysteries of a human world hidden within its secluding walls. From the city of Constantine we turned back through the Sea of Marmora, past Gallipoli, where the hulls of half-sunken British ships were grim reminders of the World War. We came on in view of the plains of ancient Troy and arrived at Smyrna. There we saw our first camel train. The long procession of stately camels, led by a little donkey, was bringing the first figs of the season to market. Carriages took us out to the American College, one of the half dozen Christian schools of the Near East which are like towers of light in all those lands. There the youth of many races gather to learn modern arts and sciences and to be shown the meaning of the Christian religion in practical application. Agriculture, technology, domestic science, and the social sciences offer these old lands new knowledge and new possibilities for both man and nature.

At Beirut we found two of our church members, Dr. and Mrs. Leland Parr. That pastoral visit was the most distant from home of any I ever made. Dr. Parr was on the staff of the medical school and took me through the well-equipped laboratories, which in every detail indicated the invasion of modern science into the old world of superstition and magic. Among the hundreds of students were Syrians, Bedouins, Moslems, and Jews, all learning the unifying knowledge and spirit of modern culture which tends to overcome racial and national differences. We visited in the home of the Parrs, played with their two lovely children, and in less than half a day had to hurry away to Baalbek. There were the magnificent ruins of the great temple with an immense court, 441 by 369 feet, and the six remaining columns of the peristyle seven and a half feet in diameter and rising to a height of sixty feet, crowned with Corinthian capitals. Some stones in the inclosing wall are sixty-two feet long and fourteen feet square.

From Baalbek we went by train to Damascus. There was war in the land, between the Arabs and the French. The train had armored cars and a heavy guard of soldiers. Every railway station was fortified, and the air was tense with the realization of the possibility of attack or of broken rails or bridges along the way. But we looked out upon the cedars of Lebanon and remembered how accustomed they were to sights of war and revolution through the ages. In Damascus we walked in the street called Straight, saw the house of Ananias, and heard the roar of cannon and machine guns in the environs of the city. The streets were barricaded with barbed wire and sandbags. But the shops were open for business, and the women in our party could not allow even war to prevent their shopping. I confess to have felt the spell myself and to have invested in a few things at the war prices, especially offered, so the salesmen said, to our American party. They were willing to take our personal checks, or even to send any amount of goods in bond simply upon our spoken order. One of the things I bought and never regretted was a beautiful red Hilla prayer rug, which now lies upon my study floor with its design pointing toward the east in true Moslem fashion.

It is a long journey "up to Jerusalem" if you start from Chicago and travel by way of Naples, Athens, Constantinople, Beirut, and Damascus. But in the evening of the day we left Damascus by train we were in Galilee, and we slept that night in Nazareth. The peace of the little town and the hills of the countryside around it filled my soul. Here we were in the very boyhood home of Jesus. These hills were the same as when he saw them and lived quietly among them. It was harvest time, and there was the ancient thresh-ing floor, and we saw the oxen on it driven round and round trampling out the grain. We went to the carpenter shop where he worked and saw the tools and bench. There were the door lintels, the shepherd's staff, and the yokes for oxen. The old phrases gained new meaning! "Thy rod and thy staff they comfort me." "My yoke is easy and my burden is light."

There was an unspoiled reality about Nazareth, the Sea of Galilee, the fishermen with their nets and boats, the farmers in the fields, and the shepherds tending their flocks. I like what some of the scholars have said about the influence of that north country on the life and spirit of Jesus. There he led an out-of-door life, close to nature, and there he found the scenes and the traditions which he made into parables everyone could understand. His homely wisdom from the soil and the hills flavored his conversa-tions ever after and gave a vitality to his words that was not lost in transmission through many lips.

It was an easy day's ride from Nazareth to Jerusalem, and that fact set me to thinking again how small is the whole land of Pales-tine. It is only about one hundred and fifty miles in length and fifty miles in width, three hours by auto north and south and one hour east and west. The road from Nazareth passed in sight of the Plain of Esdraelon, where many famous battles were fought from the days of Sisera, Cleopatra, Pompey, and Mark Antony, down to the Crusaders and Napoleon. We saw many new houses of the Zionists, who are moving into Palestine in great numbers. Their houses are simple frame structures, often standing out in the blaz-ing sun, without trees or gardens. As we left the town of Nablus, the site of ancient Shechem, we came out between Mount Ebal on the left and Mount Gerizim on the right, saw Jacob's well and drank from it, remembering the conversation there of Jesus with the woman of Samaria.

We came into Jerusalem through the Damascus Gate. It was evening and the sun was setting in all its loveliness. Approaching the city over the road along the crest of the hills, we witnessed an incident so characteristic of the life of the country that it seemed like a scene of a pageant staged for this moment, though in reality it was just a common event of any working day. As we came around a curve, a shepherd, bringing in his sheep to the fold for the night, was slowly driving them across the road. He wore the long black robe of the Bedouin. In his right hand was the long staff with its crook, and in his bosom he carried a little lamb. There was the simple fact of a tender human providence over the little ones of the flock, upon which the imagination of the shepherd people through the ages built the conception of God as the shepherd of mankind. It is a favorite figure of the Psalmist, as in Psalm 96: "He is our God; and we are the people of his pasture, and the sheep of his hand"; or Psalm 79:13, "We thy people and sheep of thy pasture will give thee thanks forever"; Psalm 80:1, "Give ear, O Shepherd of Israel, thou that leadest Joseph like a flock"; Isaiah 40:11, "He shall feed his flock like a shepherd: he shall gather the lambs with his arm, and carry them in his bosom, and shall gently lead those that are with young."

And now we were really entering the city. There were the mountains upon which it was built, Mount Zion and Mount Moriah. It was a natural mountain fortress when David captured it from the Jebusites, more than a thousand years before Christ. Mountains encircled it on every side and gave a sense of security which generated and sustained a deep piety. "As the mountains are round about Jerusalem, so the Lord is round about his people from henceforth even forever" (Ps. 125:2). We felt something of the great thrill which has filled the hearts of millions of pilgrims—Jews, Christians, and Moslems—as they came to their holy city, exultingly singing in their hearts: "Our feet shall stand within thy gates, O Jerusalem. . . . Whither the tribes go up, the tribes of the Lord, unto the testimony of Israel, to give thanks unto the name of the Lord" (Ps. 122:2, 4). Jesus went up in that mood with the Passover throngs when he was twelve years of age, and his love for the city welled up in tears in his last days when he wept over the city because it would not respond to his appeal.

We paused at a high point on the road and looked over the sacred scene—sacred because so many hearts had been lifted up by it and trusted so profoundly in what had happened there. The temple court and its surrounding wall, in its midst the great mosque, the Dome of the Rock, stood out as the central features of interest. The great rock under the dome of the mosque was a place of sacrifice before any temple was built, and that rock had been enshrined as the most sacred spot in all the temples built and rebuilt there through the centuries. The rock is fifty-seven feet long and forty-three feet wide. It was the Jewish altar of burnt offering, and on its surface may be seen traces of the con-duits which originally carried off the blood of the sacrifices. The Moslems are said to believe that here will be erected the throne of God in the Day of Judgment! Here, as in so many other places, my feelings were very mixed: a sense of pathos for the sentiments and superstitions of the human heart, and a feeling of reverence for the longings and aspirations which the old beliefs revealed. The imagination of man embellishes every place and event that has been the scene of great emotion, especially when that emotion has been experienced by generation after generation of devout and credulous souls. That emotion is real, whatever may be said of the historicity or importance of that upon which it rests!

Throughout and around Jerusalem are too many evocative things to relate: the Mount of Olives, the Garden of Gethsemane, the Via Dolorosa, and Calvary. Scarcely any of them are authenti-cally located except the mountain, and yet all actually must have been within a given area. The details had little interest for me, but the drama and the personages of the action were moving realities. The great quarries of Solomon below the city, where the stones for the temple were hewn from the solid rock, still bear the marks of the workmen's tools. We wandered long distances through them, marveling at the toil and the devotion which those excava-tions evidenced. Outside the city, the journey to the Jordan River and the Dead Sea, to Jericho along the road where the deed of the Good Samaritan became immortal, "the little town of Bethlehem," and the hills of the shepherds keeping watch over their flocks on that memorable night of the nativity—all had nature's seal of reality and the charm of inexpressible meaning and beauty.

I was constantly surprised at how much historic ground we could cover in a few hours of travel. We went in one day from Jerusalem to Cairo, down in Egypt, through the mountains of Judea with the caves in the rocky hillside where David hid from his enemies, across the Plain of Sharon, beyond Gaza, over the desert, across the Suez Canal, through the land of Goshen, with oleanders in bloom, to Cairo. In Cairo the most vivid thought to my mind was not of this or that monument or institution but the impression of antiquity and the mystery of old civilizations, one underneath another back through thousands of years. Here, on the banks of the great river Nile, today flowing on as of old, had lived peoples with their dynasties, courts, armies, sages, prophets, and artists, long before the nomadic Hebrews had reached the first steps of civilization. If David captured the site of Jerusalem as a rough, rocky stronghold in the eleventh century B.C., that was about two and a half centuries after the glorious reign of King Tutankhamen in Egypt, and his was the eighteenth dynasty of ancient Egypt. The museum in Cairo exhibits the marvelous treasures taken from his tomb, and they are the material evidence of the high civilization in which he ruled. There are six hundred groups of objects in that exhibit. They include the elaborately wrought gold sarcophagus in which his mummy was found, his gold chariot, and a wealth of jewels, ornaments, and treasures, marked by the most skilled workmanship. The Great Pyramids of Giza were constructed more than three thousand years before Christ, and more than two thousand years before David's time.

It was a long way home through the Mediterranean from Alexandria to Marseilles, from Marseilles to the Riviera, from Nice by the *Route des Alpes* to Grenoble and Paris, and by plane from Paris to London. It seemed like really getting home to meet old friends again; Mr. and Mrs. B. Fred Wise in Paris, and Mr. and Mrs. Archibald Cattell in London.

The two highest points of interest to me on this long swift journey were the one day in Athens and the few days in and about Jerusalem. These cities and the cultures they represent are the sources of the two most fruitful strains of our modern life. The Greeks gave themselves to wisdom and beauty, the Hebrews to religion. Our modern age has given itself to knowledge with the aid of the new methods and instruments of science, and it has given itself to religion. But it has yet to learn how to give itself to both at once, to the intellectual life with the ardor characteristic of the Greeks, and at the same time to religion with the passion of the Hebrews.

Chapter xvi | *Great Days and Lincoln's Birthday*

The minister of a non-liturgical church may sometimes long for a system and order of service through which he might have a more definite sense of being united in mind and spirit with his people. In the free churches the congregation seldom knows in advance what scriptures will be read, what prayers will be offered, or what the theme of the sermon will be. Even when the subject is previously published, I have been told that it is not always clear what the line of thought will be! In such a situation the minister has his perplexities. What shall guide him in his choice? How can he provide for any adequate rapport with those who are to hear him? I have often felt relief when Christmas and Easter came round, when the days themselves set the theme for those Sundays so securely that the minister's task was as clearly defined as that of the musicians.

But there are organized agencies in the free churches which their ministers have to reckon with. Each would like a Sunday given up to its special work. There is the Foreign Missionary Society, the Home Missionary Society, the Association of Church Colleges, the Ministers' Pension Fund, the Board of Temperance and Social Welfare, the Association for the Promotion of Christian Unity, the Benevolent Association, the Church Extension Society, the Religious Education Society, the Young Peoples' Organization, and other guilds and circles. Each of them makes its appeal to the local pastor for the observance of a special day for its interests and is generally willing to send a representative to preach the sermon. These are all good and worthy causes, and the churches should support them, but in the most well-regulated

churches there are other and better methods than that of giving
each a Sunday morning. At least it would be disastrous if the
preacher had to fit his preaching and his services into such demands year after year.

Another way of choosing subjects is to use occasions which
are of sufficient significance to make them truly religious. Many
of these recur with the years and are valuable opportunities for
the churches. Such days are New Year's, Thanksgiving, birth-
days of national figures like Lincoln and Washington, Independence Day, Armistice Day, and Labor Day. There are also the
possibilities of Chicago Day, Election Day, Mother's Day, Father's Day, St. Valentine's Day, St. Patrick's Day, and many tag
days for charities. Chicago is a great convention city, and frequently its gatherings are religious, like the Eucharistic Congress
or the conventions of Protestant denominations or great inter-
denominational meetings like those of the Federal Council of
Churches, and the International Council of Religious Education.

It is obvious that ministers of the free churches have to come
to terms with this problem of subjects. They may stick to biblical
texts, they may magnify the particular tenets of their faith, and
they may make it their chief purpose to win converts to their
faith. I know one minister who preached every Sunday evening
for a year on the second coming of Christ. Some specialize on
personal religion, some on the social gospel, some on institutional
religion. For me there has been a tendency to emphasize the nature of religion itself, its origins, growth, and continuous development, closely related to the idealistic phases of our culture, to
stress the relation of man to his world and his struggles with the
conditions of successful and happy living in a changing civilization. The two characteristics of modern life are democracy and
science. The understanding and promotion of both have been
given much attention in my pulpit. They have been dealt with in
the light of the spirit and moral aspirations of the teaching and
example of Jesus, and of other great souls whose life and work
express these things. It has seemed to me that all the basic values
must be included in any adequate presentation of the religious life:
health, friendship, economic security, knowledge, art, recreation,
love, life ambitions, social and civic idealism, morality, and religion. All of these belong to the goals of Christianity. Their real-

ization is the proper end of religious faith and endeavor. The pursuit of them gives meaning and satisfaction, whatever the degree of their attainment. To achieve them even partially, self-denying co-operation is necessary, and in the comradeship of their pursuit may be found the highest and the best that life affords.

There is also a mystical quality here. Men and women reach out for more than they can grasp. Their souls have an insatiable hunger for things above their heads, for justice, wisdom, beauty, and love. An experience of one of these good things brings a moment apart, idealized in memory and appreciation. If an individual heroically works for justice, wisdom, beauty, and love, and displays them notably in his character or in some form of art, he may be praised and exalted as extraordinary and unique. His example is emulated and magnified. We easily become hero worshipers, glorifying the good traits of our heroes and overlooking their faults. Thus the mystical longings of our souls enhance the good we find and fashion the world around us into something nearer the heart's desire. We crave perfection, and we resent a critical analysis of the idols we cherish. It is difficult to get people to see plain facts about their children or their intimate friends or themselves. Weaknesses are glossed over and the better traits remembered. This mystical tendency works in reverse where the heart is filled with hatred or envy. Then it exaggerates the evil and becomes blind to the good.

The great days of the year illustrate this mystical appraisal. Every great day is made greater and more potent by celebration. We strive to impress its meaning and to increase its influence by re-enacting it, dramatizing its personalities, and enlarging its place in history. All the arts are drawn upon to make the day vivid and appealing. Witness the Passover of the Hebrews, and Thanksgiving Day in America. Christmas is such a day for all Christendom. Into this birthday of Christ are poured all the affection, gratitude, and joy of the Christian world.

In our church, for many years, we had a lovely pageant at Christmastime, and we never lacked enthusiasm for the annunciation, for the lowly manger scene, for the shepherds, the wise men, the kings, the angels, and the "Hallelujah Chorus." With feasting and dancing we celebrated the coming of redeeming love to bring peace and goodwill to our hearts and to all mankind.

The pageant is more than the original event. It is the accumulated wonder and awe of the wistful soul of man, building up out
of its deep natural love and hope a drama of redemption against
all the sin and evil that has been or that is to be. Nothing can
destroy the power and the reality of that drama. Though it may
be proved that there was never in Judea such a series of literal
events, it cannot be doubted that the elements upon which the
drama and pageant were founded are true to human experience.
In many homes of the very poor, a mother broods over her infant
son and dreams of great and noble things he will do for his race
and for the world. Shepherds and peasants look at the stars and
hope for deliverance from bondage and want. Wise men pay
tribute to ancient prophecies and work and wait for their fulfilment. The life of Jesus has been made the focus and embodiment
of the values essential to the highest human life. His name is the
name of a flesh-and-blood person, and it is also the name of the
ideal man who, by faith and aspiration, is in every soul that strives
toward his way of life. Christmas is the anniversary of the birth
of the earthly Jesus, but every Christmastime is also the real and
recurring birthday of the heavenly Christ in human hearts. We
sing in the words of Phillips Brooks:

> O holy Child of Bethlehem!
> Descend to us, we pray;
> Cast out our sin, and enter in;
> Be born in us today.

Every year for forty years we celebrated this great day of the
year, and I preached upon its inexhaustible theme. It was for us
in the church, as in our homes, a pivotal day, and upon its message and experience our whole religious life turned. But do what
we will, interpret it as best we can, there remains something in it
so beyond us and so mysterious that its meaning and its beauty
baffle us. We feel the need of other days, of more common days,
that may enable us to realize and grasp in simpler terms the wonder and the mystery of this Christmas day. The same experience,
closer to our time and circumstance, I have tried to present
through a day given now and then to appreciation of some neighbor or friend whose life has been lived among us in our own
streets and neighborhood or within reach of our daily contacts.

My neighbor and friend, Professor Fred Merrifield, was such a man. He was simple, unassuming, and gave himself with a questing mind to search out the heart of religion with freedom and courage in the face of opposition and misunderstanding. In teaching biblical literature in the university, he was a friend of students awaking from dogmatic slumber, and in a quiet way he gave material help to many in need. He left an illuminating anthology of great religious poetry whose selections represent his own convictions and aspirations and the thoughts upon which his own soul fed.

Henry Justin Smith, managing editor for many years of the *Chicago Daily News*, was another to whose memory a Sunday was given. In the maelstrom of a great newspaper office he kept his mind clear and his soul alive. Modest and retiring in personal contacts, he was bold and strong with his pen on behalf of high ideals and a deep, though unconventional, religious faith. He was accomplished at the piano, and he wrote about the great city which he loved, revealing in telling phrases both its sordidness and its nobility.

But it was to the life of Abraham Lincoln that I returned most often when the great day of his birth came around. On eleven Sundays in different years he was the subject of my sermons, and usually the choir sang Negro spirituals. Many poems about him were printed in the calendar. We put a plaque on the wall of the church library, bearing his likeness and his immortal Gettysburg speech. (The plaque was the work of the artist Mrs. Henry K. Holsman.) And on February 10, 1924, I received Abraham Lincoln into the fellowship of the church. In the sermon of that day I spoke of his deep religious nature, of his faith in a ruling providence, of his unaffected habit of prayer and his dependence upon prayer in the great crises of his life. I quoted particularly his declaration in answer to the question why he was not a member of a church: "When any church will inscribe over its altar as its sole qualifications for membership, the Savior's condensed statement of the substance of both law and gospel, 'Thou shalt love the Lord thy God with all thy heart, and with all thy soul, and with all thy mind, and thy neighbor as thyself'; that church will I join with all my heart and all my soul." We placed a bronze bust of Lincoln beside the pulpit and I turned to him and welcomed him into our fellowship on that declaration of faith, as I would have welcomed the man himself, had he actually been present in the flesh. That was just a way of dramatizing my conviction that the church should receive into its fellowship any person who might offer himself for membership upon Lincoln's terms. He said he was perplexed by the long creeds of the churches and their theological differences, which did not seem to him intelligible or important. His great mind saw into the depths of the Christian religion, and he rightly assessed what was most essential in it.

In a letter to Abraham Lincoln, used as a sermon in 1920, I said:

In religion, you are typical of a new order of saints. Was it your inheritance from a long line of Quakers and the impress upon your soul of the simple faith of pioneers face to face with reality which fitted you to be a prophet to these later times? Your parents belonged to a church which renounced creeds and sought to rely upon the Bible for guidance and consolation. Was it from them you caught the faith of a religion which should be free from all external rites and authority? What a challenge you thrust before all ministers and religious organizations! One often wonders that some of them did not respond. . . . Your words are still vibrant with a searching test. Perhaps the day will come when it will be submitted by men of your spirit in a manner to determine what religious societies in this country truly face the deep issues of a sane and practical faith. It may be proposed that all churches which are willing to receive you on your declaration of conviction shall have a ceremony in which, after recounting your life of earnest, unaffected piety, you shall be welcomed into their inner company of believers.

This challenge Lincoln's religion still presents to the churches. That challenge becomes more acute as the old religious doctrines lose their influence, and a more practical faith emerges. The real problem is whether the prevailing institutional forms of religion are necessary or vital. Many religious leaders frankly face the issue and would be willing to accept into fellowship any man with a spirit like Lincoln's, who professed his faith in the two great principles of love to God and love to man. So far as is known, no preacher or church of Lincoln's time offered to receive him on that declaration. That fact is a sad commentary on the Christianity of those days, but unfortunately the same attitude largely prevails in the churches since his time. One reason I have been glad to celebrate so often the day of his birth, with sermons about his life and character, is because we had long ago settled in this church the problem involved in his case. There has been satisfaction in registering ourselves on the side of the kind of fellowship which he approved and which he would have accepted. I do not suppose it makes any difference to him now, but if it should happen that the souls of the dead remember their earthly estate and think of the injustices they suffered while in the flesh, it may be some comfort to him to know that a church finally took him in, even if it was long after his death, and even if the church that did it was just a little "Campbellite" church in Chicago!

But the celebrations of Lincoln Sundays have been more than the expression of our own liberalism. They have meant to set forth the greatness of Lincoln's mind and heart, and his significance for American democracy and religion. These are important for the rest of the world, too. The development of a democratic government and of a vital Christianity in the United States is destined ultimately to have its influence on all nations and peoples, and no one man so surely embodies the spirit of these United States as does Abraham Lincoln. In my letter to him (from which I have already quoted) I said:

> The lowliest and the mightiest will forever be drawn to you when they suffer. You are felt to be a comrade to the common folk. If you had endeavored to symbolize democracy through your personal habits, you could not have succeeded so well in any other way as you did by your unfeigned manner and unconscious conduct. We like to think of the way you lived in Springfield even after you had been in Congress and were widely known. We read with surpise, but with admiration, of the fact that you were accustomed to hunt your cow at evening on the commons and drive her home. It seems never to have occurred to you that milking the cow, grooming the horse, and cutting wood for the kitchen stove could be undignified or degrading labor. It becomes an impressive lesson to our time to read of your keeping up those homely chores to the very evening when you were nominated for the Presidency. It is little wonder that you never became used to servants and attendants. Nor is it difficult to imagine the astonishment of the gentleman from a foreign court who discovered that when President you still polished your own boots. He exclaimed, "Why, Mr. President, do you shine your own boots?" You replied, "Yes, whose do you shine?" No wonder you did not desire a military escort in the streets of Washington but walked and rode unattended whenever possible.

It is interesting to see how his personal experience became an illuminating source and symbol of democracy. Democracy radiated from his feeling and from his theory of life and government as from his very dress and manner. His homely stories circulated over the dry-goods boxes where the plain citizens formed their impressions of matters of state. But it was in signing the proclamation emancipating millions of slaves that he symbolized most dramatically the full meaning and measure of democracy. He had used telling arguments. If a Negro is a man his slavery is wrong. A Negro woman "in her natural right to eat the bread she earns with her own hands without asking leave of anyone else . . . is my equal, and the equal of all others."

There is still another reason why Abraham Lincoln's birthday has so often been celebrated in the Hyde Park Church. There was always about him a strange wraith of mysterious simplicity, yet of grandeur; of awkwardness, yet of grace; of earthiness, yet of something celestial. His life touched the coarse, rough textures and also the delicate shades and patterns. Unheralded by prophets, unannounced by angels, he came in obscurity, poverty, and rusticity. He grew to greatness in the open prairies and in the midst of men and women of the village and the countryside. As an unknown poet said, "Some power was in his splendid, perfect heart / Which e'en the humblest found within their reach." It is my hope that the plain, even the uncouth, facts about Lincoln's circumstances and personality will never be forgotten. We are especially indebted now to Carl Sandburg for his monumental six-volume life of Lincoln. It frankly faces all sides of his character and behavior. Even the gross cartoons, doggerel verses, and homely stories are given, but Sandburg has also the poet's eye for the greatness, kindliness, and sincerity of Lincoln.

One difficulty with popular religion in our day is that it makes too much of perfection. The Old Testament religion was not like that. It tells the truth about its heroes, about Abraham, Moses, David, Solomon, and the rest. Even God does things of which he repenteth himself! It always strengthens the appeal of the story of Jesus to remember that he was human enough to become weary and hungry and thirsty, and that he had to escape from the multitudes many times and go to the other side of the lake or to the mountains, before all the sick were healed or before all the people were converted. He was tempted in all points just as we are. He was ignorant about some things and was mistaken about others. All this the New Testament tells us, but these things make his greatness all the greater. His divinity was a growth, not a gift. The record says he grew in wisdom. But many of his theological interpreters treat the human side of Christ as unreal, a kind of appearance and not a reality. They want his divine perfection uncompromised in any way with the soil and substance of this lowly earth. But men are aware of their own imperfections, and anyone who is to be an example and inspiration to them must know from experience what it is to gain strength over weakness and triumph over loss and defeat. If the success of Jesus Christ was guaranteed from the beginning, then his whole life is of a different order, but if he won it by effort, by teaching, by deeds, and by courageous death upon the cross in fidelity to his faith, then we may be inspired by his example to undertake his kind of life.

This seems to me one of the great reasons why Lincoln's life is so appealing. No one can deny or destroy the evidence of his human frailties, nor can they deny or destroy his spiritual greatness and power. He lived here in the state of Illinois, and so recently that people we have known knew him. The daily papers of his city, and of the national capital, reported his words and deeds at length, and the historians and biographers are in no doubt about essential features of his life. His stature continues to increase, as the Chicago cartoonist John T. McCutcheon showed by representing Lincoln in life as a little taller than most men, then after some decades as of heroic size, and finally as gigantic. Understanding Abraham Lincoln should help us to understand Jesus Christ. Neither one should displace the other. Both have the same significance, though in vastly different degrees, one from the far past, and one from our own time and country. Whoever truly follows one of them will find his way to the heart of the other, and there he will find the real meaning of the religious life.

Many poets have sensed the soul of Lincoln's greatness. Richard Watson Gilder wrote:

A power was his beyond the touch of art
Or armèd strength—his pure and mighty heart.[1]

[1] Richard Watson Gilder, "On the Life-Mask of Abraham Lincoln," *Five Books of Song* (Boston: Houghton Mifflin Co., 1903), p. 115.

James Russell Lowell said in his famous ode:

> His was no lonely mountain-peak of mind,
> Thrusting to thin air o'er our cloudy bars,
> A sea mark now, now lost in vapors blind:
> Broad prairie rather, genial, level-lined,
> Fruitful and friendly for all human kind,
> Yet also nigh to heaven and loved of loftiest stars.[2]

The Disciple poet, my friend Thomas Curtis Clark of Chicago, has written:

> . . . The Diadem
> Upon his brow should be no piece of gold,
> But, like his lowly Lord's, a thorny crown.
> Upon his cross he died; they took him down,
> And lo! they found, before the day was old,
> That they had crucified their one true friend;
> Despite their hate, he loved them to the end.[3]

[2] James Russell Lowell, "Ode Recited at the Harvard Commemoration" (Boston: Houghton, Mifflin, 1848, 1924), p. 344.

[3] Thomas Curtis Clark, "The Miracle," *Lincoln and Others* (New York: George H. Doran Co., 1923), p. 16 (by permission of Doubleday & Co.).

Chapter xvii | The Disciples Divinity House

My active participation in the work of the Disciples Divinity House of the University of Chicago has covered a longer span of years than my ministry in the University Church of Disciples. I was made an instructor in the house in January, 1896, when I was also set to raise money to purchase the land upon which it stands. It was a slow and difficult task to secure ten thousand dollars to buy the hundred-foot frontage on what is now University Avenue at the corner of Fifty-seventh Street, right by the university (as I have related in chapter v).

President Harper was the radiating center of enthusiasm in the development of the university. The general public could appreciate his energy in gathering millions and erecting buildings more readily than his genius for bringing great scholars from the ends of the earth for his faculty. Most people could have little understanding for his ability to teach Hebrew and to enlist and excite numerous students in the study of that language. Those of us who were in the university marveled as much at his energy in getting men for history and chemistry and all other departments. But no interest was greater with him than his interest in religion. It was his own professional field, and he cherished novel plans for its promotion. He had taken over the Baptist seminary at Morgan Park as the divinity school of the new University, and he sought to bring other denominations into co-operation with it. Eventually he hoped to create a central scientific school of religion in place of the traditional seminary and to group around it other colleges or "houses" representing the various denominations, including the Baptist. At the time of his death in 1906, he had projected ar-

rangements for the central school of religion and had made some
plans toward its faculty. Since his death the divinity school has
become undenominational in fact as it was then in spirit. It now
has a Methodist dean, and on its teaching staff are representatives
of the Presbyterians, Congregationalists, Disciples, Methodists,
and Baptists.

From the first, President Harper encouraged the founding of
houses for the students of different religious bodies. The Disciples
of Christ were the first to co-operate in this way. This was partly
due to the fact that Herbert Lockwood Willett was a graduate
student in Dr. Harper's own field of Semitic languages and literature, and, as a Disciple, was at once interested in the possibility
of a Disciples house. Scarcely less important was the fact that
another Disciple, Professor W. D. MacClintock, was a close
friend of President Harper and one of the first men the president
appointed to the faculty of the university. Professor MacClintock
was in the department of English and had had ministerial training
and some experience in the pastorate. He realized fully the significance of such a training center for the Disciple ministry as the
house might be. The organization was effected and its work begun in October, 1894. Dr. Willett was the dean from that date
until 1921.

On October 20, 1894, at the second meeting of the trustees, I
was elected head of the house. This is a student position, and the
duties have been more definite and appreciable since a building
was erected. In those first years it might be said to have been
solely a "spiritual" office, concerned with promoting student fellowship and dispensing informal advice. The term "house" itself
had constantly to be explained. People would visit the university
and ask, "Where is the Disciples Divinity House?" We would
have to answer, "The house is not something you can see; it is
not yet something made with hands. It is an idea, an association.
You get into it by becoming a student for the Disciple ministry
or other religious work. It does things to the minds and hearts of
students, and its influence is attracting men and women here to
study."

For thirty-four years we lived and worked in that kind of
house, for the visible building did not arise until 1928. The house
was an association for graduate students preparing for the min-

istry. A few came for the academic year, and many more came for the famous "summer quarter," which was one of the innovating inventions of President Harper. Instead of the usual popular school conducted for a few weeks, as in many institutions, this was a regular quarter of the academic year, and the courses were the same as those offered in other quarters. The instruction was given by the faculty members themselves in all departments and subjects. Great numbers of teachers came for the summers, from colleges and public schools all over the country. Ministers also came during their vacations. The larger part of the Disciple students came in the summer, for there was little opportunity for them to defray their expenses in the city for longer periods.

The Disciples had very few churches in and around Chicago, and if any of these employed students the remuneration was pitifully small. This fact always had to be explained. The church colleges from which our students came were located in sections of the country where Disciple churches were numerous and often happy to have student preaching. Around Transylvania in Kentucky, Hiram in Ohio, Butler in Indiana, Culver-Stockton in Missouri, Eureka in Illinois, and Drake in Iowa, nearly any ministerial student of ability and enterprise could pay his college expenses by supplying churches. Such work is not likely to be conducive to the best scholastic attainments, but it was often that plan or none.

The difficulty in Chicago was geographical. The Disciples started in southeast Pennsylvania and West Virginia, and their migration was westward through southern Ohio, Indiana, Illinois, and northern Kentucky. The northern part of Illinois was scarcely touched by the Disciple pioneers, compared with the middle zone of the state. Besides, Chicago had a predominantly foreign population, with large numbers of Roman Catholics and Lutherans. Further, the Disciples were a rural people and had neither the men, money, nor imagination to plant themselves successfully in Chicago. A number of men who preached for small churches in the city, while students, left the city upon graduation or soon after and built up or became pastors of larger churches elsewhere. Among them were J. H. Goldner of Cleveland, George A. Campbell of St. Louis, W. F. Rothenburger of Indianapolis, John Ray Ewers of Pittsburgh, A. W. Fortune of Lexington, Kentucky.

But, even under these circumstances, from twenty-five to fifty Disciples would be registered in the course of a year. There were no funds for scholarships, and students often had a very strenuous time to make their way. Yet the divinity school of the university gave free tuition to all ministerial students in those days, and occasionally the house was able to provide a hundred dollars a year to assist a man.

The problems of the house continued for many years to be mainly financial. Dr. Willett served for twenty-seven years without salary. Dr. Errett Gates and Dr. Charles M. Sharpe were given modest salaries for teaching and for raising funds for endowment and toward a building fund. Ground was leased to the church for its temporary building in 1899, and from that time the local church became more and more able to co-operate with the house financially.

During the deanship of Dr. W. E. Garrison from 1921 to 1927, the fund from the sale of half the land of the house to the church was augmented to nearly one hundred thousand dollars, and the visible house of stone was dedicated in October, 1928. The three-story building provided on the first floor for a library, a large common room, offices, and an unfinished space within the walls for a chapel. The Herbert Lockwood Willett Library was named in honor of the first dean. The second and third floors were dormitory rooms to accommodate twenty-three students in single rooms. In the basement were a recreation room, a dining hall, and kitchen. The substantial and beautiful furnishings for the whole house were the gift of Mrs. Gary Sutcliffe, who had become a member of the University Church in 1927.

Mrs. Sutcliffe soon became interested in the completion of the chapel, in the unfinished space at the north end of the first floor, and offered to bear the cost up to fifty thousand dollars. Professor MacClintock was particularly enthusiastic in working with us on the plans for a Gothic interior, and the final result in the hands of the architect, Mr. Henry K. Holsman, is one of the loveliest chapels anywhere in this country. A heavy stone arch, rising from the floor to the ceiling, sets off the chancel with its rich altar. On either side of the altar is a seven-branched candelabrum, and in the center an old and precious gold chalice and paten. Over the altar is a beautiful stained-glass window, the work of Charles J.

Connick of Boston, depicting scenes from the story of the quest for the Holy Grail. In the square sections of the ceiling, with a lovely blue ground, are warm-colored symbols of the bread and the wine, in the form of a paten and a chalice, which, with the cross, form geometrical patterns. On the stone corbels, supporting the heavy beams above, are finely sculptured biblical symbols of the vine and grape, the anchor, and the dove. Around the door of the entrance is a series of small sculptures of other symbols: the lamb, the tree of life, a cherub, a lion, a rose, a pomegranate, a lily, and an olive branch. But the most conspicuous symbol throughout is the cross. In the windows and in the glass of the doors are the Latin and the Greek crosses and many of the variations of these developed among the Crusaders and in heraldry. The choir stalls and other woodwork are finished in a beautiful walnut veneer whose grained patterns almost make landscape scenes. Along the entire length of the floor from the chancel to the narthex is a tile rug in French style with the fleur-de-lis prominent in its symbolism. Two rows of seats on each side of the chapel face the center aisle and accommodate fifty people. In the loft at the back is a beautifully toned Aeolian pipe organ which was installed at a cost of ten thousand dollars.

This physical building affords many forms of association which enhance and deepen the spiritual value of the house as an educational religious institution. The building facilitates the fellowship and fraternity of its residents, in different forms of association, in the living rooms, the dining room, the library, and the common room or lounge. But the comradeship of a chapel is different from that of other places; as I explained in my address at the dedication:

The chapel is set in the pattern of a face-to-face group, the oldest and the most enduring pattern of associated human life. The chapel, more than any other room, symbolizes the objectives of the men who will be trained here. A very important part of their work will be to conduct services in places akin to this in their purposes and in their symbolism. Scientists are trained in laboratories, mechanics in shops, artists in studios, and ministers should be trained in the activities and attitudes that belong to a chapel.

The technical disciplines of students preparing for the ministry make it important to have common participation in the life of meditation and devotion. Classrooms are likely to be analytical and fact-finding. Churches are inclusive and appreciative. The intellectual attitude tends toward the abstract and the detached; the religious inclines toward the ceremonial, the near, and the personal. If a student does not feel drawn to what a chapel symbolizes, it is difficult to understand how he will be happy and efficient in a life devoted to such things. If he is not habituated to intelligent and appropriate use of such a place for himself and others, while in his formative period, it is not likely that he will ever gain that spirit of reverence and devotion which will enable him to radiate religious attitudes into the lives of others.

We shall therefore hope that our students will be drawn to this chapel for what its loveliness and meaning may do for them. Through all its uses, when we listen to elevating music, or observe the Communion, or celebrate marriage, there will run the unifying comradeship of those great experiences upon which religion itself rests and which it endeavors to cherish and illuminate. Therefore here, more than in any other part of the building, men whose minds and hearts have been stirred to the great and delicate tasks of the ministry of the church of Jesus Christ will feel themselves drawn together upon the highest levels of association, by the bonds of that faith and zeal which they in turn will be called upon to cultivate in other groups of men and women in the churches which they may later serve.

It would be difficult, and perhaps quite superfluous, to give any account of the endless details and unexpected obstacles which were encountered in carrying through the building and operating policy of the Disciples Divinity House. For thirty-four years the only place the house had for the dean's office and place of consultation was a room gratuitously granted by the university in one of the men's dormitories. I have served as a member of the board of trustees since 1901, and as secretary of the board from 1910 until elected dean in 1927. One of the most tense and surprising discussions arose in 1926 as to whether a building should be erected at all for the house. Mr. Leon Loehr, the treasurer and one of the best businessmen on the board, opposed any plans for a building. He voted against the transfer of funds from other available accounts to the building fund. His remarks were carefully recorded in the minutes. He contended that we did not need dormitories for our students, that the teaching function of the house had been a failure for thirty years, as shown by the small number of students electing its courses. He argued that the funds of the house should be used to promote attendance of Disciple students in the divinity school of the university by providing scholarships. He was answered by other trustees that the house was obligated by its original agreement with the university to erect a building and that the building was needed to provide a home and habitation for our students.

Conservative ministers and papers among the Disciples throughout the country persistently criticized the house for what they called its radical liberal leadership. Most of this criticism was directed against Dean Willett because of his lectures and writings setting forth the new views of the Scriptures as formulated by the "higher critics," of whom President Harper was one of the most prominent. A favorite method of attack by writers in the *Christian Standard* was to quote a line or two from a paper or an address by President Harper or Dr. Willett and then give a whole paragraph in refutation. Dr. Willett told of meeting a farmer out in Kansas who had been reading the *Standard*. He remarked to Dr. Willett, "So far as I can tell from the brief quotations they make from his words, President Harper rather has the best of it." That remark is an indication of the lack of force in the conservative attacks. Yet they had influence in making it hard to raise money among the churches for the house, and in securing students who might otherwise have come.

One witty opponent expressed his feeling about the enterprise by saying: "Now the Disciples Divinity House is all Divinity and no House; after a while it will be all House and no Divinity." But in spite of opposition, men came in greater numbers to prepare themselves for the ministry, for college positions, and for missionary work under Disciple auspices. When Dr. W. E. Garrison was dean, he published a promotional statement in the interest of securing further funds for the building then in prospect, saying: "The need for a building is urgent and grows constantly more so. The failure to provide it is scarcely keeping faith with the university." As evidence that the house was justified in its appeal for funds to equip and develop its work, he said:

About five hundred men have taken graduate work in the Divinity School of the University of Chicago and have utilized in varying measure the resources of the Disciples Divinity House. They are men of widely different types of thought, for no attempt is made here to run everyone into the same theological mold, but they have all gained in breadth of view and in appreciation of the things most vital in religion. Of these five hundred . . . the majority are now on the list of our active ministers in the United States. Sixty-five others are foreign missionaries. Almost as many are professors in our colleges.

The completion of the building, with its superb equipment, was the one kind of answer that all its critics could understand. It was evidence that the house had become a permanent institution and that its work and influence were growing stronger. But funds were still needed for scholarships to bring selected graduates from the colleges for the three years of training in the divinity school. The building was completed with the finishing of the chapel in 1929, when the great business depression began. The house at that time had an endowment of less than one hundred thousand dollars, the income from which was scarcely adequate to the necessary costs of providing one part-time professor and the expenses of maintenance and promotion.

In 1931 Mrs. Sutcliffe began her magnificent contributions for the endowment. She received her wealth from the income on funds placed in trust for her by her father, the late Judge Elbert Gary, organizer and chairman of the United States Steel Corporation. She made the Disciples Divinity House the special object of her benefactions and took a keen personal interest in its work and in the men who came as students. She knew how easily even large means may be disbursed among many causes without achieving distinctive and permanent results. She therefore adopted the policy of saying to all college solicitors, and to representatives of many other enterprises, that she would let others care for those interests while she concentrated on doing what she could for the Disciples Divinity House. It was her generosity which gave the house the resources to do its work on a magnificent scale, and this she did most modestly, without desire for public praise or for power to shape the policies of the house. The scholarships now provide necessary expenses for single men living in the dormitory. Each year there are many more applicants for these scholarships than can be accommodated with either rooms or funds. The students come chiefly from the twelve Disciple colleges throughout the country. Some come from state universities and other non-Disciple institutions and, upon completion of their work, usually return to the localities from which they came. The scholarships are awarded to men not simply because they want to be ministers but because they have already achieved some distinction.

With the house at last so well equipped, it is a satisfaction to see its main purposes coming into full realization. Instruction in the history of the Disciples of Christ goes on in the classes of Dr. Garrison as an integral part of the curriculum of the divinity school, and his students receive university credit. He also carries on research in this history and has published books and various articles in this field. His books are *Alexander Campbell's Theology* and *Religion Follows the Frontier*. Many students have written theses in this general subject of problems concerning the Disciples, such as Christian union, Christian education, and Christian doctrine. The house pioneered the way in these historical studies, and now such studies are a part of the training of ministerial students in practically all Disciple colleges.

The Herbert Lockwood Willett Library contains a rare collection of Disciple literature to which many important works have been added by Dr. Willett himself. All significant Disciple periodicals, books of sermons by Disciple ministers, and other related writings are carefully gathered and preserved in this library, and a similar plan has been followed in recent years in several other places. New problems constantly arise in every great religious movement, and it is increasingly important that records of many kinds be kept to guide those who are to have the responsibility of shaping the future.

Discussions of current problems are carried on informally in the house around the luncheon table each week. Often distinguished visitors are present with whom free conversations are of great value. Missionaries from foreign lands, editors of religious journals, laymen of wide experience and religious interest, travelers from many cities and countries, and leaders in various denominations have all contributed freely. Occasionally, when the house has had the funds and students of superior ability, traveling fellowships have been granted for a year's study abroad. Dr. Irvin E. Lunger and Dr. W. Barnett Blakemore have held this fellowship and have brought back to their comrades most informing and stimulating reports. The house has a total value in land, building, and endowment of three-quarters of a million dollars. This means that, with the church buildings adjoining, more than a million dollars has been invested on our corner.

When I look back over this long history and think how we launched out in our youth upon so great a project with little but our faith and hope to justify us, I am impressed with the fact that

The Disciples Divinity House | *181*

even in such a world as this a good cause can be made to prosper if we do not become weary in well-doing. A group of us have come through the years together to see the fruits of our labors—especially Dr. Willett and Professor MacClintock (now gone from us), Dr. Garrison, and I. For longer or shorter periods there were also associated with the house as instructors Dr. Errett Gates, Dr. Hiram Van Kirk and Dr. Charles M. Sharpe. On the board of trustees have been men of first-class business ability and position and men of high rank in the ministry and in religious leadership. Among the businessmen to be specially mentioned for length of service and for responsibility carried are E. M. Bowman, Leon L. Loehr, Kinter Berkebile, Dan Norman, S. M. Jasper, H. C. Taylor, Harry Moore, Archibald Cattell, and A. B. Keller. Among the religious leaders have been Dr. J. H. Garrison, A. McLean, Orvis F. Jordan, H. T. Morrison, Perry J. Rice, Samuel C. Kincheloe, Roy G. Ross, and William Clayton Bower. These names are themselves guarantees of the sound and fruitful policies of the house both on the practical side of business management and on the side of sincere and intelligent religious faith.

The Disciples Divinity House is a noble creation from small beginnings to substantial and enduring influence, not only in the lives of hundreds of students but also in the whole brotherhood of the Disciples of Christ, and to some extent in the whole religious world. It would seem reasonable to believe that it is to have a still greater future in a world that so much needs what it so freely offers.

Chapter xviii | Religious Values

Religious values are the values cherished by religious people in their beliefs, ceremonials, and conduct. If we examine the hymns, scriptures, prayers, and sermons of any religious group, we shall find there the things they prize, the values to which they are devoted. Take any modern church and it will appear that its members believe in God and in Jesus Christ, in the moral life, in the forgiveness of sin, and in the hope of the coming of the kingdom of heaven. The general impression is of men and women seeking to find security against the evils of life, and comfort in their suffering and bafflement. They pray to be kept from disease and death, from enmity and strife, from false pride and self-deceit. The sources of their joy are in a sense of fellowship with one another, in peace of mind through the love of God, and in hope of fulfilment for their faith and works. They sing songs of the seasons, springtime and harvest, of national days of thanksgiving, of peace among the nations, of aspiration for a noble life, and of courage and patience in discouragement and disaster, also songs of childhood, of love, and of death.

The sermons are more specific. They meet the minute as well as the grand occasions of daily life with counsels of prudence, concerning health and honesty, business and politics, marriage and training of children, care of the poor and sympathy for the unfortunate. In the minister's personal contacts he often has reason to be still more direct. He is called upon to advise about lawyers, doctors, and nursemaids, about houses to rent, schools to attend, and candidates to elect. Every agency for the good of the community feels that it is his duty as a religious representative to help with every kind of cause that is meant to do anybody any good. He is expected to be concerned about everything that is of importance to anyone within his reach, to know how to get a man into a hospital, to help find a wife or husband, to get jobs for people, to explain why good people have troubles, and to just sit by the side of the road and be a friend to man. Everything that pinches hard upon humanity, from toothache to anxiety about a future life, comes for solution to a minister, and comes to him legitimately because of the inclusive interests with which he is concerned as a spokesman for the religious life. Perhaps if he were adequate to these claims upon him, he would have in his office files card indexes of the best references to all the sources of information for human needs that the world affords. This is to say that the minister and the church might appropriately bring within reach of the individual the knowledge of all kinds of ways and means of meeting every kind of problem that life presents.

Something like this was in my mind when we began to create a church library thirty years ago. It was the intention to get beyond the conventional collection of books usually found in a church library. We purchased several hundred volumes selected with reference to the great departments of human interest. There were books on philosophy and religion, sociology, education, natural science, biography, critical works on modern interpretation of the Old and New Testaments, and works of general literature. There should have been encyclopedias and compendiums of scientific works, outlines of history, anthologies of poetry and literature, digests of medical science, guidebooks for love and marriage, and indexes to all the things that every man, woman, and child should know. This plan for a library arose not from any mere academic interest in having all sorts of books around but from the practical idea that the church should offer to everyone the opportunity for satisfying the craving for answers to all kinds of questions that arise in any person's life, about himself and about the world he lives in. Educated people are likely to be informed about one or two rather limited areas of life and are constantly in need of information in most other matters as much as those who have little if any of the so-called higher education.

The religious values are as numerous as the volumes in a great library, and the task of understanding them may seem as over-

whelming as that of reading all the books. But libraries are sim-
plified by classification, and so are the religious values. Life shapes
up under a few headings or systems of interest, and the main
concerns of a moral or a religious person may be summarized in
a few words. These words indicate what are the major departments of the good life. They are health, work, love, knowledge,
art, and government. All of these are names of groups of values,
and all of these groups are interrelated like families woven together by intermarriage. A man's life work, his vocation or profession, requires for its prosecution knowledge and skill, friends,
and health. Love flowers normally into family and circles of
friends. Care of children brings relations to neighbor children, to
school, to medical science, to the world of fancy and art, to problems of morals and social behavior. In similar ways the fields of
knowledge, art, and social relations branch out into each other
and into endless practical problems. No interest lives unto itself
or is in any way self-sufficient. Religious values are all these values
taken together, organized into a living whole, like the human
body and its parts. "The heart cannot say unto the hand, I have no
need of thee: nor again the head to the feet, I have no need of
you." As I have often said, religious values are at the same time
other kinds of values, educational, social, economic, scientific, and
artistic. Whenever religion tries to be something separate, it is
like a head without feet or like a heart without hands. For the
same reasons there are no separate secular values. Business cannot
live by itself. It needs alliance with newspapers, with politics, with
the laws of the land. The morals of honesty, promptness, industry,
and friendliness are essential to its success. A successful salesman
needs patience, good nature, fairness, and good address. An ad-
vertising man should have imagination and taste, and must have
the human touch.

The only real secularism in a bad sense is isolation from the full
stream of natural interests. When business tries to go its own way
in defiance of the common good, it tends to become secular. But
the same is also true of religion. When the church withdraws into
its sanctuary and denies its organic relation to scientific knowledge or to the institutions of society around it, there results a
deadly secularization of religion. Too often this has happened,
and far too widely it is happening today. It happens not only

with those sects which cultivate an intense emotionalism, like the Holy Rollers, or the sects that stress other-worldliness, but to many old and settled churches whose theologians speak in dialectical tongues and declare that the God in whom they believe is beyond the reach of man's best efforts.

It is passing strange that an age which has the means for the best understanding of Jesus that any age ever had should have many learned and influential theologians who completely secularize his religion by separating it from common sense and common experience. The parables of Jesus were about farming, house cleaning, wedding parties, vineyards, merchandising, highway robberies, wasted patrimonies, catching fish, laying foundations for houses, mending clothing, tending sheep, and giving relief. The people who heard him were astonished because they could understand him. Multitudes in our time, after listening to some of our theologians, would be still more astonished if they were to hear Jesus speak today. Would he not talk in terms of radios and telephones, of automobiles and airplanes, of stocks and bonds, of political conventions and movies and best sellers, of Hollywood and Wall Street? He would find parables in them. He would illuminate these things, as he did the common things in his world, by revealing the lessons in them. And they would be the same lessons, doubtless, of the need of sympathy, of foresight, of forgiveness, and of faith, both in our fellow men and in the kingdom of heaven.

One might say that the great quality in the teaching of Jesus was his ability to see things in their relations, to show that the simplest deeds bear religious meaning when the artificial distinctions between different departments of life are removed. A cup of cold water given in the name of brotherhood would save the soul of the giver. Too many times the cup of water is just given, carelessly or thoughtlessly given, and not in the name of anyone or anything. That is secular. When it is given in kindliness and sympathy, it becomes religious. It becomes religious because it then has a wider meaning. The difference is easily recognized, especially when we ourselves are the recipients. A proffered gift may be the cruelest affront to our honor and self-respect, but the same gift, when warm with love and unselfish purpose, may bind the world together for us. It is never the size of the gift but the name in which it is given that makes it religious or secular. The value of the deed is measured by the way the doer thinks and feels about it, and this points to a further important character of religious values.

Only in recent years have the philosophers themselves devoted their attention to the nature of value in any critical and thorough way. Only within the last two or three decades have books on the general subject of value begun to appear. It was my fortune for many years to give courses in ethics, aesthetics, and the philosophy of religion. In all these subjects the question constantly arose as to the nature of the standards by which we determine what is the good, the beautiful, and the true, but the question of value was not treated by itself.

About ten years ago I began to offer a course in theories of value, treating of the nature of values and standards wherever found. The problem is common to ethics, aesthetics, logic, and religion and is of basic importance in all of them. How can we know what is right, what is beautiful, what is true? Are there absolute standards above and outside man's own experience? Or are we limited everywhere to fallible human judgments, to individual taste, and to changing measures and appraisals? Is man the measure of all things? If he is, what is to save us from chaos and confusion over the dearest things in the world? How can one person justly denounce another's behavior or moral code? It is obvious that here is a crucial demand upon us. The war of 1914 made it very urgent and insistent. Here were the greatest nations of the world at each other's throats over their respective cultures. With new ferocity people began to assert that might makes right, while others said that right makes might. The former magnified force and terror; the latter clung to the belief that real power at last is on the side of justice and honor. Students took the keenest interest in studies bearing upon such questions, ranging over the conditions of life here and now, and all the way from nations seeking territory to individuals trying to make their fortunes or to satisfy other ambitions.

Two contrasted schools of thought are to be found in every moral, aesthetic, and religious discussion. One holds that there are absolute standards, said to be given us from some source outside our own conscious selves. They are divinely given, or they come through some power of intuition within us as a kind of conscience to guide us if we listen for its voice. The other school holds that our judgments of value depend upon the society to which we belong, upon our individual training, upon our experience, and upon our efforts to reach higher levels of life. It is this empirical school which has been convincing to me. It surveys all orders of existence and notes that in the lowest forms of life there are types of action that look very much as if the organism welcomed some things and rejected others. The tiny little amoeba, when coming into contact with minute particles of matter in the water about it, absorbs some into itself by extending the substance of its body to envelop them; but in the presence of other particles it withdraws and remains aloof.

These two gestures run through all the ascending organisms in the biological scale, the two gestures of acceptance and refusal. The dog eats one kind of food and refuses what the horse would eat. Man too has his likes and dislikes, but these are more diversified and more various than in the lower forms. On the highest levels individual differences appear. The Englishman will have his beef and mutton, and the Hindu will eat no meat. The Anglican churchman likes an elaborate ritual, and the Puritan prefers simplicity. The aristocrat enjoys a class society, and the democrat seeks to estimate all men by their proved ability and achievement.

The empiricist believes that these differences are largely the result of custom and tradition. He contends that very high and refined forms of life may be developed in this way and regards our prevailing social standards as gradual growths under the pressure of institutions and laws which have had a long history and persist under the influence of use and wont. In modern society, under the world-wide contacts of cultures and in the light of evolution, thoughtful people as never before—unless it was among the intellectuals of ancient Greece—are questioning their standards and wondering whether they are entitled to authority and finality. Values, the empiricists hold, are standards that have been subjected to examination, to criticism, being reassessed in the course of time. The conventions of society have indorsed and justified, in terms of age and wide use, the practice of slavery, the subjection of women, and the exploitation of children. Religious people frequently claim revelation as an absolute authority for belief and conduct and take the Bible as the embodiment of this revelation. But it becomes apparent that the Bible has to be viewed as a series of revelations. In the earlier stages it makes no denunciation of slavery, and in the New Testament the great Apostle Paul accepts the subordination of a wife to her husband. He also returns the slave Onesimus to his master Philemon, and only counsels the master to be kind to the slave.

It may be said that the supreme revelation is to be found in Jesus Christ and that all the rest of the Bible leads up to him. Yet there are two ways of accepting the words and example of Jesus. One is to take what he says as true because he says it, and another is to believe it because it stands the test of reflection and experience. When his way of life has been confirmed by the demands of intelligence and of practical life, it has gained the deepest security and made its strongest claims upon our loyalty. Certain of his principles confirm themselves to our best thought and to our deepest experience. He makes human life itself a supreme value, and this is substantiated scientifically by evidence for the greater power and capacity for growth of man as compared with all the lower forms. Man alone is self-conscious and critical of values. He has the ability to make elaborate and significant inventions, to develop arts and sciences. He alone plans for a long future and organizes great societies to carry on the records of the past and to promote co-operative work toward the conquest of disease and the improvement of the human race itself.

Jesus based his hopes upon the great possibilities of man, including that of building a kingdom of heaven on the earth. The sciences of man, the experiments in democracy, justify this evaluation of human beings. Nothing yet proves that continued progress is inevitable, but that it is possible no one but an extreme skeptic or pessimist can doubt. Education proceeds upon the assumption that human beings can be trained and developed into greater understanding and efficiency for a wholesome society. Hope of a better world is itself a value, and, in spite of all wars and tragedies, the long course of history lends reasonable justification to that hope. This hope of a better future is one form of the love of life itself, and the love of life is a basic value, for without the will to live the nerve of effort is destroyed and nothing significant can be accomplished. The religious pessimists of our time who belittle man's endeavor to improve his estate are dangerous foes of the most precious thing in this world.

Values, strangely enough, are enhanced by their degree of precariousness. If all the goods of life were guaranteed to us by infinite power and wisdom, so that we had no responsibility for them, life would lose its meaning and interest. The greatest moment of danger is the moment of complacency, both for the individual and for any social enterprise. The values we have made our own have thereby an added quality, and it is doubtful whether we are in a position to appreciate values of any kind for which we have not in some sense worked and longed.

A surprising discovery has come upon some of the most sensitive and righteous men of our time concerning the traditional faith in God. They have found that belief in an Infinite Being, who is to right all wrong and make all things work together for good, may be a very weakening faith. They find that there is something more inspiring in the idea of a finite God who works with us on the front lines of battle and risks his cause and all, just as mortals do. William James was one of those great souls who felt that men must have a real part in determining what *may be*. He said,

> God himself, in short, may draw vital strength and increase of very being from our fidelity. For my own part, I do not know what the sweat and blood and tragedy of this life mean, if they mean anything short of this. If this life be not a real fight, in which something is eternally gained for the universe by success, it is no better than a game of private theatricals from which one may withdraw at will. But it *feels* like a real fight,— as if there were something really wild in the universe which we, with all our idealities and faithfulnesses, are needed to redeem; and first of all to redeem our own hearts from atheisms and fears.[1]

It is sometimes thought that it requires a service of the church to make the high values of life truly religious. Something is felt to be added to the sanctity of an infant by baptism or christening. Would it not be truer to regard such a ceremony as a recognition and celebration of the value already present in the newborn child?

[1] William James, "Is Life Worth Living?" in *The Will to Believe* (New York: Longmans, Green, 1897), p. 61.

We speak of marriage being solemnized in the church. It is a recognition of one of the greatest events in human life. The love and understanding, which make the union of two lives so wonderful, are already present as the occasion of the ceremony. And when death comes, the rites observed are not to add meaning to the life that is ended but to mark with dignity and honor and remembrance the values which that life has realized.

These three great events of birth, marriage, and death are of religious value because they touch life at such great depths and lift it to such great heights. The ceremonials serve to catch and hold and magnify the values arising in life itself. They are religious values because they are so deep and so vital in human experience. It is important that they be socially celebrated and emphasized as brought to the altars of religion rather than found there. In early religions it was the sacrifice that sanctified the altar, and not the altar that made the offering sacred. So for years I put on the calendar: "This Church practices union, has no creed, seeks to make religion as intelligent as science, as appealing as art, as vital as the day's work, as intimate as home, and as inspiring as love."

Religion has had the natural function of celebrating the aspects of life which are *events*, and it should still honor all of them, not only in contemplation but in active participation and in the idealizing work of reconstruction. I have put it this way: "A religion is needed which discovers . . . values in experience, not one that endeavors to import and impose them from without. If religion does not have its proper field in clarifying and furthering the values of the economic, political and social life, then its inner attitudes and sentiments lose substance and significance." We now realize how much science can help religion make the most of life, but science is only part of it: "there are also appreciation, love, and the quest for beauty. Religion is a living experience of the great values found in the rich and growing life of the world, and in the realization of what philosophers have called the kingdom of ends." The function of religion, then, is "to discover the meaning and beauty in all spheres of life, and not to limit itself to those special experiences which we have traditionally conceived as religious." It is not enough for ministers to "make religion scientific and aesthetic, but they must endeavor to make it hospitable, radiant, and friendly for particular individuals according to their need."[2]

Values arise out of life itself. They become religious when they are felt and known to be important for the whole of life. Jesus saw this. Little children belonged to his kingdom of heaven without special consecration. He shared in the joy of the marriage in Cana of Galilee. He was shaken to tears by the death of Lazarus. The love of a father that will not give his son a stone when he asks for bread, or a serpent when he asks for a fish, was for Jesus religious in itself. The great key word of his gospel was love, and he found love already active in the world, even among publicans and sinners. He said to his disciples: "For if ye love them which love you, what thank have ye? for sinners also love those that love them. . . . But love ye your enemies, and do good . . . hoping for nothing again; and your reward shall be great, and ye shall be the children of the Highest" (Luke 6:32, 35).

He was simply encouraging them to take the little flower of love that grew wild all about them and cultivate it into a flower still larger and more fragrant. That is a process which is everywhere making over our world today. Men like Burbank are taking wild flowers and making them into a new order of beauty; they are taking wild grains and enlarging them and multiplying them into more productive and richer wheat; and it is possible to take the common run of mankind and make them over into "children of the Highest."

In practical life men have a sensible appreciation of these possibilities of new developments, but in religion they often miss the best available things because they do not have patience with imperfection. Years ago (1921), in working out a paper for the presidential address of the western division of the American Philosophical Association,[3] I made what was to me a discovery of lasting importance about this matter of religious values. I found that in the great concerns of life men acted upon the best knowledge they had, as if it were final and perfect. Then if they found

---

[2] "Theory in Practice," in *Contemporary American Theology: Theological Autobiographies* (2d series), ed. Vergilius Ferm (New York: Round Table Press, 1933), pp. 12, 17, 20, 26.

[3] Published with the title "Religious Values and the Practical Absolute," *International Journal of Ethics*, Vol. XXXII, No. 4 (July, 1922).

something better by further experiment and inquiry, they willingly adopted the new standard and acted upon it with all their power. They trusted themselves to fallible physicians in operations that were matters of life and death. They staked their fortunes on inventions and speculations that were the work of the wisest and best human beings they knew. They undertook vast social experiments, like American democracy, without any further guarantees than the best judgment of the best people they knew. And in such reflections I came to the conclusion that the greatest and finest standards we have are the standards or values of the best people. And if I were asked who were the best people, my answer was: The best people are the people who have the best standards or the highest values.

I found a lovely illustration of the way we human beings work when I observed the trademark on a little oil stove in my summer cottage: New Perfection No. 62. Obviously the inventor was so elated with his first model that he called it Perfection, and when he discovered improvements he did not hesitate to call each better one another perfection. That is what sensible people do with their religious values. We have to act upon what we have as if it were the very best, and when we find something better, it becomes perfection of a new order. Jesus urged his disciples to be perfect, but with Judas, Peter, the two Sons of Thunder, and other fallible mortals around him, he must have known that the attainment of any very great perfection would be a long and difficult process. Yet he did not lose faith in the coming of his kingdom of love and wisdom, nor should we.

Chapter xix | The Campbell Institute

The Campbell Institute is a voluntary organization of ministers, teachers, and laymen among the Disciples of Christ. They are men of college and university training who have banded together in the interest of religious ideas and work. The threefold purpose of the organization was stated in its constitution at the time of its beginning, in 1896:

(1) To encourage and keep alive a scholarly spirit and to enable its members to help each other to a riper scholarship by the free discussion of vital problems. (2) To promote quiet self-culture and the development of a higher spirituality among the members and among the churches with which they shall come in contact. (3) To encourage positive productive work with a view to making contributions of permanent value to the literature and thought of the Disciples of Christ.

This was a kind of youth movement among university students and instructors, for among the fourteen charter members only one or two were yet thirty years of age. The moving spirits were five men who had been students in the Yale Divinity School and who as early as 1892 had talked of some such organization. Some of them met with others from Harvard and the University of Chicago in Springfield, Illinois, during the national convention of the Disciples in October, 1896, to organize, with a simple constitution, by-laws, and a roster of thirteen men and one woman as charter members. She was the only woman ever elected to membership. Six charter members still living in 1940 are Burris A. Jenkins, Herbert L. Willett, George A. Campbell, Clinton Lockhart, W. E. Garrison, and I.

Other names were soon added, but the number of university-trained men in the Disciple ministry at that time was small. At the end of twenty years there were two hundred members of the institute, after forty years there were four hundred, and at present there are five hundred. Very few graduates of Disciple colleges before 1900 went to the great universities for further professional training. Since that time the number has greatly increased, partly through the example and influence of members of the institute.

The religious spirit and purpose of the organization were clear from the first. It sought a higher spirituality for its members and for the churches they served, and it encouraged the effort to produce writings that would contribute to the religious literature and thought of the Disciples. No one could be associated with these men in their meetings, or share their thought in any way, without feeling their sincerity and unselfishness. They gave a great deal of time and no little money for expenses, without thought of any financial remuneration. There was no attempt to place members in positions of power or influence, and certainly there was no disposition to manipulate organized agencies of the churches for any ulterior ends.

It was early felt that a publication of some kind was needed to keep the members in touch with one another and to give a means of self-expression to anyone who wished to write. For nearly forty years a modest quarterly or monthly publication has been maintained to promote acquaintance and fellowship among members to report important works of modern scholarship and to reinterpret the teachings of the Disciples on Christian union and other religious subjects in the light of the rapid development of biblical and historical research. The institute set up for itself a number of departments or chambers to give reviews of literature and discussions. Each member was invited to identify himself with one of these, according to his interest and to make contributions from his reading and study. These departments were in the fields of the Old Testament, the New Testament, sociology, philosophy and education, and church history. This plan was operated for several years very profitably but finally was given up as the men felt the increasing demands of their ministerial or professorial duties.

In 1907 the institute publication was begun as a monthly, and the name adopted for it was the *Scroll*. It fell to me to be the editor, as I had been of its predecessor. The first article in the first issue shows the spirit of the writers. The Campbell Institute was named for Alexander Campbell, the intellectual leader of the Disciples. He was president of Bethany College, editor of a monthly publication called the *Millennial Harbinger*, and he was constantly traveling, preaching, and lecturing. We were anxious to honor him for his leadership, for his standards and ideals of education, and for his fresh and vital interpretation of Christianity.

When we designed a seal for the *Scroll* and for other publications of the institute, it was fun to discover how I could fit into a cross, the great Christian symbol of love and righteousness, the Greek for our motto, "The truth shall make you free": ΑΛΗΘΕΙΑ ΕΛΕΥΘΕΡΙΑ. A single *theta*, the first letter in the Greek word for God, central in the intersection, was in the middle of each word, and the whole was surrounded by the Greek symbol of perfection, the circle. The crossed words in the circular design have continued to appear on the brown cover of our little magazine:

Several articles in the first volume of the *Scroll* indicate the temper and spirit of the men of the institute. Some quotations from the articles I asked them to write are of interest for several reasons, after the lapse of more than thirty years. The first was by H. D. C. Maclachlan, a rare soul among us. He was a Scotchman, a Master of Arts of the University of Glasgow. His youthful wanderlust had brought him to America and to the free life of a cowboy out on the Panhandle of western Texas. One Saturday afternoon he dropped into the office of the Disciple minister in Amarillo, intoxicated and talkative. He picked up a Greek New Testament from the table and fell to reading it, much to the surprise of the minister, for it was not often that the cowboys could read Greek. Maclachlan told of his home in Scotland and particularly of his mother and her deeply religious life.

That visit to the Disciple minister had great consequences. It resulted in the cowboy's going to the College of the Bible, in Lexington, Kentucky, and in his becoming one of the most brilliant ministers among the Disciples. At the time of his death he had been the minister of the Seventh Street Christian Church in Richmond, Virginia, for twenty years. He was one of the finest and most loyal members of the institute.

His opening article in the first issue of the *Scroll* in 1907 was "The Disciples and Modern Culture." He discussed the need for progress in religion, emphasized the great opportunity of the times and the fact that the Disciples had made large claims for freedom from every kind of dogmatism, especially creedal. He summed up the article in these words:

We stand at the parting of the ways. On the one hand the spirit of progress is calling us to join the great forces that are everywhere leading men out of the fog of ignorance and prejudice into the tonic atmosphere of clear thinking and exact endeavor. This is the spirit of free investigation, of reverence for truth, of humble waiting for the light, of unselfish aims and ideals, to be of which is to be borne along on the stream of time into larger spheres of usefulness. The alternative is the spirit of dogmatism, of sectarianism, the legalism of the letter, the dwarfing of vision, the pathetic rigidity of the death-mask. This is the mummification of faith, and to surrender to it can only mean for us that, like the traveler lost in the desert, we shall keep aimlessly circling round our extinguished camp fires, while the great world caravan moves on without us.

The second article in that first issue of the *Scroll* was by Charles Clayton Morrison. Even then his sentences had the ring and force with which the religious world was to become familiar through his editorials in the *Christian Century*. His article was "Essential Infidelity." He said:

The word "infidelity" covers a wide variety of meanings in the different ages or countries or denominations of Christendom. Names of men once used as synonyms for infidelity have been rescued from contempt by the subsequent success of their heresies. . . . It does not follow that a man is an infidel because he does not agree with the fathers or councils in the precise words with which they made their confession of faith. . . . Our fathers would have us keep their faith, not by complimenting them in the mere adoption and teaching of their ideas, but by meeting our problems with the same originality and courage as they met theirs. It is well to remember that these fathers had fathers. They certainly were not disloyal to their fathers when they broke away from the set of ideas in which they were reared. It was just this courage of theirs that makes us glad to be called their sons, and at the same time makes them worthy sons of their fathers. Their seeming infidelity to their fathers' belief is, at root, the deepest fidelity, the best proof of their possession of their fathers' faith. . . . Nor is doubt of the dogmatic authority of the scripture a ground for branding a man an infidel. The Bible is honored by the man, who, in reading, asks himself fearlessly what scriptures ring commandingly in his soul, or steal comfortingly into his heart, or light up areas of his world with sudden shafts of insight. In this attitude he puts himself in possession of the faith of the men who wrote the Bible. . . . The denial of the divinity of Christ has been taken as warrant for calling a man an infidel. . . . We do not read that Christ anywhere made the utterance of any such set of words a test of discipleship. Infidelity, to Jesus, is the lack of his spirit, his attitude toward life and the world. . . . On the deeper level of theistic discussion, too, there is room for intellectual liberty, without the use of the epithet, infidel. Innumerable are the conceptions to which the name God is applied. The gist of the whole matter is that we must go back of the intellect to get the real creed of a man. His life, his behavior, is the real confession of his faith.

There were many other articles by Dr. Morrison that also show the fruitful and promising currents of his thought and illustrate the kind of free and virile thinking characteristic of members of the institute.

In that first year of the *Scroll,* Dr. Herbert L. Willett contributed a paper on "Prophets for the Time." Among many other significant words, he said:

There is no hint in the Scriptures that prophecy expired in biblical days. Both in the Old Testament and the New it is recognized as a living and perpetual function. . . . The prophet of Hebrew and apostolic times was a man of his age, touching it at every possible point, understanding its life and thought. Therein lay the effectiveness of his message. No less timely must be the life and message of the modern prophet of God.

A further quotation from Dr. Willett brings out the application of his view to the prophet or minister of today:

Such a man will avail himself of all the aids to education which our age so abundantly furnishes. He will be a university man if he finds it possible, not because he regards such an experience as indispensable, nor because the man who lacks such training is a failure, nor because this discipline initiates him into a select and exclusive fraternity in which he would be glad to have a place. He knows that none of these things is true. But he recognizes that the university has been for many centuries the center from which the greatest reforms and the most urgent impulses toward religious awakening have come. He knows that most of the great leaders and prophets of the church have been university men. He knows that in the university truth is sought with a devotion which has braved all censure of authority in church and state, and has opened the way to the very freedom and power which the church of Christ has attained.

Dr. A. W. Fortune justified this progressive attitude by writing:

The glory of the Disciples has been that we have been able to keep our creed unwritten. We have been able to keep it from becoming ironclad. It has been able to grow as we have grown. . . . The world is moving. Each succeeding generation is looking out from the heights attained by those who have gone before. That being true it is natural that it shall have a larger conception of God and the Bible.

Other articles in the *Scroll* of 1907 emphasize devotion to Christian union, to missions, to religious education, to better-trained ministers, and to greater freedom of thought, in keeping with the spirit of Alexander Campbell and his father, Thomas Campbell. The question of church federation was beginning to be discussed in Disciple papers and conventions. The social gospel was also a new and rising interest, and a modification of the traditional insistence on immersion as a condition of church membership was advocated now and then, on behalf of a more consistent position on union and federation. The institute was ten years old but now for the first time presented the writings of its members in published form. Naturally it drew criticisms from conservative quarters, usually in terms long familiar in religious controversy.

One contention was that the institute was "a little coterie of young men," an esoteric group. Time gave the effective answer to the matter of youth. The original leaders of the institute came to be older than the new editor of the *Christian Standard*. Also the gradual growth of its membership refuted the charge that the institute was little. The charge that the organization was an esoteric group was denied by the fact that its publication was open to public subscription and that the annual meetings could be attended by anyone interested. The membership list published in the *Scroll* was republished in the *Standard*, but still there was no great defection. One college president was asked by his board of trustees to give up his membership in the institute. His reply was that he would resign the presidency if they wished, but he would not withdraw from the institute, and they allowed him to continue in both. The *Scroll* constantly insisted that the writers of its articles were alone responsible for the ideas expressed and that no individual assumed to speak on any question for the whole institute. It was admitted that there was great diversity of opinion among the members, but all agreed on the right of free thought and uncensored writing.

The charge that the institute was in a sense a selected group was truer, for it had been its policy to admit only college graduates, except in certain instances where a man's attainments and spirit commended him. But the same charge of exclusiveness might as justifiably be brought against an alumni association or against any ministerial association or any professional society whose membership is open only to those specially interested in its purposes. University-trained men are in the nature of the case a minority group in the ministry of any religious body that does not insist upon such standards for its ministers. Sometimes it was suggested that there is a place for the uneducated minister. An editorial in the *Scroll* replied:

If by this is meant that there are many untrained ministers who do good work; or if it is meant that often men should not stay out of the ministry because it is impossible for them to obtain a thorough education, then all would agree. But if it is meant that men do better work in the ministry because they are uneducated; or if it is meant that any man should take less training than the greatest amount he can possibly secure, then there must be earnest dissent.

One member of the institute, commenting on the various objections to the *Scroll*, facetiously impersonating an objector, wrote:

But how to get at this new publication and persuade its publishers to discontinue it, is not clear. To ignore it is not wise; to ridicule it calls attention to it; what to do with it is perplexing. None of the old methods in use by the persecutors can be applied to it. There seems to be no financial consideration back of it. The writers all seem conscious of their freedom. But there is one thing that can always be said against it, that will arouse suspicion in every loyal, God-fearing Disciple's heart: "It is published in Chicago!" Can any good thing possibly come out of Chicago? Did not Dowie begin and end in Chicago? Did not President Harper die there? Is not that the place where Willett lives? Did not

God destroy that city once by fire in 1871, as he destroyed Sodom and Gomorrah? Will he not destroy that great and wicked city again by water, as certain prophets are now predicting?

The members of the institute had no desire to make their organization and its publication an irritant in the brotherhood of the Disciples and were willing to discontinue the *Scroll* if that would relieve the situation. About that time the *Christian Century* came under the editorship of Dr. Charles Clayton Morrison, and it was thought that this paper, with its larger constituency and program, would serve the main purposes of the institute very adequately.

For ten years the *Scroll* was discontinued and only a "bulletin" was circulated in its place in order to afford a means of exchange of news, opinion, and fellowship among the members. The membership continued to grow, annual meetings were regularly held, and the programs show the maintenance of the same free and fruitful discussion of the vital questions of religious interests. In order to secure still wider participation in such discussions for all ministers and laymen who might be interested, the institute co-operated in the organization of the Disciples Congress, which continued for several years. It made an open forum where conservatives and liberals alike were invited to present their views and to cultivate a genuine fellowship in spite of intellectual differences. But the congress lacked such definiteness of organization as the institute had, and the financial and managerial duties finally brought the congress to an end.

The institute was fortunate in having the same secretary, Mr. Perry J. Rice, through many years. His personal acquaintance, his wide and faithful correspondence, and his fine appreciation of the purpose and mission of the institute contributed incalculably to the stability and efficiency of the organization. It was his kind of devotion that brought the institute through the stress of the war and the depression that followed.

It is interesting to live with an association like this institute through a long period of years. Some members have always felt it to be of great importance. To them it is essential that the educated men of a religious group co-operate in trying to help each other with the best available knowledge and methods of work. They all need the sense of companionship against the opposition of criticism, misunderstanding, and indifference. Many Disciple ministers have said that it was the fellowship with members of the institute that held them to the ministry. The fact that other men encountered discouragement and yet went on with their work was a source of courage and faith.

Some of us have given an inordinate amount of time and energy to maintain the institute and its activities. Our friends often think we are overzealous about it. They think we belong to the class of more or less quixotic men whom Jenkin Lloyd Jones used to call "God's fools." He referred to himself that way when he went abroad on Henry Ford's "Peace Ship."

God's fools are the men who do not have worldly sense enough to calculate their enterprises in a selfish way. They throw themselves into causes with marvelous abandon and sometimes fire the imaginations of enough people to make their causes win. Out from this warm, pulsing heart of the center of any enterprise may be seen, in concentric circles according to their interest, the other members of the order. Out on the fringe of the institute have always been men whose attachment was tenuous, perhaps a bit patronizing, often delinquent in dues, but ready to move nearer the center at any sign of activity which might offer them some advantage.

There seems to be a kind of vicariousness in every association of human beings, even in churches, for there are always a few who bear an undue share of the responsibility, the work, and the expense. The others are too willing to "let George do it." But perhaps the real reason is that many members lack the imagination, the energy, and the determination to sustain important social causes when these require initiative and personal risk. Organizations are subject to much waste motion in keeping up the morale of members, which prevents the whole strength of the group being directed to its main objectives. But in spite of such lag the Campbell Institute has maintained itself through more than four decades and has made notable contributions to its members and to the religious body in which it lives and works.

From its beginning the institute has had the encouragement and counsel of many of the greatest leaders among the Disciples, some of whom in their long lives spanned the years from the lifetime of Alexander Campbell to the birth time of the institute. Among these were such veterans of the free Disciple tradition as Alexander Procter, J. H. Garrison, T. P. Haley, and A. McLean, none of whom could be suspected of any sympathy with an organization inimical to the best interests of the religious cause.

The Disciples of Christ constitute the largest religious body which has sprung up on American soil, and it is one of the half-dozen largest religious movements in all of Protestantism. In many ways it is the freest. It has never been bound by any of the old creeds or ecclesiastical systems. It has always believed in the progressive discovery of religious truth through better understanding of the Scriptures and through the growing experience of churches and individuals. The members of the institute have been urged on in their quest for better scholarship and for wider contacts with the religious and scientific world by an impulse from their own religious inheritance as well as by the influence of the new age in which we live. The men of the institute have not hesitated to enter the great universities of America and Europe in search of light. Several of them, as missionaries in the Orient, in Latin America, in India, in Africa, and in the islands of the sea, have brought us firsthand knowledge of the most important things from the oldest and from the newest cultures of the world. This fellowship of understanding sympathy broadens the outlook of those of us who tread the round of familiar church work in this country, and it sustains the relatively isolated missionaries in the far places of the earth.

The great purpose of the institute is to gain some insight into all the human needs of the world, and also to find and apply so far as possible whatever alleviating and curative remedies are available through any agency, human or divine. There are five hundred men bound together in this fellowship, and they do what they can in co-operating with the million and a half Disciples in the world. It is a challenging opportunity for this new religious order of the Campbell Institute. If it can maintain the free spirit and cultivated soul of the modern man, together with the religious zeal and devotion of the old religious orders of the church, it may contribute another long and worthy chapter to the old, old story of Jesus and his widening influence in the world.

Chapter xx | Pentwater

After some years in Chicago, doing double duty as minister and university instructor, I began to wonder if there might be some way by which I could find or make a summer retreat out of the city and not too far away. Our four little children needed space and freedom, and their mother, with the care of them and a large house, needed a change of scene and relaxation. For several summers they had gone out to Iowa, to "Grandma's Brick House." It was on the banks of 'Coon River, two miles north of De Soto, where my wife's father, Grotius Van Meter, with his two brothers, had settled in 1853 and built a flour mill.

The Van Meters were a typical family of American pioneers. They had started some generations before in Virginia and had migrated in successive generations to Elizabethtown, Kentucky; Edinburg, Indiana; De Soto, Iowa; later into Kansas and British Columbia. In a hundred years they spanned the continent, working their way as farmers, cattlemen, and millers. Those who went to Iowa arrived there before the Rock Island Railway was built and while Indians and buffalo might occasionally be seen. The town of Van Meter, three miles east of the Brick House, was named for Uncle Jacob, the oldest brother, who built a flour mill there, owned farms, fed cattle, and belonged to the church of his fathers, the church of the true faith!

He remained a great hunter, as he had been from boyhood. He told fascinating stories of the early days in Indiana. There he and his brothers worked hard through the week, but on Sundays Jacob could not resist the call of the wild and would regularly go hunting when the others went to church. As regularly, his father would take him to the woodshed and administer the rod for his correction. He seems to have settled down to that arrangement and accepted it as a kind of inevitable bargain, hunting on Sunday and a whipping Monday morning. When I knew him in his late eighties, Uncle Jacob was a powerful old man, of massive build, with thick grey hair and beard, piercing eyes, and quick wit. He was the family referee on practical matters, One summer day I brought home from an early morning hunt along the river an animal quite unknown to me and to my mother-in-law. It was heavier and darker than a raccoon, shorter of legs than a fox, and bigger than a prairie dog. Unable to agree on it at the house, we decided to take the pelt to Uncle Jacob, with the understanding that if he said it was anything to eat I would dress it, Mother Van Meter would cook it, and all of us would feast on it. He said it was a groundhog and that people sometimes ate groundhog. So we prepared for the unfamiliar dinner but found when we sat down to the table that there was more pleasure in the pursuit than in possession.

The Brick House had been a landmark from the day it was built, across the road from the mill and the great dam. The house was ready for Grotius Van Meter to bring his bride, Damaris Dodge, to on their honeymoon. For a generation it was the center of the family life. After her husband's untimely death she lived there until her five children were grown. To this house and millsite we went from Chicago every summer until fire destroyed the mill and the miller's family were scattered. The heat of Iowa days and nights could not spoil the joy of old associations or defeat our children's pleasure in living in the midst of country life.

At length it became a settled project to get a summer place on the eastern shore of Lake Michigan. Ten or twelve of us, ministers and friends, secured a tract of thirty acres of sand with about 1,300 feet of frontage on the North Beach at Pentwater, Michigan. We called it Campbell Park, for Alexander Campbell. My only possible resource for my part of the venture was to borrow on an insurance policy which an enterprising and friendly salesman had persuaded me to take out years before. That proved to be life insurance in the best sense, for it was one of the old tontine policies which matured twenty years after it was written. From the cash settlement there was sufficient to build a simple cottage in 1911, which has been the best kind of health-and-happiness insurance.

Honesty and candor compel me to relate also the sad fact that a thousand dollars was received beyond the cost of the cottage and that this money, on the advice of a friend, was invested in an enterprise from which great profits were expected. That thousand dollars was a complete loss except for its lesson. What needed comforts it might have bought! And security, if wisely placed where at modest interest it would have been a resource in time of sickness or any need! That loss made a deep and lasting impression. It brought complete immunity from any temptation ever to invest again in any venture "to make a lot of money quick." It gave me understanding sympathy for others who lost their hard-earned savings in speculation or in the depression that was to come.

But we had the cottage by the lake, and every summer as soon as school was out we rented the town house to students and made our pilgrimage two hundred miles north to the woods, the dunes, and the beach by the clear cool waters of the great inland sea. Almost every year, in the family councils, we debated whether we should not send the children to the public schools for economy, instead of to the expensive University Elementary and High School. But the public schools opened right after Labor Day instead of the first of October. Arguments were always settled by the fact that all departments of the university had vacation in September. That extra month outweighed all other claims and meant that the father could have his free time with the rest of the family. I quote from some letters written twenty-five years ago for the church *Messenger*.

June 1916. I have just made a fire in the good old-fashioned fireplace. Its crackling music makes a genial, friendly spell throughout the house. Out of the windows to the west I look over Lake Michigan, which has been rather quiet for the two days since I came. That is about as long as one mood lasts, and a leaden sky now suggests a possible storm. Usually our human moods blend into the moods of nature, and by the time she seems to tire of too much warmth and soft sunshine we are also ready for thunder and the roaring waves. How a wild storm over the water acts vicariously for our pent-up human restlessness!

Last evening we had a marvelous sunset. It was one of those in which a single strip of cloud at the horizon meets the descending fire and furnishes a curtain for brilliant, dissolving views. At last the sun is half-sunk in the water. The upper edge is hid by the cloud above, and the wide stretch of waves and the sky are wondrously illuminated. A painter would need a full palette of vivid colors to reproduce it, and if he succeeded many an observer of his canvas would doubt whether such shimmering lights and profusion of tints ever really existed in nature. Tonight the spectacle seems likely to be omitted. What endless variety in the procession of days in nature and in our human hearts!

To my left, out of the window to the south, branches of oak trees heavy with leaves make a screen through which little glimpses of the sky may be seen. The wind stirs through it all with pulsing life. To my right, out of the northern window, are the pines, their high brown trunks tipped with billowy green. The pines are most sensitive to intruders. They do not endure houses built close to them. They have already given way in many spots to maples and oaks. But they still give character to these sand dune hills. They are the second growth. Here and there along our paths are the great stumps and sometimes the moss-covered fallen trunks of the mighty sentinels which stood here until forty years ago. Then the white man's invasion occurred. Ruthlessly and wastefully the old forests were shorn from the earth in the mad, unthinking rush to turn them into gold. Now, when people come from the rushing city to build little summer cottages for shelter, they have to buy pine lumber grown in the far-south state of Georgia. But the new pines have the old stateliness, the rich odor, and the deep shade. They sway over our heads like proud keepers of the earth, harboring the birds and sighing with a music which tempers all the brightness of summer with hints of autumn.

August 1921. There is a deep quiet in the woods that heals tired spirits by a kind of magic. The evenings and the mornings are cool enough to make a fire on the hearth very welcome, and what is better for the soul than to sit where with one glance you can look into the leaping flames, and with another sweep your eyes over the wide expanse of water? It is easy to get the illusion of being at sea as you sit in a cottage high on the lake front, for you can look straight out on the water with no sight of the land. So far as the eye can measure, the sea before one is infinite, and the very sight of such vastness gives one a sense of the greatness of the world in which the poor, tired little self can forget and be absorbed. It helps in throwing off responsibility to behold something so vast that the self seems to become infinitesimally small and unimportant.

This is a good place to read great books. There is no telephone, no doorbell, no public walk in front of the house, no road for passers-by, no streetcars, no policemen on their beats, no dogs, no ragmen, no venders, no dressing up, no impending speeches, no meetings, no alarm clocks. Only the music of the lake, sometimes a low crooning and, when the wind plays over it, a grand chorus of many deep-toned waves. The other day I saw from our porch two little girls running on the beach and playing in the sand. When they moved about they did not walk, they skipped. Their arms waved lightly with gestures of grace and nimbleness. It was a picture of the spirit of these shores. It was a kind of symbol of the wonderful renewal of life which comes through these waters and the winds of heaven, to all of us who come here, weary and discouraged, to gather strength and blithesomeness, to move with new energy upon the tasks and events which await us. Every year the lesson is borne in anew upon me that the secret of effective living and working in this world is not so much to have our way smoothed out for us as it is to gain the strength to conquer the lions in the way ahead. . . . The little pines I planted seven years ago have grown to my own height.[1] The face of the dune, which ten years ago was just shifting sand, has covered itself with grass and flowers, sand berries and juniper. It is proof that with time and labor the face of the world can be changed and be fashioned nearer to the heart's desire.

What I have quoted may sound as if the solitude sought was that of escape into rest and quiet, freedom from people and from responsibility. There is justification at times for that kind of solitude. The human machine, like any other, must have periods for repair and reconditioning. The engine has to be cooled down, the dust and waste removed, and the action of all the parts adjusted and tuned into harmony. Such solitude is not only an end in itself but a necessary stage for further and better work. To prolong it unduly means stagnation. The cottage by the lake was, then, first of all a kind of repair shop, a retreat for a rest cure, a calm haven to restore worn nerves and replenish depleted energy.

This solitude did not mean loneliness. It meant freedom to select and enjoy the finest and most stimulating associations. Here I could gather around me in imagination, or by means of books, the greatest souls I had ever known or heard of, and commune with them without interruption until their words and thoughts became more fully my own. Most of my working year was too hurried, too much broken by time schedules and imperious duties. But in the woods by the lake every suggestion was of a steadier and longer rhythm. The waves washed little grains of sand up on the beach, and the wind carried them farther up until great dunes had formed. At night, in the clear atmosphere, the unwearied stars

[1] On the kitchen door E. S. A. recorded the dates of setting out little pines in different years; and always the inches of tender new growth on their tips, when he first arrived in the summer, delighted him.

shone above it all, as they had done for unnumbered ages. It was good to feel oneself part of a world like that, active and moving but unhurried. Just as the stars, after long contemplation, appear in patterns and constellations, so the events of the human world, viewed through untroubled atmosphere, take on order and relation and deeper meaning. Our regular summer neighbors and visiting friends, sharing this same great life of nature, deepened the joy of it as we sat together around the fire or watched the spectacle of the setting sun at the day's end.

After reading newspapers, with their sensations of a day, it is a broadening of mind and spirit to become aware of the headlines of cosmic events, written in the stratifications of the earth and in the milleniums of history. Thirty years ago I was much occupied with the records of the early religions of mankind, and with the development of the great cultural faiths of Confucius, Buddha, and Jesus. They were like mighty forests that had risen from the seed thoughts of great individuals and had spread through the soil best suited to them, until millions upon millions of men and women had grown into maturity by those same thoughts. Now the seed thoughts from those forests had been carried by winds and tides across the whole world, until any person who tried to trace and understand the development of his own religion had to take account also of all the other religions of the world. The ancient forms of religion had grown up within the customs of the peoples to whom they were indigenous, much as the languages and fashions of dress had grown up, largely in isolation, self-contained and self-sufficient. But now languages were being translated one into the other and history traced to the elemental roots and forms, finally to the needs and qualities of human nature itself.

At last scholars were bringing to light, with painstaking labors, the common elements and the distinguishing traits of the various faiths. New reverence for them all was felt by those who studied them, and a far profounder faith was coming to be felt in the essentially religious nature of men of all races and times. A new tolerance emerged among the enlightened people of all lands. Missionaries began to bring back more charitable views of the religions of China, Japan, and India. Christian scholars became aware that missionary work could no longer be most effective with an attitude of exclusiveness and denunciation toward other religions, but must be conceived more as appreciation of the good traits in them all and as an exchange of cultures at their best. Such new vistas in the realms of religion could be seen better away from the duties of a parish church, and more courage and more effective methods found for bringing such discoveries back into the life of such a church.

In the solitude of my tower study in Harper Library at the university, and even more in the solitude of greater detachment in the summer, I pondered the world-wide religious significance of the development of the human mind in the period of modern science. In the last three hundred years the cake of custom has been broken up, or at least cracked, for all who have been trained in the natural sciences. But it has been the growth of the social sciences in the last fifty years that has brought all religions and cultures face to face with the most searching self-examination of all time.

In 1933 the Haskell Lectureship Foundation, of the University of Chicago, organized a series of lectures on different phases of the application of scientific studies to the world religions. One section was on the significance of the scientific method in relation to these religions. Representatives of Islam, Judaism, Christianity, Buddhism, Confucianism, and Hinduism spoke. Professor A. E. Haydon, editor of the published volume of these lectures, says in his Introduction:

> Today the great historic religions are compelled to come to terms with revolutionary forces unknown to any earlier era. Patterns of thought and custom which have remained relatively stable for centuries are now being challenged, neglected, or discarded. It may be that the religions of the world are in this generation passing through the greatest transformation of all time. . . . The influence of modern scientific thought is far-reaching and the implications profoundly disturbing for traditional religions. The natural sciences give an entirely new picture of the universe, of man's place in it, and of the nature of human nature.[2]

Professor Haydon pointed out that the result of this is that over all the world the noblest spirits are for the moment bewildered and grope fumblingly to find their way.

---

[2] A. E. Haydon (ed.), *Modern Trends in World-Religions* (Chicago: University of Chicago Press, 1934), pp. vii–viii.

I had the honor to give the lecture on "Christianity and Scientific Thinking," showing that at first science was developed outside religious subjects and that two world views soon stood over against each other:

... science holding to the conception of geological processes and epochs, and religion to the idea of the action at every stage of supernatural power. ... It was of the very nature of science to go its own way and to do all it could to achieve an understanding of the world in its own terms. Religion was on the defensive and undertook by various interpretations to maintain its claim of the working of a supernatural power. ... Religion itself was discovered to be involved with the total culture, rather than being something distinct or superimposed from outside the human scene. Every people, including the Hebrews, had their cosmologies and myths, their inviolable taboos and commandments, their heroes and sacred ceremonials. In all cultures there were tribal gods, inspired sages, miracle workers, mysterious medicine men, and marvelous magicians. The final realm of scientific study has been the inquiry into the psychology of religion, a searching quest into human nature itself to discover, if possible, the inner sources of religious attitudes and behavior. ... It turns out that science, on its own method and in its own terms, discovers the reality of religion as a vital and universal aspect of human life. It finds that religion is concerned with the celebration, dramatization, and artistic representation of the felt values of any given society, as a means of enjoying and realizing these values in the common life. Thus science is able to give an account of the nature and function of religion and to explain its ceremonials, its beliefs, and its significance, including the character of its deities.[3]

I confess that these views of nature and of religion required solitude for their formulation and appreciation. Not many ministers or theologians of my acquaintance shared them. I had come to them by scientific and philosophical paths, and often at the cost of radical disagreement with friends as well as unfriendly critics. The distances that separated my conceptions from those of the traditional patterns sometimes overawed me, for I realized that to many people such views were incompatible with current religious thought and especially with the performance of the tasks of a Christian minister. But there were many wise and sincere men of my acquaintance, and among the authors of books, whose ideas gave me confirmation and courage. Most heartening of all was the loyalty of the members of my church, for, while I realized that many of them took little interest in the steps by which I had

[3] *Ibid.*, pp. 26, 28.

come to my positions, they frequently expressed their satisfaction in the attempt to make religion intelligible and practical, and consistent with the best we experienced in other phases of life.

It was in such reflections as these that I came to appreciate more highly the religious inheritance I had received from the Disciples of Christ. Their religion was that of laymen. In their "pure" days, for three-quarters of a century, they had no "doctors of divinity," and they did not call their ministers "reverend." I did not know for a long time that Bethany College, founded by Alexander Campbell, forbade in its charter the teaching of theology, although the institution sought to train ministers for the churches, nor did I know that our very oldest college was launched on its career by the indorsement and approval of the scientific views and spirit of Francis Bacon.[4] But in the course of time I realized the consistency of these things with the freedom and common-sense religion I had known from childhood. In spite of any criticism or opposition from latter-day conservatives within these churches, I am more than ever convinced that a thoroughly scientific and non-theological[5] interpretation of religion is the logical and fruitful fulfilment of the beginnings which the Disciples made in the early part of the nineteenth century, leading to a great religious movement among the middle classes of the United States.

Now, after thirty years of annual solitude in the woods by the lake, its value is greater than ever. The little children have grown up. The little boy has come to be a philosopher and author, proud husband and father, with his own cottage under the pines.[6] Two

---

[4] Transylvania was originally Francis Bacon College.

[5] E. S. A. thought it crucial that the creeds of the Reformation were formulated in medieval terms, because Luther died in 1546 and Calvin in 1564, the year Galileo was born and most of a century before the birth of Locke and Newton. Alexander Campbell moved beyond orthodox Protestantism in launching the Disciples in the nineteenth century, because he had the benefit of the Enlightenment fathered by Locke. So E. S. A. would put theology with alchemy and astrology as compared with modern science and a co-scientific philosophy of religion. He regretted the naming of the University of Chicago's Federated Theological Faculty and would have preferred having "philosophy of religion" or "religious studies" in the name. Though recognizing that "theology" might be modernized, he associated the word with what Alexander Campbell thought the Disciples should leave behind.

[6] Van Meter Ames and Betty Breneman were married by his father in her home in Cincinnati, June 12, 1930.

of his sisters are married and happy in their homes in Chicago.[7] The youngest sister is following the career of an artist in New York City.[8] All still cherish the blessed memories of the free vacation days of the long summers and return each year with new appreciation. Their Grandma Van Meter came every year as long as she lived. She sang quaint songs for us, told stories of the old frontier, and wove rag rugs for the bedrooms. She would stay until her birthday on the fifth of September, when she and her granddaughter Damaris, named for her, celebrated their same birthday together.

During the last two summers our solitude has been enlivened by a marvelous grandson, on whom all family attention centers.[9] His first steps and first words, his unconscious sweetness and joy have been as wonderful as if he were the only child ever born. Certainly no child could ever have had a healthier, happier, more intelligently devoted mother, a prouder father, or a more adoring and understanding paternal grandmother. He is the only child to carry on in this branch of the family tree the name of Ames. In a reasonably long lifetime he will be able to celebrate early in the next century the centennial of the building of his grandfather's life-insurance cottage.

I have given a rosy picture of this summer solitude, without exaggerating its charm or practical value. Perhaps the shadows should not be painted in, but it will all be more real if I tell you that the roof leaks, carpenter ants work on the timbers, field mice and polecats pay their visits, and many of the lovely pines turn brown and die. One summer (1936) my wife came down with pneumonia (before the antibiotics tamed it) and lay for ten weeks in the hospital, between life and death.

[7] Damaris Ames was married to the historian Bernadotte E. Schmitt by her father in the house he lived in for neary fifty years, at 5722 Kimbark Avenue, November 22, 1939. They have been living in Alexandria, Virginia. Adelaide Ames was married to the Danish painter Harald Schade in Copenhagen, August 22, 1938, where they have made their home.

[8] Polly Scribner Ames moved her studio to Chicago in 1953 to live with her father and look after him.

[9] Sanford Scribner Ames was born March 1, 1938. His sisters also arrived in time to be enjoyed by their grandparents at Pentwater: Christine, born March 15, 1940, five days after the completion of this manuscript; and Damaris, born January 31, 1944.

At such a time all that a loved one means will come to the fore with almost too much intensity. Then one of our church services was broadcast and recorded, with the singing of the choir (which had always been a joy to me) and the sermon. The subject was "Living Religiously." When we played the record later, I knew why there was a moment when my voice broke. She loved our summer life, although most of what she did in the city, aside from church work and entertaining, went on: housekeeping, sewing, remodeling, walking farther to market. Always she was listening, advising, caring.

Our "Pine Terrace" has been our refuge from heat and care, a place where it is easy to believe in the possibility of a kingdom of heaven on this earth. There I have increasing appreciation of the words of Jesus, when he said to his disciples: "Let us go over unto the other side of the lake."

Chapter xxi | My Faith

Many times in the past forty years I have tried to state my religious faith in a single sermon. Very early there was a "Confession of Faith." Another attempt was on "The Essentials of Christianity," another on "The Three Great Words: Faith, Hope, and Charity." Quite recently I tried it with the subject "My Religion." Now the title is "My Faith." In these successive sermons there was an endeavor to get beyond special questions, such as biblical criticism, evolution, theological speculations, and to reach a deeper, simpler, and more living insight into the nature and central experiences of religion. It was an endeavor to reach the heart of the religious life of mankind and to see how this could be more adequately and directly expressed. There was also the constant desire to see religion in relation to the whole life of man, integral with all the processes of culture, including the scientific spirit of the modern age.

These statements were my answers to church members and students who often asked about specific problems or who wondered what kind of church I represented and how I could be a minister at all. Such questions were the most interesting to me because they were frequently the very questions I asked myself. In a very real sense my statements have been directed to myself even more than to anyone else. No one else could possibly be more concerned with their appeal or validity. The answers could not ignore the expert knowledge and criticism of people in the university on one side of the street or the practical interest and daily problems of the great variety of people on the other side of the street. It was my fortune to live on both sides and to share in the life and thought of both. In reality they were not so different as many individuals thought who, so to speak, lived only on one side or the other.

The times in which we have been living for the last four decades have sharpened all the basic problems of life—economic, political, educational, moral, and religious. Many persons have given up the hope of significant answers, especially in the religious field. Others have reverted to the unquestioning beliefs of their childhood. Some are trying new cults seven fold worse than the old, and a few are finding their way into more intelligible and satisfying religious convictions. My own ideas have been tried in the fires of doubt and wonder. Some of them have passed away like smoke, but my religious faith is clearer and more secure after the purge, and more confident of the larger place religion is to hold in the society of the future.

By faith I mean trust, confidence, assurance. Faith is a psychological attitude. We may have faith in a person, in a principle, in a practical project, and in life itself. It means belief that a person, a principle, a project, will not disappoint us in action or in eventuation. Faith has reference to possibilities as well as to present realities, and it is with possibilities that religious interests are especially concerned. Can we make something of our lives? Can we hope that a spirit of good will and of intelligent devotion will produce desirable results and some measure of satisfaction in this world? Faith is an affirmative answer to such questions. Faith is a thrust into the future, based upon more or less knowledge and rewarding experience in the past. It is not entirely blind or chimerical, but it is seldom absolutely guaranteed. If a course of action has no uncertainties whatever, it does not require faith, but most of man's life is cast in a complex of events leaving every venture somewhat hazardous. We never quite know what a day may bring forth. The great venture of religious faith is on behalf of the possibility of a better society, which religious people commonly call the kingdom of heaven. This kingdom already exists in some degree, for, as Jesus said to those about him, "The kingdom of heaven is within you." To bring it into fuller realization is the great task of religious people.

There are two principles essential to that fulfilment, and these are love and wisdom. These are qualities present in some measure in all normal human beings. The specific religious problem is therefore how to develop this love and wisdom among men. The crucial and searching question is whether we have faith in these two principles, whether we believe it is possible to increase them and extend them in all relations of life. It has been an increasing conviction with me in recent years that here is the concrete and tangible soul of the religious life and that appreciation of this would bring the meaning and purpose of religion within the reach of every man's understanding and within his ability to do something about it. These qualities of love and wisdom are self-evidencing. They are not speculative or theological. They are immediately present in experience, and their cultivation is the obvious need of the world.

Whoever seeks love and wisdom together need have no anxieties about religious realities under other names. He may rest assured that a life of love is a life in God. God is love. Every one that loveth is born of God, and knoweth God. If we love one another, God dwelleth in us. Love is the fulfilling of the Law and the Prophets. It is the supreme principle of the teaching of Jesus. For Paul it is greater than faith and hope, because faith and hope move toward love and find their realization only in love.

Wisdom is essential to the development and fulfilment of love. It is the means of finding the way for making love effective. Love furnishes the "drive," while wisdom gives instruments and methods. As in every other kind of significant desire or ambition, wisdom affords intelligent direction. All wishes of the heart remain blind and unfruitful unless guided by knowledge and skill. Wisdom is accumulated experience in the life of the individual or in that of other people. The ambition of youth to be a merchant or lawyer or artist requires training. "Wisdom is justified of her children" in any calling, and not least in the great, delicate, and far-reaching experiences of love.

In my teaching of courses in ethics and in theories of value, this fact of the importance of intelligence appeared in its full meaning. Love has an instinctive basis, and in its instinctive forms love is blind; yet from its blind strivings effects arise which sensitive beings may remember and profit by. Never have the psychologists and philosophers given so much attention to understanding, analyzing, and interpreting love as in recent years. One of them, Professor DeWitt H. Parker, defines love as "any activity which finds its end and value in the maintenance and increase of value in another mind."[1] Thus the mother identifies herself with her child, feels his happiness or pain, and seeks to share with him her own strength and well-being. Such also is the relation of physician and patient, of teacher and pupil, and of lovers. There are differences in the love of a man toward a woman, of a man toward his son, of a man and his friend, of a man and a cause to which he is devoted, but in all these relations he identifies himself with that which he loves. By sympathetic imagination he lives in the thought and feeling of the other. The welfare of the other is his own welfare, and any disaster to the beloved also befalls him.

Some experiences of love are more sensuous than others, but the sensuous element is scarcely absent from any of them. In Europe you see a man greet a man at the railway station with an embrace and kisses on the cheeks. In America they clasp hands and perhaps exchange a pat on the shoulder, or walk together arm in arm. In Hawaii I saw a family of Japanese bidding goodbye to a son as he was about to go aboard ship, apparently for a long journey, and they stood about him, each one clasping his own hands and bowing before the young man, while he also clasped his hands and bowed to the others. But even in this there was a sensuous factor, for the exchange of looks and the use of the same gestures made clear to all how each one felt.

It is also clear that love grows as it finds normal expression. Young lovers tend to be demonstrative with each other and impelled to caresses and tender glances. Their ecstasy is in their mingled being. Their mutuality of love broadens and deepens when they work together in the care of a child, thinking, planning, and toiling for his physical comfort, for his education, and for the refinement and strengthening of his character. The parents grow into a deeper and greater affection for each other as they discover, each in the other, powers of patience, cleverness, and wit in meeting the common problems. Their love is enlarged, too, by appreciation of other people who take an interest in the child. Teachers, doctors, neighbors, and friends, who contribute to his training and happiness, are felt to share the parents' concern, and

[1] DeWitt H. Parker, *Human Values* (New York: Harper & Bros., 1931), p. 177.

the parents are thereby drawn into a wider companionship of affectionate understanding. Beyond and beneath any professionalism, or the payment of fees, is the sense of the genuine human interest necessary to the best co-operation.

We give various names to love in its different expressions, but in all of them is the quality of mutuality, of reciprocal outgoing of affection and understanding. Friendship is a form of love, "cooled of its elements of passion." A friend is one whose company we enjoy, one with whom to talk and play without constraint and with no fear of betrayal or double-dealing. Working together at common tasks generates friendship. In the shop or laboratory men working side by side, if at all congenial, are likely to become close friends because each is able to appreciate the skill, the resourcefulness, and the power of the other. If one is overcrowded at his job or has fallen upon some misfortune, the other will take over extra toil in the generous exchange of helpfulness in which friendship delights.

The friendships formed in college days are often the most enduring and refreshing that youths ever form. The chum I gained in those days, by working with him on vacation ventures to make some money for academic expenses, remains one of my closest friends. We talked over our ambitions, laid bare our hearts' fondest dreams of life and love, and, although years sometimes pass without our meeting or even exchanging letters, yet we do not lose our sense of intimacy. When we do meet, the old attitudes of cordial comradeship revive, and we go on in the old spirit. We have lived in cities distant from each other, pursued very different vocations, and his scale of living is altogether out of my reach; yet we feel no strangeness and have no difficulty in taking up the happy role of our youthful companionship when occasion offers. We often think of planning another vacation together, believing that it would be a supreme happiness to both of us, but the occasion has never come.

There is also a kind of love that grows up in the pursuit of great causes. Patriotic societies, lodges, reform movements, scientific associations, and religious movements are deep soil for the growth of love among those bound together in these common endeavors. Of these none welds closer or more powerful bonds than religious orders. Where every element of self-seeking is absent and a common ideal is shared, love binds hearts in marvelous fellowship. Not only is there mutual sympathy among the members, but there is also a living relation between each one and the ideal person who is the spiritual head of the church.

A powerful mystical love arises in the soul of most Christians toward Christ, and a sense of companionship with him may transcend all other ties. With him there are intimate conversations in the form of prayers, and often he appears to the imagination speaking his counsels and his comfort. Many a hermit or monk in his cell is sustained by the sense of the living presence of the divine lover. To millions of Christian people in the world the love of Christ is a more vital influence than that of any other friend. It becomes a conscience against temptation and refuge in times of stress. The same psychology is evident in the other great religions that develop allegiance to their founders. Buddhism and Islam have their devout adherents, the solidarity of great brotherhoods.

No one of intelligence doubts that the surest possible cure for many of the ills that afflict humanity would be the spread of love for our fellow men beyond all nationalistic and racial lines of separation. It is not enough to impose political control over people by statutes designed to compel them to be just and unselfish. It is necessary that there be bred into the hearts and cultivated in the minds of individuals a spontaneous and urgent desire for justice and brotherhood. And when there is this desire for peaceful and mutual co-operation, there must be wisdom available for individuals to express and operate successfully their good will. It is no longer simply pity and charity that the poor and underprivileged need. In a world of increasing plenty, love seeks reasonable and just means by which all may deserve and be able to achieve by fair means a share in the material and the spiritual goods of life.

Love and good will toward all men is something to be understood and cultivated just as much as the desire to have a universal postal system or a world-wide system of credit and exchange. No system of universal co-operation has come by merely wishing for it. The means and methods of it have had to be learned in each instance, and if universal peace and good will ever take possession of mankind, it will be through agencies like the League of Nations and through processes of national education and family training.

This is my religious faith—faith in the possibilities of developing love and wisdom. The reasons for my faith are that we already have convincing evidences of the reality and power of love and wisdom in our world. These have their basis in the nature and experience of mankind. Conjugal love is a reality among all races and conditions of men, often flowering into beautiful and sacred harmonies in least suspected places. Parental affection also shines through all the great literature of the world and has been made the key to the conception of God as the Father of men. Friendships like that of Jonathan and David spring up in all cultures, and the ties that bind men together in loyalties to their groups and communities are stronger than death.

There is also a heartening fact in the way in which the day's work of the world goes on. Children are in schools under the care and instruction of trained and genial teachers. Scientists are quietly and patiently at work in their laboratories, gathering facts, making experiments, and alert for some idea or hypothesis to open a new window upon the scene. The great industries, factories, farms, trade and commerce, domestic operations, go on at the hands of millions of men and women, most of them happy in their work.

Occasional quarrels, now and then a tragedy, and in exceptional times a war, interrupt and blacken the course of human life; but to make these exceptions the main features of the picture distorts it and defames it. The one fact that hatreds and their consequences make the "news" of the daily press is proof of this view. If the sensible, peaceful pursuits of the world made the news, this would be evidence that the regular and characteristic thing was murder, arson, infidelity, and war. I do not mean to belittle or ignore the tragic side of life, but I refuse to make it the primary index to an interpretation of the whole. I know, too, how mixed our human nature is, how men clothed with a little brief authority often go wrong, how jealousy and envy and baseless gossip may corrupt the inner springs of the souls of men and women, as they did the heart of Othello.

Schopenhauer, the arch pessimist, has been to me one of the most stimulating authors since my college days, partly because his powerful arraignment of this world has made ordinary pessimists seem so futile in comparison. When he magnifies the evils and weaknesses of human nature, and the strange perversities of good people, my faith in the possibilities of improvement is strengthened. For is it not reasonable to think that, if there is so much good in such a bad world, there is a good chance of achieving more good when we seriously set ourselves to do it? The miracles wrought in the history of medicine and surgery increase our faith in further triumph over disease. Corresponding improvement seems credible in the highest ranges of human life and society, and the faith is growing that in the future we shall be better able to develop more wholesome and intelligent, more moral and religious, persons, because that is the supreme need and the most commanding desire of our hearts.

Faith in love and wisdom seems reasonable to me also because it comes home so directly to the deepest interests of every individual. Every man may have a share in fulfilling this faith. The kingdom of love and wisdom has its anchorage in the minds and hearts of individuals, and it has its field of operation in the natural companionships of the home, of fellow workmen, neighbors, and friends. This makes religion concrete and near at hand.

We in America have believed for a long time in democracy, and we have believed that every citizen has some responsibility for its effective working. Each person is called upon as a sacred duty to be informed about politics and to vote according to his honest convictions. Our educational system has been developed in the common schools in order to support our love of country by the fullest possible wisdom. We need to strengthen education and to safeguard what has been achieved.

And we still have the problem of developing a democratic religion. We are yet largely bound to the old style of a monarchical religion, whose laws and institutions are referred to revelation and to divine authority. My faith is democratic, because it is my conviction that the forms of religious faith, when they are vital, go hand in hand with the forms of the society to which they belong. To endeavor to preserve the forms, the vocabulary, and the attitudes of a monarchical religion in a democratic society is to have a people divided at heart and torn by a constant conflict in striving to maintain two kinds of supreme allegiance, political and religious, which deal by divergent methods with the moral and spiritual life.

It is my faith that we are all privileged to be co-workers with God in building his kingdom of love. This co-working does not mean that we are simply to follow blueprints laid down, but that we may also be called upon to re-think important features of the entire project. This puts heavy demands upon the individual. Many persons are keenly troubled not to have more time for any intelligent part in politics. They may well ask how they could possibly participate in democratic politics and also in democratic religion. The answer is that if we are to maintain a democratic political and religious society, we need to realize that we must give more time and thought to these ideal interests.

We have overdeveloped the individualism that arose in a pioneer country. We are destined to become more co-operative, more collectivistic, and to find in this direction still greater opportunity for the individual, not so much restricted and defeated by competition but enlarged and enhanced by the support of a common will. It may be that the problem of material goods—of the necessary but yet external goods of food, clothing, shelter, and money—is about to be solved through new discoveries and developments, with the energies of men left freer than they have ever been to cultivate on higher levels the sharable goods of life, such as love and wisdom. These values grow with use and multiply by being freely shared.

In connection with a sermon fifteen years ago, "Our Changing Religion," I printed in the calendar a poem by John Drinkwater, "The New Miracle." It expresses a note still cherished in my faith in these lines:

> Of old men wrought strange gods for mystery,
> Implored miraculous tokens in the skies,
> And lips that most were strange in prophecy
> Were most accounted wise.
>
> And so they built them altars of retreat
> Where life's familiar use was overthrown,
> And left the shining world about their feet,
> To travel worlds unknown.

We hunger still. But wonder has come down
　From alien skies upon the midst of us;
The sparkling hedgerow and the clamorous town
　Have grown miraculous.

And man from his far travelling returns
　To find yet stranger wisdom than he sought,
Where in the habit of his threshold burns
　Unfathomable thought.[2]

[2] John Drinkwater, "The New Miracle," *The Collected Poems of John Drinkwater* (London: Sidgwick & Jackson, Ltd., 1923), I, 140–41. Reprinted by permission of the author's representatives and of the publishers.